Where to
Reti[...]
in Britain

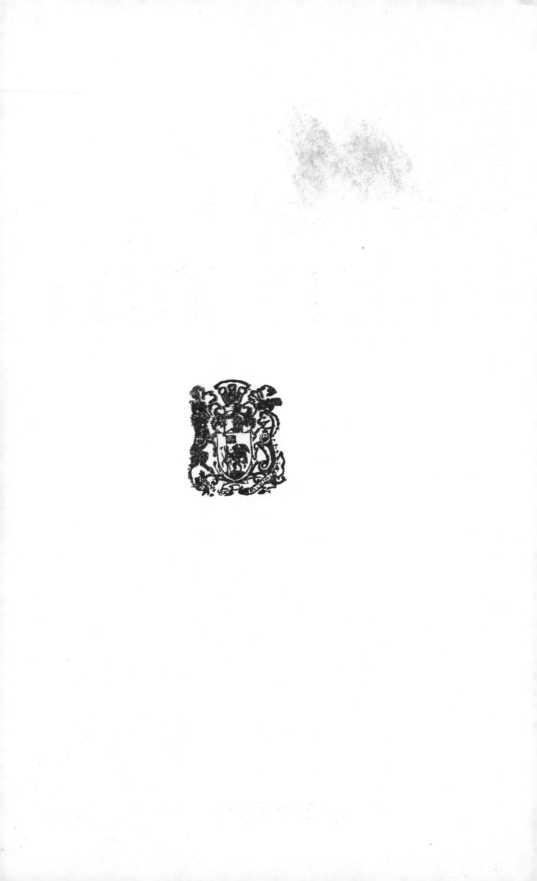

Where to Retire in Britain

Victoria Pybus

crimson

Holiday
RETIRE WITH STYLE

Shouldn't life be one long holiday when you retire? Not just time to rest and relax but time to do the things you enjoy most, a choice of activities to inspire you and fill your days with pleasure and good company.

We all have higher expectations of life these days and we offer you more from your retirement and an environment where you can experience security, companionship and excellent service.

This unique lifestyle is founded on the principles of respect, dignity and choice - living in a safe environment within your own home. You have peace of mind whilst keeping your independence enabling you to enjoy the best living experience of your life for an affordable, all inclusive, monthly rental.

Our philosophy of creating light, space and elegance is immediately apparent on entering the atrium of the reception area. Communal areas within each of the developments are for you and your visitors – enjoy the coffee lounge for hot drinks, fresh fruit or home-made treats, or the library for times of quiet contemplation. There is a TV lounge for sociable viewing and film evenings. The billiards and games room, gym, unisex hairdressers, beauty salon and multi activity room, used for classes, exhibitions and Sunday prayers, are all there for your use.

Delicious, nutritionally balanced meals, freshly prepared by our chefs are served for breakfast,

Shouldn't life

be one long holiday

when you retire?

dinner and supper in the light, bright dining room by your waiting staff. There is also a private dining room available when your family and friends come to visit and a guest suite available should they wish to stay.

You have a choice of one or two bedroom apartments or a spacious studio. A balcony or patio option is available. All carpets and curtains are fitted, and towels, linen and bed can be supplied. Apartments have built-in or walk-in wardrobes, a small tea bar with sink and fridge and your bathroom has a shower unit.

You will make new friends and your family and current friends will be warmly welcomed. There are plenty of activities each week that may interest you, from day trips, theatre evenings to tai chi and art classes. There is also a daily coach service to take you to and from town. Free parking is available should you wish to bring your own car.

Holiday prides itself on its excellent service. Our Housekeeping team change your linen and towels on a weekly basis, and also surface clean your apartment. There is a residential management team and a manager on duty 24 hours a day who will be happy to help you in any way they can.

With all the necessities taken care of, you are free to enjoy your own home and life to the full. We are very proud of our facilities and would love to have the opportunity to show you around.

You have peace of mind whilst keeping your independence.

This edition first published in Great Britain 2008 by
Crimson Publishing
Westminster House
Kew Road
Richmond
Surrey
TW9 2ND

A catalogue record for this book is available from the British Library.

ISBN 978 1 85458 407 6
Printed and bound by Mega Printing, Turkey

NOTE: the author and publishers of this book have every reason to believe in the accuracy of the information given in this book and the authenticity and correct practices of all organisations, companies, agencies, etc. mentioned; however, situations may change and telephone numbers etc. can alter. Readers are strongly advised to check facts and credentials for themselves. Readers are invited to write to Crimson Publishing, Westminster House, Kew Road, Richmond, Surrey TW9 2ND or email info@crimsonpublishing.co.uk with any comments or corrections.

Cover and internal images: iStock

Preface

In recent times, a significant number of Britons have been retiring in their 50s, buoyed up financially by the high value of property in Britain and generous occupational pensions. The recently introduced (A-day) pension rules have relaxed restrictions on how much money can be added to personal pensions and the possibility exists of drawing down on pension funds from age 50. Better off Britons are using this pension flexibility and their property assets to fund early or partial retirement. Significant numbers of people also take earlier involuntary retirement through redundancy or for health reasons. Of course the majority of people are still retiring at official retirement age and the government wants to increase the age at which those in the private sector receive a state pension to 67.

Considering retirement in another part of Britain with better value for money and beautiful surroundings may help those with the financial means to make the best of their situation. Although the better off will have more choices when going about this, there are still strategies for living in amazing places in Britain and there are still spots where property does not yet cost a king's ransom. Whatever your reasons, if you are approaching retirement, this book will help you to find a place in England, Wales or Scotland that suits your plans.

ACKNOWLEDGEMENTS

The author acknowledges a debt of thanks to Lianne Slavin for interviewing dozens of retirees, and to Alice Halliday and Lois Stuart Black for help finding interviewees in their respective towns. Also the people mentioned by name in the text who willingly gave their time to be interviewed and to all the astoundingly beautiful places in Britain for making siren calls to those approaching their retirement, and thus a reason for this book.

Contents

Where To Retire In Britain
some useful comparisons

5 most expensive places for buying property

Place	Average price of two-bedroom property
The New Forest	£540,000
Bath Spa	£450,000
Holt	£365,000
Sidmouth	£350,000–£400,000
Poole	£345,000

5 least expensive places for buying property

Place	Average price of two-bedroom property
Whitehaven	£105,000
Spalding	£116,000
Rhyl	£124,000
Mablethorpe	£152,000
Southend-on-Sea	£164,684

5 most accessible retirement places in Britain

Place	Accessibility
Bath Spa	Fast access to Bristol, Wales and the West Country and good access to London
Leamington Spa	Centrally situated in England and on main transport routes to London, Midlands, etc
Southport	17 miles from Liverpool
The South Coast	Easy access to London and Channel ports
The New Forest	Easy access to London and Channel ports

5 least accessible retirement places in Britain

Place	Remoteness
Builth Wells	12 miles from nearest large town
Isle of Wight	45 minutes by ferry from the mainland
Scilly	28 miles off Land's End
Shetland Isles	130 miles off the north of Scotland
Tenby	57 miles from Swansea

Highest population of over-60s

Place	Percentage of over-60s
Moelfre	75%
Worthing	45%
Mablethorpe	40%
Swanage	34%
Chichester and Christchurch	33%

Lowest population of over-60s

Place	Percentage of over-60s
Shrewsbury	14%
Perth and Southport	16%
Herne Bay	16.2%
Cheltenham	17%
Harrogate and Scarborough	17.4%

Part I
The Decision to Retire

Retirement in the 21st century

WHY RETIREMENT NO LONGER MEANS OPTING OUT OF LIFE

It is said that 60 is the new 40. Greater longevity means that middle age, when you slow down, is now likely to be around 70 rather than 50. While the government is keen to make sure that the over-50s should be economically participating in the labour market, the over-50s have other ideas of what to do with their lives after 50. They are making their own choices, according to what their circumstances will allow. At the start of the 21st century we are in the midst of a major social transformation. The postwar notion of retirement as a time to put your slippers on and settle in front of the telly with a nice cup of tea is fast becoming obsolete. The very word 'retirement', not to mention the images of encroaching decrepitude that it conjures, no longer fits the reality of how people are living their lives after full-time employment. Today's retirees are often younger, fitter and wealthier than their forebears and together they are reshaping the very meaning of 'old age' and 'retirement'.

RETIREMENT TRENDS

- In 1950s Britain, the average retirement age for men was 67. By 1995 it was between 62 and 63.
- At the start of the 21st century, the average retirement age in Britain is 64 for men and 61 for women.
- The retirement age for women is due to increase gradually to 65 from 2010.

Many social commentators suggest that these changes are being wrought by the 'baby boomer' generation. Born between 1945 and 1965, baby boomers are a force to be reckoned with, making up almost a third of the UK population and responsible for nearly 80% of all financial wealth. The baby boomers grew up in an era of postwar optimism and new social freedoms, and as such have always represented a force for social change. Indeed, they have spent a lifetime reconstructing social norms. Now the first wave of this generation has reached retirement age, and with such political and financial clout their approach to growing old is profoundly different. As *The Times* recently put it:

> The pioneers of the consumer society are unlikely to settle for an electric fire and a can of soup.

One of the main reasons that the concept of retirement is changing is that people are living far longer. Life expectancy in the 20th century rose by 20 years due to better healthcare and greater health awareness. Around 18 million people in the UK are over 60. Not only are people living longer, they are also leaving the workforce younger. Many are giving up work in their early 50s when they are still fit and active, in order to enjoy a new stage in life – not their 'retirement', according to the American website www.2young2retire.com, but their 'renaissance'.

A recent report by *Demos*, a democracy think tank, claims that the baby boomers are intent on having their time again; of creating a new life phase in which they can revisit their own desire for personal fulfilment, free from the pressures of overwork and childrearing. The report identifies a new 'experience economy' of travel, food, learning and lifestyle. The baby boomers do not want to retreat from the world as the word 'retirement' suggests, but to head out into it with renewed vigour.

The new retirement is all about finding a better life balance. This may not necessarily include giving up work – around half of the people who leave permanent 'career' jobs before state pension age move initially into part-time, temporary or self-employed work. It would seem that people are no longer happy to compartmentalise their lives into linear stages – school, work, parenthood – with retirement at the end of the line. Retirees these days are demanding greater flexibility; preferring to see life as a never-ending cycle, in which they can choose to dip in and out of periods of work, education and leisure. Others have the funds behind them to pursue a hobby or interest full-time. It would appear that the prevailing gloom that people once felt about the ageing process is slowly being replaced by a sunny optimism. People no longer dread reaching retirement age. They eagerly anticipate a new life stage, in which, released from the shackles of full-time work, they can seek out new cultural experiences, new adventures, cram as many things as they enjoyably can into the day, and maybe spend the children's inheritance!

NATIONAL ATTITUDES TO RETIREMENT

The British attitude towards retirement – or the Third Age as it is often called – is that it is a well-earned period of non-economic productivity that should permit individuals to live the latest period of their lives to the full and with financial security. However, salary-related pension schemes, which have until recently been the financial bedrock of a comfortable retirement are not what they used to be. Mounting costs have caused a backlash among providers; fewer than half of such pensions in the private sector are open to new members, or pension companies have upped the age at which they become accessible. The government, in its efforts to deal with the 'pensions time bomb' caused by not enough savings, not enough births and a rapidly ageing population, wants us all to work until we drop, or at least until we are 67, before we can draw a state pension. This effort to force people by social/economic engineering goes much against the grain. Most people in Britain still retire before state pension age, some voluntarily, but a significant number do so for health reasons or to care for ageing parents and relatives. The majority of those who are not retired would like to retire in their 50s while they are fit and well enough to enjoy their retirement to the full, but many will not feel financially secure enough to do so. Under current HM Revenue and Customs regulations it is possible to begin drawing on a private pension at age 50 (this will rise to 55 in 2010). Only a very small minority reach normal retirement age and want to continue working.

A DWP poll taken in 2005 showed that nearly 60% of responders were against working beyond retirement age. The government is thus forcing the less well off to continue working, while those who can afford to, will retire earlier.

The security of the retired in Britain is funded by the state from employer/ employee deductions, which citizens have paid from employment earnings. It is estimated that one in four British pensioners lives below the poverty line and it is not hard to see why. The UK state pension is far less generous than in many other countries including France, Germany, Sweden and Italy where contributions are higher. For instance in France, not only are contributions higher (especially employer contributions) but compulsory supplemental occupational pension schemes are paid for by additional automatic wage deductions. In other countries such measures ensure that the retirement pension is enough to live on comfortably. Conversely, in Britain a considerable number of people rely on the state pension as their sole income in retirement, and there is enormous government expenditure on additional long-term social benefits for the least well off. A smaller tax burden in the UK and an entirely free health service (in some countries there is a personal contribution element) are no compensation for a lack of creature comfort in retirement. The free NHS provision is not all it seems when divided up into regional health authorities, which are responsible for managing their own budgets. This means that some treatments, particularly for chronic diseases, are available in one health authority area but not in another area where they may be deemed too expensive. This situation is unheard of in most European countries.

The quality of retirement in the UK (if defined by the standard of living and a sufficiency of facilities) can be related to the wealth (or lack of it) of the region where you retire, as well as personal wealth. In the UK there is a considerable north–south division with the south being seen as a better place to retire generally, as judged by these criteria. However, there are several regions in the north and even the Shetland Isles in the extreme north of Scotland, where a comfortable retirement lifestyle can be created with fewer resources than you would need for Jersey or Poole Harbour or any other exclusive retirement place. There are compensations for not living in the most exclusive coastal retirement places; you might for instance find somewhere on the edge of a national park with stunning scenery and less congested roads than you are used to.

RETIREMENT STATISTICS

■ Recent evidence suggests that only 37% of British men are still working at the age of 64 (compared with 57% in 1979). Only 7% of French males are actively employed after 60 and only 27% of American males.

■ Fewer than one in 10 men and one in 100 women who retire are doing so solely for the reason that they have reached statutory retirement age.

■ In the age group 55-64 55% of women are employed in the UK (35% are employed in France and 67% in Sweden).

The decision to leave work

Those lucky enough to plan how and when they will leave work and retire can give themselves time to organise their financial situation and ensure that they have the wherewithal to maintain their lifestyle after retirement from work. The wherewithal is likely to come from the value of their home, private and company pensions and savings and investments. Be aware that some of these might not fulfil their financial promises. Many people have found to their cost that assumptions based on the returns from pensions and savings for retirement have proved to be meaningless. They have had to adapt or postpone their retirement plans to take account of shortfalls in estimates.

Those whose financial circumstances have not worked out as well as they expected might have to decide whether to carry on working to maintain their current standard of living, or retire, but with a simpler lifestyle. You have to ask yourself *'how much is enough to retire on relative to my priorities in retirement?'* You will give yourself more choices if you feel that living more simply is not an issue if you can still afford to go sailing, take foreign holidays, and drink decent wines – even though you may have to manage with one car and grow your own vegetables. Those who are most likely to experience problems with finances are those whose exit from employment is not planned and happens abruptly. It is therefore advisable to start your financial planning early so that you have sufficient savings or have paid off the mortgage on your property, which in the meantime has risen in value. You can then use these to counteract the unpredicted sharp fall in income that comes with a forced early retirement. Some people will not have this option because of low average earnings during their lifetime, which means that they will probably depend on state benefits for the rest of their lives. For such people, planning for the future is not a priority. Financial factors therefore play a considerable part in the decision to leave work earlier or later than retirement age, but there is no doubt that most people would retire early to do other things, if they could afford to.

WHY MOVE IN BRITAIN FOR RETIREMENT?

Planning to move to another place in Britain gives you a project and a welcome distraction from the fear that you may stagnate should you stop work. 'Change is good for the soul' and moving to another British area gives you a sense of an adventure and revitalises your outlook on life. It will help you if you are starting to have negative thoughts about how you are going to fill your time during your forthcoming retirement and stop you doing anything rash like buying a ruin on a Greek hillside, that you may regret later. If circumstances permit, before you retire and before you move, you should take holidays in different parts of Britain with a view to assessing their retirement potential. Consider that new places mean new faces and observe how you feel about different places and the type of people living there. Although you will not want to lose touch with your old friends, moving gives you the opportunity to make new ones (without finding yourself subjected to the same merry-go-round of faces, as often happens in a British expat 'colony' abroad.) Moving to another part of Britain gives you a chance to enjoy new or your favourite activities in a fresh environment. Peak time traffic congestion in Britain may be at crisis level, but once you are retired, your travel times are more flexible and, with a little planning, you can usually avoid the busiest times.

Moving in Britain means you can find the best place for your favourite pastimes. If you are a golfing fanatic then you might like to consider moving where there is a course on your doorstep, like Rye or Tenby. If you are a surfing dude or babe then you will probably want to move to North Devon or Cornwall, or if you love swimming in rivers and lakes (wild swimming) then you had better move to Wales where rivers are clean enough and this has long been popular in the rivers Wye and Usk and even the inland town of Brecon has its own bathing beach. If your passion is for the arts then somewhere with important literary and music festivals like Bath, Cheltenham or Perth would be suitable.

Other reasons for moving in Britain could be that your current residence was chosen for convenience or with investment in mind, and is not necessarily the ultimate retirement place. Perhaps you want to move to the countryside from the city or vice versa. Despite the fact that moving to another part of Britain can be stressful it is still less of a wrench than moving abroad permanently. However, there are still pitfalls such as blowing the budget on an overpriced property with fabulous views. You may have to settle for a property near great views, rather than amidst them. Another trap is to imagine that the best place to retire is the place where you were the happiest on childhood holidays, early days of marriage etc; but as the Greek philosopher Heraclitus put it 'You cannot step twice into the same river, for other waters are continually flowing on', People and places change, while your own memories of them are frozen in time.

Why stay in Britain rather than join the exodus abroad?

Perhaps a better question would be 'Why move abroad to retire?' Why move abroad and sever yourself from your roots, your loved ones and your circle of friends? You can always have extended holidays abroad and rent places in Italy, France etc. or do a house swap with expats there. If your retirement is not the result of careful planning but a sudden necessity like redundancy, retirement can be a particularly traumatic event as you are not able to plan your transition from a work culture to a leisure culture so well. You may rush into moving abroad because that is what everyone else seems to be doing, and then find it is not for you.

There has been much newsprint lavished on the retirement exodus from Britain to any number of foreign countries, the so-called 'silver flight'. Research shows that about half of British émigrés will return to Britain at a later stage, probably when a spouse has died or if their health deteriorates and they don't want to cope with a foreign health system, or if there is no old age care available. If you don't speak the language of the country where you retire you can be lonely, especially if one of you dies. Returning home brings its own problems and may not be an option if you sold your British home to fund moving abroad and your foreign property does not realise enough to buy back into Britain's exorbitant property market. Coming back after many years of absence abroad can be difficult. You may not be prepared for the reverse culture shock of finding that you, as well as the places you knew so well, have changed and leave you feeling foreign in your own land. What better way of avoiding all the above concerns, than not leaving Britain to retire abroad in the first place. You can always spend extended holidays abroad, but still remain based in Britain.

OTHER GOOD REASONS TO RETIRE IN BRITAIN

Familiarity – familiarity and fewer settling-in problems.

Small country – Britain is a small country compared with France or Spain so nowhere is unfeasibly remote, or more than a couple of hours from the coast.

Small, but amazingly varied – Britain has many incredibly beautiful places to retire to and to explore.

Choice of coast – Britain is an island and its coast is one of its greatest glories. The majority of people dream of retiring on the coast and Britain has a huge choice of places and a range of property types and prices.

Enjoy your heritage – Have the time to delve deeply into the amazing history of Britain and its cultural (especially regional) and literary heritages.

Less complicated financial planning – Save yourself the bother of complicated financial planning, especially inheritance and offshore arrangements, by not moving abroad.

Cheaper relocation costs – It is generally much cheaper to relocate to another place in the UK than to move your goods and chattels to a foreign country.

No extremes of climate – Although startling anomalies do occur, they are not on the same scale as Hurricane Katrina, that drowned New Orleans in August 2005, or the Earthquake-Tsunami in the Indian Ocean on Boxing Day 2004. Parts of Spain, Italy and the Balkans can be extremely harsh in winter. Britain tends to have only short cold snaps.

No water rationing – Britons who move abroad may experience very severe droughts and daily water rationing in summer. The latest climate change report suggests that the whole of the Mediterranean area is likely to be almost uninhabitable in summer because heatwaves with temperatures well above 30°C and droughts will become increasingly severe.

Improving public transport – After much criticism of poor services, many rail franchises have shown significant improvements. There are generous concessions for the over-60s on rail travel and local buses (see page 00)

Free National Health Service – The NHS is entirely free at the point of delivery, unlike its equivalents in many other countries. If you retire to Scotland, you are entitled to free personal and nursing care if you need it and you are over 65, whether you are at home or in a nursing home (but not in England and Wales).

Excellent road system – Britain has one of the best road systems of any country.

Closer to friends and family – If you retire in Britain, you are not removing yourself from the comfortable vicinity of family and friends, which often causes heartache if you move abroad.

Communications and technology – Computers, broadband and internet technology have made it possible to organise your life from home. Broadband coverage in Britain is close to 100%, higher than France (95%), Spain and Germany.

(Continued on following page)

(Continued)

Cost of telecoms less in Britain – Britain generally has cheaper telecoms than in many countries.

Foreign travel – You can fly to an amazing number of places from UK regional airports at budget prices so you can still enjoy foreign winter sunshine. If you live permanently abroad and return to the UK for holidays it may not feel like a holiday.

You don't become 'pickled in aspic' – Brits who move abroad to British 'colonies' tend to become exaggeratedly 'English', and stuck in a time warp of 'Englishness'. By staying in Britain you keep evolving with Britain.

Lots of uncrowded places – South-east England is very densely populated and main tourist stops in summer are overwhelmed, but there are many places throughout Britain that remain far less crowded. You can always find a haven to escape to.

More choice of pursuits – It is much easier, because there is no language barrier, to get more deeply involved in local projects, voluntary work or continuing education courses at the local college.

Retirement finances

PENSIONS

It is generally known that private and company personal pensions have experienced a sharp drop in popularity here in Britain. The catalyst was undoubtedly the virtual collapse of Equitable Life and the consequence of the resulting House of Lords ruling in 2000, which meant it would be impossibly expensive for companies to provide the generous company pensions that had been the norm up to the Millennium. Those who took out private pensions have also suffered a shock at their financial shortfall, having based their expectations on the meaningless projections of pension growth offered by their pension providers. It is not an exaggeration to say that the pensions industry has lost the faith of the British people. People don't want to be beguiled into parting with their money to enter a kind of tax contract with a government, especially a government that is always moving the goal posts. Furthermore, it is a contract that does not allow the contractee to own the wealth in their pension, except for a lump sum representing a quarter of their pension pot, which they can claim on retirement, or at the age of 50.

The remaining 75% of any private pension must be used to buy a life annuity (see annuities below).

In contrast to saving for pensions, ordinary savings among older people are on the increase probably because they are the only age group in the country who can afford to set aside regular amounts. Although gains are modest, at least they are reliable. It is estimated that about half of all savers are saving for their retirement. Individual savings accounts (ISAs) are the most popular vehicle – understandable, as the interest on them is accrued free of tax.

On 6 April 2005, the government changed the rules on state pensions allowing deferrals. This means that you can choose to put off claiming your state pension in return for a higher amount of state pension, or claim it as a one-off taxable lump sum. The cynics would say that the government is trying to make it seem attractive to work beyond retirement age in the hope that we will die (probably from overwork) before we finally claim our state pension.

Basic state pension

A person earning the British salary average of £22,000 would find their state pension paid out just 48% of that. The average state pension payout is 69% with a number of countries including Italy, Spain, Turkey and Hungary paying 75%. Luxembourg tops the pensions league table with a very generous

110% of the working wage. The British state pension lost its link to earnings while Margaret Thatcher was prime minister. The present government has suggested that the link may be restored if it can afford it, but in any case this would not be before 2012. The amount of the state pension is based on National Insurance Contributions (NICs) deducted from wages. The current basic state pension per week for a single person is £87.25 and for a couple £174.05. Various means-tested benefits are available for the least well off to supplement the basic pension. Unlike private pensions, the state pension is guaranteed provided that you qualify with the requisite number of years' contributions.

> British state pensions are among the most meagre in the western world putting Britain 26th in a rank of 30 countries (OECD, 2005).

If you retire before the state pension retirement age, you will not be able to claim your pension until state retirement age. You will usually receive less than if you had worked until retirement age and paid your full quota of NICs. If you retire early you can continue paying voluntary NICs until you reach retirement age so that you get the full amount of pension. The government has promised that the number of qualifying years needed to get a full state pension will be reduced in the future. The number of years of NICs to qualify for a full state pension will be reduced to 30 years for both men and women (currently it is 39 for women and 44 for men). This is intended primarily to benefit women, who tend to lose out on pensions because they have usually worked fewer years than men. By 2010 70% of women would be eligible for a full basic state pension (currently it is 30%).

The state pension age for men is 65 and is between 60 and 65 for women. The state pension age for women will increase incrementally from 2010 so that by 2020 it will be 65. The increase in the state pension age does not affect women born in 1950 or earlier, who can still receive their pension from age 60. The Pension Service Website has a handy pension age calculator on the State Pension section of its website. Women born on or after 6 April 1951 up to 6 April 1955, can see when they will reach state pension age. Women born on or after 6 April 1955 will have a state pension age of 65.

There is a full explanation of the state pension, how it is worked out, how you get additional state pension and benefits and conditions applying to women on The Pension Service website (www.thepensionservice.gov.uk) in the A to Z State Pension section. The site is part of the DWP (Department of Work and Pensions). If you want to know how much your pension will be, and you are more than four months away from retirement, you can get a state pension forecast online at www.thepensionservice.co.uk; telephone 0845 300 1658 and fill in the application form for a forecast over the telephone; or print out an application form from the website and post it to the Future Pension Service (The Pension Service, Tyneview Park, Whitley Road, Newcastle-upon-Tyne NE98 1BA). This forecast shows how much you will get when you retire, based on your National Insurance contributions.

State second pension

Also known as S2P/Additional State Pension the State Second Pension replaced Serps (State Earnings Related Pension Scheme) in 2002 and like Serps is a state top-up pension. S2P and Serps are calculated differently. Serps applies to those in employment between April 1978 and April 2002 and pays a maximum percentage of your average earnings and is linked to your income and NICs paid during those years. S2P is like Serps in that it is related to earnings. However, it is structured to benefit the lowest paid workers the most. If you have been in work under both regimes then you will receive a mixture of Serps and S2P. The amount of the state pension is based on NICs.

PERSONAL PENSIONS

Anyone can start a personal pension plan for retirement, even if you already have an occupational pension through your employer (see below). You set up a personal pension with a commercial provider. These include banks, building societies and insurance companies (for example, Standard Life, AXA, Virgin, Norwich Union). There are dozens on the market in slightly differing formats. The personal pension umbrella also includes the basic government-backed personal pension, the Stakeholder (see below). In April 2006 (A-day), the rules about how much you could put into a personal pension were relaxed and it is now possible to save as much as you like into more than one personal pension. However, this Chancellor specialises in U-turns (remember the SIPPS fiasco) so it is highly unwise to rely on one set of rules lasting the course of your pension.

> Anyone can start a personal pension plan even if they already have an occupational pension through their employer.

What you will get from a personal pension provider is an estimate of what your pension might be worth at retirement age based on a hypothetical growth rate, based on a hypothetical stock market. In other words, an estimate that is meaningless. You could end up with more, or less than the estimate. At worst, the pension provider could go bankrupt, as happened with Equitable Life. The thing to remember about personal pension plans is that there are no guarantees and it is a leap in the dark for your money. It would appear that this belief is supported by the consumer. According to market research, new personal pension contracts have fallen by 70% in the last five years.

If all goes well with your pension plan, it will provide you with a pension pot during retirement. This can be at any age from 50 (rising to 55 by 2010) up to 75. You can draw a tax-free lump sum on retirement of a quarter of the pension fund and interest or bonuses paid by the provider (depending on the terms of the pension). Financial provision out of your pension fund is made for your spouse or other dependants should you die before retirement.

A stakeholder pension is a low-cost pension that conforms to government set standards and conditions – mostly related to the annual charge for administering the plan and the flexibility in stopping and starting, or raising and lowering contributions, without penalty. Stakeholder pensions are available from companies that provide personal pensions. Some employers and trades unions offer stakeholder pensions to their employees/members.

Occupational and company pensions

Occupational pensions are provided by employers to provide pensions and life assurance to their employees in addition to any other pensions that the employee may have. They fall broadly into two main types. Less common in these times of job mobility is the final salary scheme by which the pension is a percentage of your salary at or just prior to retirement. It is related to the number of years you have been employed by a particular employer. The other version is the money purchase scheme where the pension is based on the total value at the time of retirement of the money you have paid into the scheme and on the investment performance of the scheme. Until recently, occupational pension schemes have proved to be one of the best forms of pension. Many employers are abandoning these schemes or closing them to new members as they have become too expensive to guarantee.

Alternatives to retirement/phased retirement

Alternatives to retirement at retirement age may be an option if you have a personal pension. The A-day rules introduced by then Chancellor Gordon Brown on 6 April 2006 have made retirement a much more fluid concept by allowing those with personal pensions to draw down 25% as a lump sum from the age of 50. The remaining 75% of the pension can be left untouched to grow in a tax-sheltered environment until you buy an annuity. Pension holders can use the 25% lump sum from their pension however they wish. It could, for instance, be used to pre-empt retirement. The lump sum could be used to pay off your existing mortgage, or take out a mortgage on a second home in the area where you want to retire. Others might prefer to use it to fund a partial retirement, whereby you reduce your hours in your main occupation to pursue other interests or activities. The latter option would depend on your employment circumstances. For instance some employers might not like the idea of a phased withdrawal from work; others might be more open-minded about it.

Annuities

If you have a personal pension of the type that pays 25% at age 50, you will have to buy a compulsory purchase annuity with the remaining 75%. Details of the various types of annuities can be found in 'Pensions websites' below.

An annuity provides a regular, usually monthly, income in retirement in exchange for a lump sum. There is an open market for these and it is advisable to shop around for the best deal, just as you would with your savings, as you can be hundreds of pounds better off if you do. There are different types of annuity arrangements for different requirements, including enhanced annuities for reduced life expectancy (usually because of a medical condition rather than because you take part in dangerous sports) or joint life last survivor, if you want the annuity to be passed on to your surviving spouse or partner. In fact, being sickly is one of the best ways to boost your income from an annuity.

Enhanced annuities provide a higher rate of income as providers are calculating them based on a lower life expectancy. These operate in a similar way to impaired life annuities for those with the most serious medical conditions, such as cancer. On average enhanced annuities pay out about 20% more than standard annuities so if you think you might qualify for the enhanced rate you should hunt around for a provider. On the other hand, you will enjoy your retirement better if you just devote yourself to keeping as fit and well as possible.

State pension from another country

When you are working out how to finance your retirement, be careful not to overlook any possible sources of income that you may have forgotten about. If you have ever paid into another country's social security system during a period abroad, you may be entitled to regular payouts in retirement provided that you have retained the paperwork that you were given at the time with your social security number on it. Many, but not all countries have reciprocal agreements with the UK. If you think you are due any such retirement payments it is nearly always up to you to chase it yourself. You may not consider it worth pursuing but even for periods of a year or two abroad, the resulting payments of £30–£50 per month could be very useful. Your first port of call should be the relevant country's embassy.

Pension shortfall?

If your pension will not be enough to cover your retirement you will probably need to consider your options. You can increase your contributions into your personal or company pension by as much as you like under the 6 April 2006 pension rules.

Alternatively, if you have lost faith in your pension's performance, you can start saving in a tax-efficient investment, of which the ISA is the most popular. Most banks and building societies offer these. Interest rates above 5% are quite easy to find. Other options include equity release schemes, remortgaging your house or downsizing to a smaller and cheaper home. You can get more advice and information on the government website www.direct.gov.uk.

Pensions websites

Financial Services Authority (www.moneymadeclear.fsa.gov.uk)
The FSA is the official watchdog of the financial services industry and gives general advice to consumers of financial products.

The Pensions Advisory Service (www.pensionsadvisoryservice.org.uk)
TPAS provides information and advice about personal pensions including stakeholder pensions. It does not give specific financial advice, for this you need an independent financial adviser.

The Pension Service (www.thepensionerservice.gov.uk)
Official site; part of the DWP (Department of Work and Pensions).

The Pensions Regulator (www.thepensionsregulator.gov.uk)
Regulates work-based pension schemes. Information for pension holders and trustees.

National Pensioners Convention (www.npcuk.org)
The UK's biggest pensioner organisation and lobby group. Lots of useful news and information.

This is money (www.thisismoney.co.uk)
Useful commercial website.

Money Facts (www.moneyfacts.co.uk)
Another useful commercial website.

YOUR PROPERTY AS A RETIREMENT FUND

Your home, your biggest asset?

When planning finances for retirement, many people have found that their home is the single largest financial component involved. That is, unless they have discovered a priceless treasure in the attic that they can sell at Sotheby's, or they have a fabulous pension fund. How you manage your biggest asset will be related to the part you see it playing in your retirement plans. It is also possible that you will want to use it to finance a move elsewhere in Britain. This in turn may be related to finding out how you can best avoid paying inheritance tax. For 2007/08 the inheritance tax threshold is £300,000 and the current tax rate is 40% of estates valued above that. Many people are only too well aware that their home, for which they paid a modest price decades ago, is now above the threshold at which the tax is levied.

> If your finances do not allow much room for manoeuvre then you may be able to raise funds from your property by downsizing to a smaller home.

You may decide to downsize, release equity or remortgage depending on your circumstances and also decide how much any consideration of your future beneficiaries welfare will play in your decisions. By moving to a smaller home, you may be able to kill two birds with one stone: have funds with which to enjoy retirement, and make gifts to your heirs in your lifetime, on a drip-feed basis. If inheritance tax still looms over your estate after you have put some of your retirement plans into action, you can reduce your taxable estate by setting up a trust. You will need some expert, independent financial and legal advice as it is an expensive alternative and so only usually financially worthwhile for large estates. A trust will help you tie up all the loose legal and tax ends and help you find the best way of avoiding paying unnecessary tax.

An alternative to creating a trust is to own things jointly with your spouse or life partner. This means that you are assessed for taxes only on the part of the share you have received. The usual way to do this is to have yourselves made tenants in common; a legal arrangement that can help avoid inheritance tax. The drawback is that if one of you dies, the beneficiaries of that person may put pressure on you to sell your part of the property.

Equity release

Many people are tempted to raise money for their retirement by releasing equity in their home via an equity release scheme provider. It was calculated that in 2006 over a billion pounds was drawn on through equity release in the UK. However, financial experts have been sounding warning bells that this could be another financial product mis-selling scandal in the making. This is because many such schemes are expensive and there may be cheaper alternatives. Say your house is worth £250,000 and you want to release equity of £50,000. According to calculations on one scheme it could cost you £7,500 a year just to stay in your own house, and after 20 years this would amount to £120,000. Other schemes that release equity include home reversion and lifetime mortgages. The problem with equity release schemes in general, is that it is very difficult to work out how much it will end up costing you.

The amount varies depending on your longevity, and what happens to house prices during your lifetime.

Equity release is the easy option in that it enables you to stay put in a house to which you may be very attached. However, it only works if you are not worried about who is profiting most from this arrangement, and that you may be reducing what could be left to your heirs. If you have no heirs or beneficiaries to worry about, then equity release could be appropriate. What the companies that sell equity release schemes – including lifetime mortgages and home reversion – won't tell you is that it could be cheaper to downsize to a smaller property. This of course, gives you the perfect reason to consider buying a retirement property in another part of the country. You can get advice from financial organisations. Homewise (www.homewise.co.uk) specialise in retirement property and finance, and can offer you a range of options to release equity in your property and help you afford a property that you find acceptable.

Alternatives to equity release schemes

One other way of raising equity from your property without taking out a loan against it is to sell part of your garden. This could be done to remedy a pension shortfall or help raise funds for retirement. You may have a neighbour who is interested in buying part of your garden to enlarge theirs, or, if you can get planning permission, a developer may be interested. The latter is potentially more lucrative. Developers tend to target properties with large gardens in exclusive streets so that they can buy a row of ends of gardens and thus acquire a swathe of land on which to build several houses, or one big section of garden to build two homes where previously there was one. However, there are caveats. Be careful that you do not reduce the value of your home by making the garden disproportionately small in relation to the size of the house, or by removing one of its best features, or by allowing badly planned development to rob the house of light and privacy. Depending on the size of the plot, developers have paid prices upwards of £40,000 for plots. However, you may be liable for capital gains tax (up to 40% of the sale price). Sales of a section of garden should be done before you sell the house and remaining garden.

RETIREMENT BUSINESSES

Start a small business

Some people decide to start a small business in retirement, particularly if they have retired early and their finances are not adequate to sustain their non-economic activity. There are a number of factors that prompt someone to consider becoming a mature entrepreneur, but they boil down to needing more money, a fear of intellectual atrophy/boredom, or a combination of these. However, it is also crucial that you enjoy operating your business, and that you are prepared to invest some of your retirement savings in it. Investment is most likely to be needed in materials and equipment, but at least if you are running your business from home, your overheads will be minimal.

Not everyone is cut out to be an entrepreneur. You have to be passionate about what you are doing, and you have to identify what motivates you – is it creativity, a sense of accomplishment, personal recognition and respect, money, or perhaps a mixture of these? Also bear in mind that just because you were an excellent employee, it doesn't mean that you will good at running a business. You can begin with shadowing someone who is already running a retirement business to see what it entails. Often, keeping the books is a challenge if you have never had to do it before. If you have no head at all for figures, you may need to hire a part-time bookkeeper to do this for you. There are some valuable tax incentives when you are self-employed and running a business. You will be able to claim all your operating costs and loan interest against your income. The website www.50connect.co.uk has a section *Start a Business* aimed at the over-50s.

. A potential problem for early retirees who have been forced into retirement is a lack of confidence. It may be necessary to rebuild confidence first before you can sell yourself and your business to the public. A lot of people have reported that exercise and sports are a great way to rebuild self-esteem, so membership of the local gym could be the first investment you make in your business. Another likely problem, if you have been used to having colleagues around you at work, is the loneliness of owning your own business. For this reason it is essential to join local small business networks and the chamber of commerce so that you have regular interaction with other business people.

Ideas for retirement entrepreneurs

To a certain extent retirement entrepreneurs create their own workplace, having identified a need in the market and their ability to fill it. There are many possibilities, depending on where you retire. Below are a handful of ideas that have worked for some retired people.

Antiques restoration. This could be something that you have previously done as a hobby. People are always finding bargains at car boot and flea markets or in their local antiques market, such as Victorian chairs, stools and footrests. If you are skilled at re-upholstering, mending cane seats, or carpentry and wood repair, you will soon get a name locally and people will bring their bits and pieces to you for mending or restoring. If you haven't previously developed the skill, now could be a time to start. Many community centres around the country run courses on upholstering furniture and mending china.

Running a bed and breakfast. This is one of the most popular ways of supplementing your retirement income, or using your home to raise its own maintenance fund, but it is not for everyone. You have to like welcoming strangers into your home and you have to be living somewhere on the beaten track or a well-worn tourist circuit, so that customers can find you easily. One of the benefits of this type of business is its flexibility. You can choose just to operate during the summer or if your customer base comes from local businesses, theatre folk or summer English students, then it can adapt to these needs. This means that although it can be a lot of work, it need only be for a few months at a time. You will almost certainly need to provide en-suite accommodation, as this is what most guests expect as standard. The main attraction is likely to be the breakfast, which should be full English or, depending on your clientele, a wholefood spread. If you are getting it right, word of mouth will expand your customer base. You may not need to advertise if the word spreads, but if you want a wider, perhaps international clientele you will need to be included in guidebooks or on websites, or have your own website. At the least you should have some cards and leaflets with the contact details of your B&B. You can get more useful information at www.howtorunabandb.com. Useful publications include *How to Start and Run a B&B* (Louise and David Weston, How To Books, 2006) and *Starting and Running a B&B: A Practical Guide to Setting up and Managing a Bed and Breakfast Business* (Stewart Whyte and Nigel Jess, *The Daily Telegraph* Books, 2006).

Consultant. It is quite common for retirees to become consultants in the field that they have been working all their lives. Many companies use former employees who have retired, as consultants on a part-time or *ad hoc* basis. This can apply to all types of industries from the technical ones such as engineering to the hospitality industry such as restaurants and bars. It is ideal if you still want to feel the buzz, but no longer wish to have full-time responsibility. You will probably be paid an hourly or daily rate plus expenses.

Desktop publishing. This is a versatile possibility for anyone with the requisite computer know-how. Home-based desktop publishing is expanding globally with the ever present human need to produce leaflets, flyers, newsletters, graphic materials and even books. Your client base is likely to include local businesses, schools, clubs and organisations. The problem is that if you may find yourself spending excessive hours in front of the computer, especially if you are successful at finding customers, so it is probably a good option for those who are less mobile. If you are an active person you would probably prefer to be out and about with daily human contact when you are working.

Dog care. This is a great little earner for someone who loves working with canines. The good news is that there is such a demand for the services of dog groomers and behaviourists that there are City & Guilds qualifications in dog grooming and canine studies. Short animal behaviour courses are a little harder to come by but you can do a one-day taster course organised by The Centre of Applied Pet Ethology (www.coape.co.uk), which also does correspondence courses in pet behaviour. Also look at the Association of Pet Behaviour Counsellors (www.apbc.org.uk) for more information on full-time degree courses in animal behaviour. Plenty of franchises involve work with animals. Home-based and flexible, they include:

- Bugsie's Mobile Dog Wash (0870 042 4610)
- Barking Mad (01524 276476) provides temporary pet care (you will need space in your own home for dogs).
- Oscar (0800 068 1106)
- Trophy Pet Foods (www.trophypetfoods.co.uk) delivers pet food to customers' doors (you can take your own pet with you).

Gardening and garden maintenance. Many people do not have the time or inclination to keep their lawns cut, their bushes pruned and their flowerbeds weeded, so there is a great demand for gardening services and potential year-round employment concentrated in a small area. Garden work is also healthy, outdoor work ideal for keeping your fitness levels up. Most people have their own garden tools and mowers, so you will not have to invest in a lot of equipment. Hourly rates of pay are usually from about £5 upwards. If you live in an upwardly mobile area you will probably get asked about garden design so you may have to keep up with what is fashionable, or limit yourself to lawn maintenance, weeding, planting and digging.

Handyman and household repairs. There are endless small repairs needing to be done in any house: small DIY jobs or mending/rewiring small electrical gadgets. If you have a lot of experience fixing things, you can advertise your services. Word soon gets around if you are good. You will need a small, equipped workshop at home for items that cannot be repaired on the spot and it would be useful to live near a DIY superstore or builders' merchants for supplies.

Life coach. This is a rapidly expanding field and is a great way to do something worthwhile and use your experience to good effect. The coach helps the client find out what their goals are in work or life and shows them how to work towards them. This kind of occupation is appealing to many mid-life career changers and executive types retiring from high-powered careers. It provides two-way satisfaction for coach and client. Executive coaches in particular can bring all their own executive experience of the workplace together in a positive and useful way, to which their executive clients can relate. Your client base is therefore likely to reflect your previous career and your contacts can provide a useful starting point.

Life coaching is not currently regulated in the UK and there are no minimum academic qualifications. You will almost certainly need to do a course and it is up to you to satisfy yourself about the integrity of any course on which you enrol. The Coaching Academy (www.the-coaching-academy.com) offers training courses in the UK. You can join the ICF (International Coach Federation) (www.coachfederation.org), which has branches worldwide. A useful UK website is www.achievementspecialists.co.uk. Retirement coaching is an area beginning to take off and is a niche market waiting to be filled with entrepreneurs. If you have the right background, and have organised your own retirement successfully, now might be the time to pass on your wisdom to others and earn nice fees from consultations or lectures.

Tutor. Someone who has worked in education as a teacher or lecturer will find there is a demand for part-time tutors or coaches. This can be on a one-to-one basis such as piano teaching or coaching a student for GCSEs, A-Levels or retakes of these. There is also the possibility of crammer courses for groups before the summer exams, held in private colleges and schools. The only problem is that you have to spend a lot of time touting for new business. It would help if you could get on a local tutors' register. Music shops often keep lists of singing tutors and teachers of piano and other instruments, while schools and colleges keep lists of private tutors.

FINANCIAL CONCESSIONS

In asssessing how well your finances will match your aspirations in retirement, a potentially invaluable contribution to your quality of life are the various price concessions for those over 60. These are dominated by travel concessions, including local concessionary bus travel schemes. Such concessions provide free off-peak travel between 9.30am and 11pm Monday to Friday and all day at weekends and on bank holidays, especially (but not exclusively) in urban areas. This is a legal requirement funded by government. In addition, local authorities may offer their own supplementary concessions, which could include travel before 9.30am, and free travel on other modes of transport such as trams, tokens for taxis and community-provided transport. Other national travel concessions include a third off National Rail fares, and half fare travel on scheduled coach travel throughout the UK. For culture vultures there are various reductions for the over-60s on ticket prices for arts and culture events, senior screenings at cinemas, or various theatre and musical events. Arts concessions vary considerably from place to place, so when looking for a place to retire you can enquire further.

The long-planned new development on the concessions front is the Concessionary Bus Travel Bill, launched in November 2006 to provide free bus travel nationally from 2008 for older and disabled people. Nationwide free bus travel for Scotland was implemented on 31 March 2006. Anyone over 60 and disabled people can apply for a National Entitlement Card to access the Scottish scheme. This card is also used to access local services such as libraries. Wales and Northern Ireland launched their own free national schemes in 2002. From April 2008, local entitlement to free bus travel will be extended to allow bus travel throughout the country. This is the Nationwide Free Bus Scheme for Over-60s and Disabled People. More information is available at www.transportscotland.gov.uk for the Scottish scheme, and the Department for Transport website www.dft.gov.uk for England and Wales.

Concessions for the over-60s are not limited to local public transport. Many county councils in England, Scotland and Wales now have a policy of free swimming for the over-60s at municipal swimming pools, and colleges and universities also offer cheaper tuition fees to pensioner students.

Specialised retirement property

RETIREMENT DEVELOPMENTS

Why you might choose a retirement development

Calculating how much you can afford to spend on a retirement property and still have enough to live on is essential. Thinking about what type of property will suit your needs is almost as important. For the majority of people, the size of property they need for their retirement is smaller than the one where they brought up their children, although you will probably still want a guest bedroom. However, if you are going to run a small retirement business you may need extra rooms for B&B, workshops or a workroom or possibly an outbuilding. Another consideration is whether or not you intend to spend the rest of your life in the new house, in which case you may need to think ahead. How suitable it will be in 20 or 30 years' time if your agility is compromised?

> Specialised retirement property is a valuable option available to those contemplating retirement as it allows both completely independent living initially and forward planning for later anticipated care needs to be provided for.

Steep steps up to the front door or cutaway stairs between floors, a huge garden, or an isolated position down a bumpy track are all fine when you are in your nifty 50s and 60s, but you may not be able to take them in your stride in your 70s and 80s. You may be forced into moving again at an advanced age when you least feel you want the bother of moving house. A solution to this potential problem is to live in a retirement development or retirement village that has been created to take away most of the problems of running a home and leave you free to enjoy yourself. What is more, they are aimed at those in their 50s who are thinking ahead about what services they may need in 20 or 30 years' time. This kind of ready-made older community does not appeal to everyone, but it may be worth looking into. Not all retirement developments and retirement villages attract the same kind of people, so it is a case of finding one where you feel you will fit in.

Prices from
£149,950

24 Hour Security
Independent Living
5 Star Leisure Facilities
Optional Assistance

- Lifestyle
- Choice
- Security
- Care

Middleton Towers, situated off the Lancashire coast, is the largest retirement village in the UK **exclusively for people over the age of 55.**

The full site has beach access and stretches across 80 acres. It is an example of where people can live an independent, active lifestyle being safe in the knowledge that first class care is available 24 hours a day, 7 days a week if required.

Middleton Towers Retirement Village
Carr Lane, Middleton, Lancashire, LA3 3LH
For a brochure & further information please call

01925 822352
www.prestigiousvillages.com

PRESTIGIOUS
REMENT VILLAGES PLC

Tingdene Homes – The One-stop-shop for all your Park Home needs

Tingdene Homes, leading manufacturer of Park and Leisure Homes, have been in business for 39 years and with that have a broad range of experience in providing their customers with not only a quality built home but also with excellence of service. They pride themselves in providing new benchmarks in modular construction year on year developed by a young enthusiastic management team whose ethos is based on having the customer at the heart of its operations.

Park Homes are ideal retirement/semi-retirement homes, providing couples the opportunity to downsize from their bricks and mortar home and release a substantial amount of equity which in turn allows them to then enjoy a more relaxed lifestyle, time and funds with which to take holidays, or even buy a holiday home from which to indulge during their newly acquired spare time. Many have taken up new hobbies such as boating, a new lease of life. Park Developments are generally set in a tranquil environment away from the hustle and bustle of the centre of the town, however normally close enough to benefit from community amenities.

Tingdene's design team have developed a portfolio of innovative homes that reflect customer's requirements, some modern and contemporary, some with a traditional feel like the Deene Cottage. Some with a study, many with en-suite facilities, others with a utility room, the choice is yours from a top of the range luxurious park home, to a more cost conscious home to suit all budgets, tastes and styles. Each and every home has been designed with attention to detail to ensure that the customer has a home that they can enjoy living in for many years to come.

All homes are fully furnished, double glazed, centrally heated, fitted throughout with kitchen and bathroom fitments, being individually built to exact customer requirements.

Tingdene's Exhibition Centre was set up to allow customers to browse and explore the homes and lifestyle available in comfort. A visit is a must for anyone considering the Park Home or Leisure Lifestyle and is truly a one-stop-shop for all visitor needs. The Exhibition Centre offers, 10 show homes on display, Park information via Tingdene's Estate Agency, Factory Tours, advice on Home Exchange, Finance and any other aspect regarding the homes or the Lifestyle available.

To find out more about Tingdene, call us today for your free comprehensive brochure on **0845 803 7703** (local rate charge) or visit the website – **www.tingdene.co.uk**

Taken from 'best practice' developments from around the world St. George's Park takes the concept of retirement villages to a new level – making it one of the leaders throughout Europe.

All St. George's Park apartments are spacious and the latest standards for access and mobility have been incorporated throughout the internal and external design. Extensive Communal facilities include a restaurant, bar, shop, library, gym, games room, visitor suite and 24 hour concierge. In the later phases a leisure complex will include an indoor pool, fitness room, sauna and steam room, a bowling green and tennis court will also help to encourage the residents to 'live life to the full'.

The current residents have already arranged many clubs and outings and the numerous themed nights held in the restaurant have helped to form a real sense of community. St George's Park is therefore living up to its original concept of offering a secure environment with a vibrant and diverse community.

NorthDales
LEISURE PARKS

Retire to the country
in style!

Bridgend, exclusive new Park Homes in majestic Northumberland.

Bridgend is an exclusive development of beautifully appointed Park Homes on the outskirts of the friendly border town of Wooler where you will enjoy country living combined with security and a much less taxing lifestyle.

The park has excellent facilities including a lounge bar, shop and indoor pool with endless walks, nice local pubs and restaurants, golf and fishing on the doorstep. It's only 20 minutes to Lindisfarne, glorious beaches at Bamburgh, the Scottish Borders, Alnwick Gardens, the busy coastal towns of Berwick and Eyemouth. Newcastle and Edinburgh are all within easy reach.

...ing this Advert for top deals

Contact Karin or Kim on 01668 281294
sales@northdales.co.uk   www.northdales.co.uk
SALES OFFICE, BRIDGEND, BREWERY ROAD, WOOLER, NORTHUMBERLAND, NE71 6QG

Shaw Extra Care –
Innovative Retirement Properties + Care

Extra Care is becoming the commonly accepted term for retirement housing developments where care is available. Housing with care is a more descriptive term; other names include assisted living, continuing care, and close care.

Shaw healthcare, in partnership with Herefordshire Council are delighted to announce the recent opening of its new Extra Care Centre; Leadon Bank, in Ledbury, Herefordshire.

The new facility delivers a £7 million Extra Care scheme that is operated in partnership with Herefordshire Council's Adult Services Team. This Extra Care Scheme provides the opportunity to acquire an assisted living type of property which is both a secured legacy and continued investment in the property market.

Leadon Bank

Leadon Bank offers a range of optional support services which are available 24 hours a day with personal care and support on hand 7 days a week.

Our Extra Care Properties have bright, spacious living spaces and include a fully fitted kitchen, hall, store cupboard, wheelchair accessible shower room, lounge/diner and a host of features to assist your daily living needs. Leadon Bank also includes a communal lounge, restaurant, café-bar and other hotel type facilities, along with specialist assisted bathrooms, computer and library facilities, and even overnight accommodation for guests.

Innovative retirement properties + Care

Shaw extra care schemes offer the next generation of retirement housing as a real alternative to, and a step up from traditional sheltered housing schemes which do not provide personal support and care. The schemes offer a new lifestyle choice and opportunity designed for those active in retirement, who also want the security of care services on hand whenever they are required.

The Shaw healthcare (Group) Ltd

The Shaw healthcare Group was established in 1988 and is now an award winning independent healthcare organisation with over 80 Care Homes and Specialist Care Centres across the Country. Shaw design, develop and operate quality accommodation and clinical care facilities providing mainly for older people in 2386 registered care home beds.

For more information:
Tel: **0800 7318470**
www.Shaw.co.uk

Increasing numbers of people are seeking fulfilling lives in retirement and turning to age-exclusive lifestyle villages which offer the benefits of private property ownership yet freedom from many of the chores associated with it. That means more free time to enjoy life to the full. Here is one couple's story…

We wish we had made the move ten years earlier…

MOVING to a retirement village is a major lifestyle decision – but the Williams wish they'd done it 10 years earlier.

"We'd have had more energy then to enjoy the wonderful surroundings and village life," admitted Valerie, who with husband George recently bought a property at Blagdon Village in Taunton, Somerset.

The couple are among the first to move into this brand new retirement village for the over 60's. Saying goodbye to their four-bedroom home and third of an acre of garden was a wrench but one they do not regret. They are not alone – there is a growing trend of single people as well as couples looking for a more fulfilling life as they hit 60.

"Attitudes are changing," explained Sarah Burgess for developer Retirement Villages Ltd. "People want to enjoy themselves and get as much out of this stage of their life as possible. They want to have their house in order, so to speak, with no worries and a secure situation. This lifestyle provides exactly that."

Retirement Villages Ltd has been building lifestyle villages for over 25 years. Blagdon Village offers 85 apartments, cottages and chalet bungalows built around the central Blagdon Lodge clubhouse which features restaurant, bar, function room, library and managed reception. A fitness room and hair salon is also planned.

The village is next to the famous Vivary Park and within walking distance of Taunton town centre and mainline railway station.

Retirement Villages currently has developments in Cornwall, Devon, Somerset, Warwickshire, Oxfordshire, Surrey, Lincolnshire and Hertfordshire. For more details call **01372 731888** or visit the website: **www.retirementvillages.co.uk**

RETIREMENT SUCCESS COACHING

"The 'new retirement' is not an ending, it's a new beginning, the start of a new life journey of vastly expanded proportion." – Dr. Richard P. Johnson

Would you like to:
- Know what your ideal retirement looks like?
- Learn about the 15 factors that contribute to a successful retirement?
- Create a life of meaning and purpose?

Why is this so important?
With the average age of retirement in the UK now 61 and with increased life expectancy meaning that you could live at least another 20 years – planning and personal awareness are essential for a happy, fulfilled and satisfying retirement.

How will you benefit from this programme?
- Explore your attitudes, expectations and beliefs about retirement
- Discover what is really important to you
- Formulate a personal plan for creating a satisfying retirement
- Learn how to make a positive transition into this new stage of your life

For further information, visit www.transitionslifecoaching.co.uk
and contact Jackie Fletcher on 01425 472354
or email Jackie@transitionslifecoaching.co.uk

Transitions
Life Coaching

Getting it right in the golden years

The chances are you'll spend almost as long in retirement as you did in work. As more of us live longer and stay active into old age, the more important it is that we invest in and plan for what is effectively the second, and for many, the more fulfilling half of life. Whether or not our jobs or careers were successful and satisfying, we all have the chance to invest and plan to ensure our years in retirement will be.

Experienced life coach, Jackie Fletcher, offers the *Retirement Success Coaching Programme* to help people to do exactly that. "Just as career coaching can help us to make the right choices in our working lives, coaching can empower us to create the best quality of life for our later years" says Jackie. "We all need help clarifying what we really want and planning the best way to achieve it."

For more information, call Jackie on 01425 472354
or email Jackie@transitionslifecoaching.co.uk

Retire close to all you need.

Churchill Retirement Living has built a reputation as fine as our apartments for locating them close to all you need.

Thinking of retirement...
Think Churchill Retirement Living

Award winning one and two bedroom retirement apartments

Lodge Manager • Lift • 24hr support & help
Video entry • Guest Suite • Owners' Lounge

DEVON: Fishponds (Bristol)
BERKSHIRE: Old Sandhurst*
BUCKINGHAMSHIRE: Princes Borough*
CORNWALL: Falmouth*
DORSET: Lilliput (Poole), Gillingham
EAST SUSSEX: Bexhill-on-Sea
ESSEX: Chelmsford
GLOUCESTERSHIRE: Gloucester
HAMPSHIRE: Portswood (Southampton), Bitterne, Cowplain, Titchworth, Parkgate*, Southampton (Central)*
KENT: Broadstairs, Cliftonville, Hersham, Tunbridge Wells, Hythe, Chington
MANCHESTER: Sale*
MONMOUTHSHIRE: Caldicot
SOMERSET: Glastonbury

SOUTH YORKSHIRE: Armthorpe*
SURREY: Lightwater (nr Camberley), Sutton, Camberley, Addlestone, Epsom, Farnham*, Hindhead, Tadworth (nr Epsom), Woking, Wallington
SOUTH GLOUCESTERSHIRE: Filton (Bristol)*
SOUTH WALES: Caerphilly*
STAFFORDSHIRE: Uttoxeter, Stafford*
WEST MIDLANDS: Solihull (Cornyx Lane), Solihull (Warwick Road), Stourbridge, Sutton Coldfield (Boldmere), Sutton Coldfield (Reddicap)
WEST SUSSEX: Bognor Regis, Chichester, Petworth*, Worthing*
WILTSHIRE: Chippenham
WORCESTERSHIRE: Stourport-on-Severn, Malvern

* Subject to planning permission

Call FREE 0800 458 1847

www.churchillretirement.co.uk

Churchill
retirement living

Independence • Safety • Security

Churchill Retirement Living Customers choose an easier way to move

Mr and Mrs Palmer found the 'Home Exchange Service' suited them perfectly when they moved from their Basingstoke home to a new Churchill Retirement Living apartment in Hampshire.

Selling a house and buying a new home is a stressful procedure at any time of life. For those of retirement age, who may have been out of the property market for some years, it can be rather more of a shock to the system. Understanding this, Churchill Retirement Living has devised a number of services to help make the move as smooth and hassle free as possible. One of these, called 'Home Exchange', was an option which Richard and Barbara Palmer were happy to take up when they downsized and purchased a new one bedroom apartment from Churchill Retirement Living.

Early retirement for Richard and Barbara Palmer led to a complete re-think of their lifestyle. The couple had been living in a bungalow in Basingstoke for 14 years but were beginning to find the upkeep of the house and garden more of a chore than a pleasure. With their four children grown up the Palmers were free to go where they chose - and they picked a small coastal market town in Hampshire.

Through Churchill Retirement Living's 'Home Exchange Service', Richard and Barbara elected to use the services of Quick Move Properties who purchased their bungalow in Basingstoke after three valuations and a survey.

"This was very useful in removing the anxiety of selling the property without the business of chasing the agents to secure the sale," said Richard. "This really appealed to my wife as she did not want the hassle of having the necessary viewings."

This service also offers financial help by eliminating estate agents fees – a very welcome saving in the expensive moving process.

Another service provided by Churchill Retirement Living was the 'Moving Made Easy' provision for the packing, removal and delivery of all household goods. With this service, the Company looks after the whole moving process from booking the removal company right through to unpacking your possessions including fragile items as required. The Customer does not need to pack anything, get any quotes, worry about any costs or panic over the removal date. Everything is taken care of by Churchill Retirement Living.

However Richard Palmer, an ex army man says, "We are well used to packing and did 80% of the packing ourselves." The Company also recommended a local solicitor which the Palmers found extremely useful.

The Palmers were in their new home in a surprisingly fast seven weeks from first deciding to purchase, with a sale achieved satisfactorily on their old home. "We were genuinely amazed at how quickly it all happened," says Richard. He describes the apartment as "spacious and comfortable, with a fully equipped kitchen. We chose the apartment especially for its view over the gardens and the playing fields," he says.

Churchill Retirement Living developments can be found in carefully selected locations in the UK all of which offer the very best of local amenities and shopping, together with independence, security and 24-hour support and help when required. This aspect is one that the Palmers appreciate, although, as Richard says with some amusement, "I think the family worry more about our security than we do! But it is nice to know we can go on holiday, close the door and be assured that everything will be looked after. There's a good social life here too, a friendly group of similar age people with coffee mornings and games afternoons."

Fore more information on Churchill Retirement Living please visit **www.churchillretirement.co.uk** or alternatively call **0800 458 1839**.

What is a retirement development?

Dedicated retirement property can range from a historic building conversion to a new apartment building, and from a small housing estate to an entirely self-contained complex with a range of shops, amenities and care facilities.

For older people, there are an increasing number of property options aimed at promoting independence, providing choices and an emphasis on quality of life and attractive surroundings. These include the totally independent retirement developments, which are essentially blocks of flats, built in small and larger country towns or in coastal situations.

Specialised retirement properties are usually aimed at the over-55s, although some may start at a lower or higher qualifying age. For instance, Firhall Retirement Village on the Moray Firth is for the over-45s who are 'thinking about retirement', while some McCarthy & Stone retirement flats are for the over-60s.

These are marketed to the over-55s and appeal to those who are happy to be in the midst of people of similar ages and interests as themselves. Some 50 and 60 year-olds would probably find them too staid, but others revel in the range of social and leisure activities that are laid on, or amusements that are easy to organise locally. For the very aged or infirm there are developments with an onsite care service and 24-hour assistance. The cost for these depends on the number and level of care services needed.

There is a niche market in retirement building and it is a rapidly expanding sector. Developers have cottoned on to the fact that one in six of the population is over 65 and that an increasing number of the over-50s need to downsize from their current home to cash in on some of its value and boost their retirement income. Retirement apartments can be very luxurious and expensive, but prices start at about £160,000, making them potentially an affordable and attractive option. Many of the retirement developments are run by management companies and service charges for maintenance of the grounds and property can be high. Most developments allow companion animals to live with their owners but there are strict regulations to eliminate the nuisance factor to neighbours and other residents. Another big advantage of retirement developments is that they usually have 24-hour security and closed-circuit television (CCTV) which means that if you want to go travelling you can 'lock and leave' without a moment's concern for your apartment and its contents. One of the best-known retirement builders/developers is McCarthy & Stone who specialise in apartments for the over-60s. Currently, they have over 180 developments in England, Scotland and Wales. Prices start from about £160,000. Pegasus Retirement Homes (www.pegasus-homes.co.uk) have developments throughout England including genteel seaside places. They offer attractive shared communal areas such as a lounge for socialising, guest accommodation for visitors and personal services as required.

Other big names in the sector include Churchill Retirement Living and Beechcroft Homes, which emphasise the total security of their developments, English Courtyard, which is the luxury end of the retirement development business, and an expanding newcomer in the retirement sector, Wren Homes, which so far has confined its operations to south-east England. There are also many general developers who have built one or more specialised, and possibly quite small retirement developments as part of their portfolio of developments. It is not essential to buy into a retirement development; you can also rent apartments. Girlings has been offering a choice of retirement rentals since 1990.

Retirement development: useful contacts

Beechcroft Retirement Homes (01491 825522; www.beechcroftretirementhomes. co.uk). Based in Wallingford, Oxfordshire, Beechcroft retirement developments are aimed at the over-55s. Selling points include high levels of security and low maintenance. They offer a mixture of new and conversion properties in the Home Counties and Dorset.

Churchill Retirement Living (0800 783 7661; www.churchillretirement.co.uk). Developments in England: the Midlands, south-west and south-east. Dozens of new developments are planned, so check their website or telephone for more details.

David Wilson Homes (0800 234455; www.davidwilsonretirementhomes.co.uk). Developments in England: Berks, Bristol, Hants, Hereford, Oxfordshire, Surrey and the West Midlands. Dozens of apartments from one to three bedrooms, starting at £180,000.

English Courtyard (0800 220 858; www.englishcourtyard.co.uk). Slough-based English Courtyard offers luxury end retirement housing including conversions of existing buildings, for the over-55s. Prices start at £300,000, 30 developments in England in 20 counties.

Girlings Retirement Options Ltd (0800 525 184; www.girlings.co.uk). Based in Taunton, Girlings has been offering assured tenancy retirement rentals to the over-55s since 1990. Database of 10,000 properties in England, Wales and Scotland, predominantly one-bedroom apartments but some larger properties too, all on purpose-built retirement developments.

Golden Living (0800 085 0855; www.goldenliving.co.uk). Based in Leeds. Assisted retirement developments in Northern England: Cumbria, Lincolnshire, Teeside and Yorkshire.

Goldsborough Estates (0800 731 6287; www.goldsboroughestates.co.uk). Part of the BUPA Group based in Leeds. Has 45 developments throughout England and Wales for those aged 55+.

McCarthy & Stone (0800 919 132; www.mccarthyandstone.co.uk). One of the best-known retirement builders/developers specialising in apartments for the over-60s. Currently, they have over 180 developments in England, Scotland and Wales. Prices start from about £160,000.

Where to retire in Britain?

'Where to retire' is a huge question to ask anyone and in Britain alone is a highly topical subject. Many factors are taken into consideration whilst pondering this conundrum. There are many different views and opinions, and with each individual's needs comes a different set and order of priorities. Typical requirements include:

- Affordability
- Location
- Security
- Lifestyle
- Choice
- Care

Prestigious Retirement Villages plc as of October 2007 have been listed on the London 'PLUS' stock market and have emerged as a dynamic brand that has catered for the majority of individual's requirements.

Middleton Towers is Prestigious Retirement Villages flag ship development, near Lancaster. This 6 year long development began construction in 2006. The former ever popular Pontins holiday camp which was acclaimed to be the largest Pontins holiday camp when open was famous for the SS Berengaria (main building designed as a ship), its cabaret acts and fond summer memories for many families.

The new village is a world apart from how it used to be in the old days due to its new luxurious make over. The brand new village is specifically designed for the over 55s and will be the largest and best equipped retirement village in the UK. The site boasts an idyllic location with its own beach and is situated on the picturesque Lancashire coast, only a few miles from Lancaster.

The 80 acre site will comprise approximately 590 new homes, leaving 20 acres of natural open space, for rural walks, gardens and landscapes such as ecology and rose gardens. The proposed layout encompasses various amenities and services that many villages will envy.

Facilities (when complete will) include:

- Health and beauty spa

- Gymnasium and pool
- Tennis court
- Bowling green
- Golf nets
- Pavilion
- Garden walks and trails
- Library and internet access facility
- Restaurant and café
- Guest suite
- Recreational areas

Prestigious Retirement Villages Properties are designed to create a relaxing comfortable environment for people to enjoy their retirement, by developing them in a way that makes them easy to manage. This is the design prerequisite for both active and less able people.

Many features and services have been applied to the village to give residents peace of mind and as much independence as they desire. The practical design and service aspects that have been taken into consideration include:

- Life style consultants who assist the village Manager in running the village by providing general assistance. They support the residents in many ways an example includes assisting them in organising events and trips. As there is a minibus on site regular organised shopping trips are arranged to various towns and villages. Lifestyle consultants also arrange any domiciliary care and any assistance that residents may require whilst at the village. In addition building and garden maintenance is managed from this office.

- Safety and security measures such as, CCTV on all of the main streets in the village that is viewed in the security lodge and by residents on their own televisions. The properties are designed with a 24 hour emergency alarm system built in. This system has pull cords fitted in each room, the cords are linked to a Security Office who will contact the necessary emergency service to assist residents. Other design features such as; waist height ovens for ease of lifting, generous number of raised sockets to reduce the amount of bending required to use them; wide doors for wheelchair accessibility; large bathrooms for disabled access; and much more.

- The guest suite permits residents to invite guests to the village and visit them. Residents may have downsized and therefore not have space in their new home for their children and grandchildren to come and stay. The guest suite is a perfect solution to this predicament if such a situation occurs. The suite consists of 2 bedrooms, reading area, bathroom and an open plan kitchen, dining and lounge area. The residents lounge provides an excellent service for residents to keep in contact with loved ones particularly those who reside too far afield to make the round trip in a day. This is just one of the many features that Prestigious Retirement Villages have taken into account when designing the village.

There is a strong community spirit on this site as residents look out for each other whilst respecting each others privacy. They endeavour to lead active independent lifestyles, some of the group sessions that are conducted in the on site Pavilion are lead by residents themselves and include classes such as line dancing.

The success of such gated communities is evident from many countries such as the US, Canada and South Africa where these complexes are popular. The wave of retirement living is just reaching our shores in Britain and the demand for such communities is rapidly rising. This is mainly due to the large demographic of 'baby boomers' who are approaching or entering retirement. The upward shift in the number of pensioners in the UK signifies that the number, style and location of retirement villages is on the up. This can only be a positive consequence as these new developments creates additional choices and options for older people.

For further information on
Middleton Towers or Prestigious Retirement Villages plc
please contact Lorraine Sinclair **01925 822352**
or via email **mail@prestigiousvillages.com**

Orbit Housing Association (www.orbit.org.uk). Housing Association that manages private retirement schemes in England, for older people who want their own property with the benefit of a range of services. Schemes in the Midlands, south-west, south-east and East Anglia.

Pegasus Retirement Homes plc (0800 583 8844; www.pegasus-homes.co.uk). Purpose-built retirement properties for the active retired throughout England. New developments planned, including Cardiff in Wales. Resales are dealt with by Peverel Management Services or local estate agents.

Raven Audley Court plc (www.audleylife.co.uk). High-end luxury retirement apartments converted from existing historic houses in England: Harrogate, Ilkley, Matlock, Newbury, Maidstone, Tunbridge Wells and South Hams.

Wren Homes plc (020 8643 4300; www.wrenhomesplc.co.uk). Surrey-based Wren homes specialises in retirement apartments in south-east England.

RETIREMENT VILLAGES

Those searching for retirement property may overlook retirement villages, believing them to be only for the well off. This is not necessarily the case as many housing charities and local housing organisations now have interests in retirement villages and some residents may be subsidised by local authorities.

Retirement villages are an idea imported from the USA and Australia where they are very popular and comprise purpose-built communities for continuing care. In the UK, they are a relatively recent addition to the options for retired living. The charitable organisation Housing Care Counsel describes them thus: *'An increasingly popular concept. Essentially anything from an estate to a full-blown village-sized development of bungalows, flats or houses'.*

The model for many such communities is Hartrigg Oaks in York, which was opened in 1998 after 10 years' planning and research by the Joseph Rowntree Housing Trust. It comprises 152 spacious one- and two-bedroom bungalows and a 42 en-suite bedroom care centre for the most dependent residents. Typically retirement villages contain more than 100 dwellings and they are aimed at the over-55s, but more usually, the over-60s. Residents may be wholly independent when they move in and the extensive care and support services on site can be brought into play as and when needed. It also suits couples where one partner is wholly independent and the other needs high-level care.

Retirement villages, therefore, appeal to those who wish to plan ahead how their future care needs will be provided while they are still fully able to look after themselves, or if one half of a couple is frail. There are now scores of retirement villages around Britain and most are in England. Many one-off villages are run by trusts or local housing associations. For instance, Staffordshire Housing Association runs Bradeley Village, consisting of 239 apartments in the village complex aimed at people over the age of 55, and aims to maintain a population of about 300.

So, are the elderly being 'pied pipered' out of sight into pleasant ghettos? Some sociology experts have reservations about segregating older people in their own communities, when perhaps there should be more emphasis on promoting balanced mixed-age communities. Economic experts also have their doubts and question the financial viability of retirement villages, especially when it comes to providing care services and high maintenance care such as that needed for those with dementia. Retirement villages claim they can get round this by having mixed tenure residents and a spread of ages and needs, but admit it is a delicate balancing act to maintain financial sustainability.

There is no doubt that many retired people want to be part of regular communities and regard the idea of living on an estate for the elderly as an unappealing option. But life within a safe, gated community is what some retired people want and if so, they should not be put off investigating the possibilities by the mistaken belief that retirement villages are only affordable by the wealthy. Although prices vary depending on the village, one-bedroom apartments start at about £84,000 at Firhall (Moray Firth), £129,000 at St Crispins (Northampton), although £179,000 is a more common starting price, especially in the south-east. Most villages offer a rental option for people who are unable to buy an apartment, or an equity scheme, whereby residents purchase 25% to 75% of their property and pay rental on the remaining percentage. Local authority housing bodies may also pick up the tab for those with social housing needs who are on the lowest incomes.

ASPECTS OF RETIREMENT VILLAGES

■ They function as a communities by encouraging a lot of resident-led activities and a spirit of good neighbourliness, such as helping each other with shopping, for the less agile residents.

■ Financially, they operate on a pooled resources basis that allows for a fixed fee that rises only with inflation so there are no unpleasant surprises. Payments and annual fees paid by each resident go into a central pool and the resulting fund provides care and support services for all residents.

■ A range of facilities is available in the village to all residents and the nature of these will vary from village to village. They are likely to include a café, a restaurant, health activity/sports facilities, library, community shop, hairdressers, beauty salon, computer room, an arts and crafts room and a communal transport vehicle such as a people carrier.

■ Residents have freedom to come and go as they please, but there is ample opportunity for communal activities and forming new friendships within the village. There is also the certainty that when you need more care this will be provided at exactly the right level you require.

(Continued on following page)

> *(Continued)*
>
> ■ Security is of paramount concern to many retired people and retirement villages provide a high level of security and reassurance of personal safety.
>
> ■ If they decide to leave (or the money goes to their estate when they die), residents are guaranteed the original purchase price of their property. Vacant properties are, however, sold at market value and all profits are reinvested in the village. Thus residents are an integral source of subsidy for the village.
>
> ■ Residents get a guarantee that they will not be forced to sell their retirement village property to fund any care needs that they may develop while resident in the village.

Retirement village groups

Caledonian Retreats (01463 227561; www.caledonianretreats.co.uk). Based in Ross-shire. One of the few retirement village developers in Scotland. Also has Firhall Retirement village on the Moray Firth near Nairn. Another site is planned.

Care Village Group (01225 721449; www.carevillagegroup.co.uk). Based in Bath, Care Village Group has five retirement villages: Bath, Cheltenham, Bristol and one in Kent and the Cotswolds.

Extracare Charitable Trust (01159 757860; 01225 721449; www.extracare.org). Based in Nottingham, the Trust has six villages in Birmingham, Sheffield, Milton Keynes, Nottingham and Hereford.

Four Seasons Healthcare (01625 417800; www.fshc.co.uk). Retirement apartments and villages in Harrogate, Galashiels, Isle of Man (two) and Belfast.

Richmond Villages (0845 607 6405; www.richmond-villages.com). Richmond Villages has retirement villages in Nantwich, Coventry, Northampton and Painswick with six future sites planned in central and south-west England. Luxury end. Very steep prices from £429,000 to £799,000 for two and three-bedroom flats. Service charge extra.

Retirement Villages (01372 731888; www.retirementvillages.co.uk). Six villages for the over-55s located in Somerset, Hertfordshire, Surrey, Warwickshire, Cornwall and Oxfordshire.

PARK HOMES

Park homes are essentially mobile homes, but those aimed at the retirement market do not usually resemble an extended caravan, which is most people's idea of a mobile home. Park homes for retirement are also known as prefabricated bungalows, outwardly they resemble bricks-and-mortar housing and are designed for year-round living. They are a popular affordable type of retirement property typically costing 50% less than regular property, and people use them to downsize and free up some income for their retirement. However, there are drawbacks as legally, they are not as secure as bricks-and-mortar housing and you do not own the land on which they are sited. You are also bound by the rules of the site, which vary from one park home site to another. You have to seek an approval from the site owner of any potential new buyer of your park home if you decide to sell it on, and this has been a source of endless legal disputes.

> The legal position of park homeowners has been improved by new legislation contained in the Housing Act 2004. However, living on a park home site, you are still bound by the rules of the site such as no animals or children staying.

New legislation is being introduced in stages to improve the position of park homeowners under the Housing Act 2004. There is also other legislation coming on stream over 2007 and 2008 regarding model standards, a change in the definition of a caravan and site licensing regulations. For further information, see the web page of the Independent Park Homes Advisory Service (www.iphas.co.uk).

ABOUT PARK HOMES AND PARK HOME SITES

- An estimated quarter of a million people live in mobile park homes, not all of them from choice; for some it is the only affordable housing in their area.

- New park homes range in price from about £30,000 to £150,000+ depending on the location and amenities. Some top-of-the-range homes can cost more than the average house price (currently £185,000) in Britain.

- Pre-owned park homes may be cheaper (prices are from £15,000) but as their basic fabric is not as durable as bricks and mortar, buying second-hand may not make financial sense.

- If you are intending to buy a second-hand park home you should have a professional survey done first.

- There are a total of about 2,000 park home sites in England, Scotland and Wales. By law, every park home site must have a licence on display. Owners and managers should be members of the British Holiday and Home Parks Association.

- Park home sites have different rules, for instance regarding keeping pets and children staying on the site, and some are for retired people or the over-50s only.

- The National Park Homes Council checks that all park homes conform to health and safety standards in force at the time of their manufacture and is the specialist representative body for the residential park home industry.

(Continued on following page)

(Continued)

■ Any park home that you buy should be covered by a warranty and conform to British safety standard (BS3632). Various warranty schemes exist including the Gold Shield Ten Year Warranty.

■ Not all park homes will last out your retirement. Some need replacement after two or three decades. However, new technology has improved the durability of modern park homes and some of these may be expected to last 50 or 60 years from manufacture provided that they are well maintained.

Park homes: useful contacts

Britannia Parks (www.britanniaparks.com). Develops and manages residential home parks across the UK. Useful website includes a sample of the new written agreement, lists specialist park home surveyors, and organises park home viewing events.

Independent Park Home Advisory Service (IPHAS) (www.iphas.co.uk). IPHAS is a non-profit voluntary organisation that gives independent advice to anyone contemplating living or who is living in a park home. Gives free advice to members and publishes a range of useful, inexpensive publications to do with all aspects, legal and otherwise of living in a park home.

National Association of Park Home Residents (www.naphr.org) Wholly voluntary advisory service for people living in residential mobile homes. £3–£5 annual membership fee.

National Park Homes Council (NPHC) (01252 336 092; www.theparkhome.net). Based in Aldershot the NPHC represents the park home industry and is a division of the National Caravan Council. Membership includes manufacturers and vendors of park homes and specialist suppliers of products and services to the industry.

Park Home and Holiday Caravan (0845 676 7778; www.phhc.co.uk). Monthly magazine dealing with all aspects of park homes and holiday caravans.

Park Home Living (www.parkhome-living.co.uk). Useful commercial website with information and contacts as well as a home and plot search facility.

Choosing a park home site

There are so many mobile home parks that it can be difficult knowing where to start. Unlike bricks-and-mortar homes, park homes have little individual character; what they do have is their setting and their inhabitants. This means that the key factor in choosing a park home site is the situation of the site, the atmosphere and the character. Some of the contacts mentioned above have a useful link to a park directory and a manufacturers section so you can check out the types of park home and their prices. Looking for a park home site for retirement narrows the choice in that not all parks are suitable or appealing to the over-50s. Most retired people want to live in an attractive park that is well maintained. As with bricks-and-mortar properties, location affects the price; for instance seaside parks come at a premium. You will also probably want to have a good selection of shops and amenities nearby. Some parks have a visiting mobile shop and you can also arrange deliveries but this does not provide the variety that most people would like. It is a good idea to visit as many parks as possible so that you get a feel for what is available and what suits you.

The parks aimed at retired people can be very much in demand. One such, Deanland Wood Park (www.deanlandpark.co.uk) in Sussex, has been established for 50 years. It has all the amenities of a small town, about 400 homes and is near Brighton and Eastbourne. Other retirement sites are much smaller, such as the new (2003) Shillingford Park (www.shillingfordpark.co.uk) near Saundersfoot in Pembrokeshire, which has 37 park homes, or Woodlands Caravan Park, Aberystwyth (woodlandsdevilsbridge.co.uk), which has just 18 retirement homes for the over-60s in a park that is part of a holiday park complex.

Buying a park home

As you do when buying bricks-and-mortar, it is advisable to engage a solicitor to carry out a local search to uncover any potential problems that affect your chosen site. If you are ordering a new park home you may want to check out a few manufacturers' websites to see the range of models virtually before seeing them physically. Larger companies include Wessex Park Homes (www. wessexparkhomes.co.uk) and Home Seeker Homes (www.homeseekerhomes. com). There are annual park home events around the country where you can actually roam around various models and get an even better idea of what you want. Details of such events can be found on the manufacturers' websites. If you are buying a pre-owned home, arrange a meeting with the park owner to introduce yourself and to ensure they are aware of the sale.

Before sealing your purchase, you should also go through the park's conditions with the site owner to make sure that you fully understand them all. You are entitled to a written agreement under the Mobile Homes Act 1983 (revised 1 October 2006), which will clearly define residents' rights and the terms and conditions of the park home site. Under the 2006 revision, a park owner has a legal obligation to recognise and consult with a residents' association and under the same ruling a minimum of 50% of homeowners must be members of the residents' association. Also note that the advertised price of a new park home does not usually reflect the total cost to you. Some of the additional costs related to park home living are given below.

EXTRA COSTS INVOLVED ON PARK HOME SITES

■ The site owner will charge a pitch fee. Under the new ruling of 2006 there are greater restrictions surrounding the review of the pitch fee, which has been misused by unscrupulous park owners in the past.

■ There may also be the cost of a transportation fee on new park homes and the costs of onsite assembly and connection to the utilities.

■ Council tax is payable on a park home in the same way as for a bricks-and-mortar property

■ A maintenance charge is made weekly or monthly towards the shared amenities. Charges vary according to the park, and probably the location, and typically they are in the region of £100–£150 per month.

Park homes: useful contacts and websites

Elderly Accommodation Counsel (advice line 020 7820 1343; www.housingcare. org). Offers free and independent advice on all types of housing for the retired and the elderly.

www.fifty5plus.com (01488 668655; www.fifty5plus.com). A property search website for all kinds of retirement property in selected counties of England.

Retirement Homesearch (0845 880 5560; www.retirementhomesearch.co.uk). Part of the Peverel Group suppliers of property services. Website for buyers and sellers of retirement properties of all types and brand new homes in England, Wales and Scotland. A property search website for all kinds of retirement property in selected counties of England.

How to choose where to retire

CHOOSING THE LOCATION

Choosing the right location can be a nerve-racking process but success is more likely if you carry out as much research as possible before reaching any decisions. Obviously, getting it right is partly about detailed planning, particularly in the financial area, and then deciding what you want from your retirement. For most people retirement is a time of emotional as well as physical upheaval and contains many new challenges and opportunities. How each person goes about dealing with this period of life is as individual as human beings themselves; many will blossom when released from the strict regime of the workplace. Others will fret and flounder when the structure of a working week is withdrawn from their lives. Choosing the area of Britain you want move to is only the first step of the retirement journey. Mapping out your course is the second step and then using the map you have prepared to get there is the third step. What happens when you arrive is where the journey really starts.

The basic criteria for choosing a location are that you need to live somewhere you find congenial, somewhere you can afford, somewhere with amenities you need and somewhere where you can have a lifestyle that will enhance your retirement. However, these fundamentals embrace a multitude of different priorities for different people. Some folk may value excellent cultural facilities and a wide choice of restaurants and bars above access to parks and other green spaces; others may put country air and healthy living at the top of their list. Non-drivers and drivers alike may want to make the most of the generous public transport and rail concessions offered to the over-60s. Then there is the all-important what-feels-right factor, which is hard to define but you know when you are experiencing it. Be prepared to spend some time over choosing the right location. Some of the main factors influencing choice of retirement location are mentioned below.

The seaside premium

Research shows that for the majority of people, retiring to the seaside is their first choice. But going for a coastal location usually means paying a premium, which varies depending on the region. For instance, in the south-west and on the South Coast a sea view can add as much as 40% or even 50% to the cost of property. However, if you go north to resorts such as Scarborough or to less fashionable Colwyn Bay in Wales, the seaside premium is half that. The coast, especially the South Coast, has long been popular with retirees, but nearly all west coast towns in England and Wales have experienced huge price rises of between 150% and 176% since 2001. The most expensive place in England and Wales is Sandbanks near Weymouth in Dorset, which has an average property price of over £500,000. Only three seaside towns in England and Wales have average prices of less than £100,000 and they are all in the north-east (Withernsea in North Humberside, Blyth in Northumberland and Hartlepool in County Cleveland). However, there are still attractive coastal towns where the average property price is reasonable as long as they are not in Cornwall, Devon or Dorset. In addition, many of the South Coast and south-west coastal towns have very high water charges and these have to cover the cost of keeping the beaches and bathing areas clean enough to meet EU standards. If the coastal town of your choice is beyond your budget, consider living in a revamped city or town centre inland, as these are also very attractive places to retire, especially as they have all the facilities you may need on your doorstep. If you get more property for your money inland, you can indulge in lengthy coastal exploration on your holidays.

> Most people in the UK would like to retire to the seaside.

Scotland has much cheaper coastal property than England and Wales but for many southerners, or 'Sassenachs' as they known by those living north of the border, Scotland seems too far away from friends and family. However, if this is not a concern, Scotland is a possibility although there is the Scottish climate to consider: *'Scotland has only two seasons, June and winter'* is a not uncommon quote. However, a recent report released by the Scottish Executive on the implications of climate change in Scotland predicted that Scotland would become warmer in winter (and wetter). You can read the full text at www. Scotland.gov.uk/cru/kd01/ccsi-07.htm. If you are prepared to move to Scotland, you will be rewarded by amazingly affordable prices from about £65,000 (an apartment in Wick) up to £210,000 (a comfortable historic town house in Fortrose). Eyemouth in the Borders has seen the highest rise in property prices and North Berwick is the most expensive coastal town in Scotland (average price £251,509). The cheapest towns are Wick, Fraserburgh, Thurso, Ardrossan and Peterhead. Unfortunately, these may not be the most attractive places. Property prices are higher, but still very reasonable in the prettier towns of Cullen and Nairn, which are popular with retirees.

One of the best sources of house price information for coastal property in England and Wales is the Halifax Building Society which publishes an Annual Seaside Town Review including price tables, on its website at www.hbosplc. com/economy/includes/28-08-06seasidetowns.doc. The Bank of Scotland published its first ever Annual Review of Seaside Towns in Scotland providing prices of property in 26 Scottish seaside towns in 2006 (www.hborsplc.com/economy/includes/27-05-06Scottishseasidetowns.doc).

FACTS AND FIGURES FOR SEASIDE HOMES

■ The 10 most expensive seaside towns in England and Wales are also some of the most popular retirement spots: Budleigh Salterton, Fowey, Lyme Regis, Lymington, Padstow, Rock, Sandbanks, St, Mawes, Sidmouth and Swanage. Of these, Lymington in Hampshire is the only one not in south-west England.

■ The 10 most inexpensive seaside towns are Blyth, Cleethorpes, Fleetwood, Hartlepool, Maryport, Morecambe, Seaham, South Shields, Whitehaven and Withernsea, which are all in northern England on both east and west coasts.

■ In the highest top 20 for the biggest price increases since 2001, one, Seaham in County Durham, has had the highest price rise in England and Wales (181%), followed by Pwllheli (Lleyn Peninsula) in Wales (176%) and Rock in Cornwall (172%).

■ Nine of the towns with the fastest rising prices are in Wales: Aberystwyth, Barry, Caernarfon, Cardigan, Colwyn Bay, Prestatyn, Rhyl, Pwllheli and Tenby.

■ The 10 seaside towns in south-east England with the lowest house prices relative to their region are Bexhill-on-Sea, Clacton-on-Sea, Dover, Folkestone, Hastings, Herne Bay, Margate, Newhaven, Ramsgate and Southend-on-Sea.

■ Seaside property in Scotland is much cheaper than in England and Wales, with starting prices of around £65,000 (Wick).

Climate

The British weather is governed by depressions bringing in wind and rain from the Atlantic which makes the weather anywhere in Britain very changeable. Within this there are general weather trends in different regions that are worth checking out if you want to find the sunniest or mildest place in Britain for your retirement. Rainfall, which seems to preoccupy most of us, is by no means uniformly distributed. The western side of the country tends to be milder and wetter than the eastern side, very high rainfall occurs over mountainous and hilly parts including the western Highlands of Scotland, the Lake District and most of Wales. Parts of Scotland are some of the most rain-soaked spots in Britain with precipitation occurring on most days of the year. The south-east of England and the eastern side of Britain have far less rain and summers can be very dry. Parts of Essex have the lowest rainfall in Britain. More detailed UK climate information can be gained from the Met Office's website www.metoffice.gov.uk. Coasts in particular are likely to be affected by climate change, with very high tides, worsening and frequency of gales, heavier rainfall and the predicted rise in sea levels. The Environment agency has information about flood risks nationally on its website www.environment-agency.gov.uk.

Healthcare provision

When choosing a place to retire it would be advisable to check what National Health Service (NHS) healthcare facilities are provided locally. Younger and fitter retirees may well be happy to live in a secluded rural location. Older people and those with ongoing health concerns will want to be near a large general hospital and to know what medical facilities it provides. These might include an accident and emergency (A&E) unit, cardiac services, intensive care, women's services, or general surgery. Driving 50 miles to receive treatment, especially if you need regular routine appointments, would be very time consuming. Older people are also more likely to anticipate having to have hip and other joint replacements. Typically, retired people moving to a new area ask what the waiting time is locally for such operations. Local dentists are another basic requirement, although they will nearly always turn out to be private. National Health Service dentists are so rare that the arrival of a new NHS dental practice in an area instantly produces a long waiting list. NHS dentists are also listed on the NHS website given below.

Although retirement is a time to anticipate new beginnings and look forward to living your life to the maximum, it is probable that many people will spare more than a few thoughts as to the likely state of their health in 10 or 20 years' time. Although the reorganisation of the NHS seems to involve closing down local hospitals and concentrating services in super hospitals in large cities, there is every likelihood that the health demands of an ageing population will mean that primary healthcare for older people will aim at keeping them healthy for as long as possible. Ideally, to avoid worry, the majority of older folk would like to make private provision for their future health needs, to ensure regular check-ups and a shorter waiting time for the types of operations that are most common in older age groups. However, for many people, private health insurance premiums are too costly, especially on a reduced retirement income, so medical intervention, if needed, will usually depend on local NHS healthcare provision. Larger towns have ample general practitioner (GP) practices, but you should check on their availability in the area where you are thinking of moving, just to make sure there is one nearby. You can find the addresses of primary care trusts (GP practices) by area, as well as information about what specialist hospital departments there are at the nearest hospital, through the NHS website www.nhs.uk which covers the whole of the UK. You can also get healthcare information for Wales on www.wales.nhs.uk and for Scotland on www.show. scot.nhs.uk.

For private care insurance www.privatehealth.com and www.bupahospitals. co.uk are two useful websites with information about private hospitals and their specialties around the UK. Some pensioners have gone abroad to places such as India and France to seek affordable necessary operations. This is always worth considering if you are subjected to a long waiting time or have other concerns about the NHS treatment you may receive. Useful websites for treatment abroad include www.people-logistics.com, www.tajmedical.com and www.treatmentabroad.net. A very useful website that gives advice and help to older people and that also carries detailed information about health services and health reforms in the UK is www.counselandcare.org/uk.

> When choosing a retirement place, people normally want to know how the area is rated for crime. If they have major concerns about security then they may consider a retirement village which has its own 24-hour security system.

Security and crime

Incipient frailty inevitably leads to thoughts about safety and security, which is one of the reasons why specialised retirement property is proving a big hit in Britain. If you are not moving into a security protected retirement complex or a retirement village with 24-hour security provision, you may want to check the crime statistics for the area where you are thinking of moving and also talk to locals about crime trends in their area. Statistically, the south-west and Essex have the lowest crime rates in England and Wales. More information on crime statistics in England and Wales can be found on the Home Office website www.homeoffice.gov.uk. You might also consider doing a self-defence or martial arts course.

RETIREMENT INTERESTS

This is the part of your retirement where the sky is the limit. You may already have well-established interests, on which you have always wanted to spend more time, or ones that you have always wanted to pursue. You might have wanted to restore a vintage car and attend rallies, learn to ride a motorbike, or tango, restore antique furniture, research your family history, take part in archaeological digs, or write and publish a book. To some extent your retirement interests may influence where you retire, for instance if you want to study astronomy, you will want to live somewhere the night skies are not drowned out by 'light pollution', which rules out large parts of England. Or if you want to study art you will want to be somewhere where there is an art college, or by the coast if you want to spend the summers sailing or sea canoeing. Perhaps you want to have a smallholding with animals, or have your own horse and live in a rural environment. Or perhaps you are lucky enough to have a well-funded retirement and want to put something back into the world by volunteering. With the internet to help you, it is possible to discover a range of possibilities, helpful websites and local contacts. Many people consider learning new things in retirement: these can embrace the practical, academic, artistic, sporting, or adventurous. Keeping the brain and body active and keeping socially engaged are the best ways to enjoy a long and fulfilling retirement.

My experience...

80-year-old **Cyril Selby** explains how he keeps himself busy.

Since arriving here, I served four years as Councillor representing the town centre on West Sussex County Council, I have been chairman of one of the local camera clubs, a town guide, and I give slide shows to local groups, among other things. Although I am supposed to be retired, I am a volunteer photographer for English Heritage, taking photographs of listed buildings in and around East and West Sussex. My other half spends two days a week running a coffee shop for the local Red Cross and is the convenor for one of the Scrabble groups in the U3A [see p43]. So we both keep very busy and have made many friends, which we feel is most important at our time of life, because if you don't get up off your backside, you will have an early date with a large wooden box.

If you know that crossword puzzles, sudoku or bridge evenings are not going to fill your ample free time, why not look around for a course or commitment that sparks your interest?

Learning in retirement

Lifelong learning is more than a social policy cliché. For many people it is a pleasurable part of their retirement that unlocks innate curiosity and gives it a direction and a quest, and often has a spin-off in enhancing social contact. Since the 1960s, distance and flexible learning opportunities for older age groups have been expanding. These embrace home-based and class-based learning and sometimes a mixture of the two. Open University studies, while pursued mainly in front of a personal computer, also include regular summer schools for its students. There is also a University of the Third Age specifically aimed at older people, which is primarily sociable and unites people with similar interests. Overall, it has never been easier for older people who have become masters of their own time to study. There are estimated to be upwards of 600,000 over-60s currently on courses of learning in England alone. Many universities that have modular degrees offer reduced fees, (often 50% less) for the over-60s on their *modular* courses. A module can be in practically any subject; do enough modules and you can clock up a degree. Or you can do a course in local history such as those run by York and Oxford universities. You can find out what modular courses the nearest university to you has by looking on their website.

> Find out what modular courses the nearest university to you has by looking on their website.

The type of learning that you want to pursue may affect your choice of retirement place. For instance, do you want to be near a city college or university with all the study resources on hand that this implies? Do you want to participate in classes and the organised trips that are an intrinsic part of many such courses? Alternatively, would you be content with home-based learning using your computer and dealing with your tutor online? Home-based learning often takes more self-discipline but it does mean that you can follow courses from anywhere in the UK, at times to suit you. Thousands of online courses are available and a useful website for these is www.learndirect.co.uk which also has regional advice centres to help you get started on a course. Living in a university city is not essential for courses with classes, but will almost certainly give you the widest choice of subject matter.

Many local authorities in cities and larger towns also run their own part-time non-vocational courses under the adult learning banner. They offer a wide range of subjects including yoga, painting, aromatherapy, French conversation, belly dancing, writing poetry and computer and IT skills. A few years ago, many such courses were free for the over-60s but progressive government cutbacks on subsidies for adult learning mean that many of these courses are now charged at the full fee to pensioners. Even so, costs are very reasonable. There is no standard pricing of such courses across the UK, or even across England, Wales or Scotland, so details will have to be obtained locally.

THE OPEN UNIVERSITY

■ The Open University was pioneered in the 1970s and was *'Open to those who do not have the traditional entry qualifications'*. The internet has changed the way that it delivers its basic tutorials to students. The OU stopped teaching via television in 2006 and is now entirely internet-based. The television programmes are still available as archive material, but have to be downloaded from the internet. Obviously, a personal computer is essential for following OU courses. You can learn more about the OU from www.open.ac.uk or telephone 0845 300 6090 for an application pack.

■ 10% of OU students are over 55 years old and the OU is now targeting the retirement age group to increase this percentage.

■ OU courses are divided into 13 subject areas including modern languages, the humanities, social sciences, information technology, computing and the web.

■ The cost of OU courses depends on how many and which ones you take. Sample costs include £395 for nine months' Spanish or an OU degree in computing and IT £3,500 (spread over five years).

■ The OU can provide financial support if you are on a household income of less than £25,645 (£15,345 if you live in Scotland). Having a dependent partner ups the threshold at which financial support is available. The OU pays some or all of your course fees and may provide help with buying a computer. Further details of all financial support and application forms can be downloaded from the website or requested on the telephone when you register.

■ Those with a disability may get extra funding regardless of financial circumstances.

■ The OU's latest initiative is Open Learning, where it has made some of its teaching material and resources available free on the internet to anyone.

■ OU qualifications are recognised as having academic validity, unlike the University of the Third Age (see below), which promotes study for recreational purposes.

THE UNIVERSITY OF THE THIRD AGE

■ Now over 22 years old, the University of the Third Age (U3A) is represented in the UK by the Third Age Trust. Other U3A groups are based in Europe, Australia, New Zealand and South Africa. The UK group is U3A UK (0208 315 0199) (www.u3aonline.org). According to their website: *'U3As are self-help, self-managed lifelong learning cooperatives for older people no longer in full-time work, providing opportunities for their members to share learning experiences in a wide range of interest groups and to pursue learning, not for qualifications, but for fun.'*

A range of age groups use the U3A and there are many members in their 80s and 90s. There are course fees and a small annual membership fee, which help fund the project. A voluntary profile of tutors and tutored is requested.

■ The U3A offers both tutored and untutored courses and subjects include creative writing, western philosophy, writing family history, maintaining independence, digital imaging astronomy, the Romans and art history.

■ There are no exams, but there are activities connected with some subjects intended to ensure progress.

■ It is possible for members to write a course for other U3A members. Professional tutors are not normally used, although some groups happen to have retired academics among their membership.

■ The U3A is based around local groups and lessons take place in members' homes or online.

■ Field trips and other visits based around the courses may be arranged.

■ The U3A is a lifeline for many pensioners and helps to keep them mentally healthy and involved in the community where they live.

■ Membership extends up to the fourth age (80s and 90s).

■ According to the U3A's own research, about a third of the membership have joined for social reasons and a significant number of these hope to meet others with similar interests.

Volunteering

After a long high-powered working life many retirees are not ready to devote themselves entirely to the golf course and round-the-world cruising, as they rightly feel that they still have much to contribute to society around them. Freed from the need to earn a fat salary to make them feel valued, their new incentive is not financial but altruistic, or a simple need to make a difference. Volunteering provides an outlet for all kinds of expertise, from giving the local charity shop boutique appeal and tripling its income, to running the local branch of a national housing charity. If you want to do some good and derive health benefits, then why not help with outdoor maintenance at a local woodland trust, or if you have business expertise advise local young entrepreneurs. There are a huge number of possibilities for immensely satisfying volunteer work.

The kind of volunteering you want to do can affect your choice of retirement place. If you are passionate about theatre or music, you may want to live in a city with vibrant theatre or big arts festivals where you can volunteer as a steward or usher and see many of the events for free. Most theatres and concert halls have a volunteer scheme whereby you work front of house or cloakroom or sell refreshments in return for free tickets. If you feel strongly that children should be encouraged to play more sports and you have coaching experience that you can put to good use, you will want to move somewhere with good sports facilities. Perhaps you see yourself volunteering in the great outdoors in a national park, heritage garden, or nature reserve.

Volunteering websites

British Trust for Conservation Volunteers (www.btcv.org). Promotes practical conservation work. Thousands of opportunities throughout the UK offered all year, every year via their website.

The National Trust (www.nationaltrust.org.uk/volunteering). Britain's best known guardian of many of the nation's greatest architectural treasures, as well as coast and countryside properties, offers thousands of volunteering opportunities from gardeners to guardians.

Retired and Senior Volunteer Programme (RSVP) (www.csv-rsvp.org.uk). RSVP is a free-standing programme within CSV (Community Service Volunteers) that utilises the experience and skills of the over-50s to benefit their local area in England, Scotland and Wales.

Retired Executives Action Clearing House (REACH) (www.reach-online.org.uk). Recruits and supports people with managerial, technical and professional expertise and places them in part-time, unpaid roles in voluntary organisations near where they live, anywhere in the UK. No age limits and no charges to the volunteer.

Timebank (www.timebank.org.uk). National charity that connects would-be volunteers with opportunities in their own community. Lots of ideas, contacts and inspiring stories.

Volunteering England (www.volunteering.org.uk). Provides regional contacts for volunteering and much more information about volunteering throughout England.

Volunteer Scotland (www.volunteerscotland.org.uk). All types of volunteer work, all over Scotland.

Volunteering Wales (www.volunteering-wales.net). Details of volunteer bureaux throughout Wales.

Part 2
Places to retire in Britain

Where to retire in Britain at a glance

Place	Good for	Less good for	Page
North-east England			
Berwick-upon-Tweed Eastern Scottish Borders and Northumbrian Coast	■ Birdwatching ■ Clean air ■ History ■ Moulting mute Swans ■ Peace and quiet ■ Scenery ■ Walking	■ Fifty miles from the nearest city ■ ASBO seagulls ■ Poor shopping ■ Very small arts/entertainments scene	110
Scarborough North York Moors	■ Lively, traditional Victorian seaside town ■ Two magnificent bays ■ Good shopping ■ Arts scene ■ Wonderful walking	■ Long way from an international airport	106
North-west England			
Chester Welsh Borders	■ Attractive, compact town ■ Beautiful surroundings ■ Affluent ■ Lifestyle ■ Transport connections ■ Walking country	■ Expensive and touristy ■ Some areas of the town are rough and should be avoided	126
Kendal Lake District	■ Affordable property ■ Holistic spirituality big in the area ■ Scenery ■ Transport connections	■ Area experiencing decline ■ Low incomes	114

(Continued on following page)

Place	Good for	Less good for	Page

North-west England *(Continued)*

Place	Good for	Less good for	Page
Southport Merseyside	■ Tremendous facilities and ambience ■ Arts scene ■ Flat and easy to get around ■ Transport connections	■ Some resentment towards incomers ■ Rise in number of storm events observed in recent winters	122
Whitehaven Lake District	■ Historic, attractive town with Georgian architecture ■ Money poured in for regeneration ■ Natural beauty and wonderful views ■ Friendly locals	■ Lacks arts scene ■ Sellafield nuclear reprocessing plant a few miles south	118

Central England

Place	Good for	Less good for	Page
Cheltenham Spa Cotswolds	■ Arts ■ Beautiful surroundings ■ Shopping	■ Popular with chavs	215
Chipping Campden Cotswolds	■ Arty ■ Friendly ■ History ■ Social life and clubs ■ Peace and quiet ■ Walking	■ Car essential ■ Parking ■ Small town	219
Harrogate Yorkshire Dales	■ Elegance ■ Upmarket amenities and facilities ■ Bustling ■ Beautiful surroundings ■ Walking	■ Higher than average property prices ■ Infrequent rail service	64
Hereford The Marches	■ Countryside ■ Flat level ■ History ■ Social life ■ Transport connections	■ Not much to keep the grandchildren amused	231

Leamington Spa East Midlands	■ Architecture ■ Green spaces ■ Shopping ■ Transport connections	■ Said to be not as friendly as many other places	223

Great Malvern
Malvern Hills
	■ Arts scene
	■ Fabulous countryside
	■ Great for active types
	■ Transport Connections
		■ People who've retired
		  there don't want
		  anyone else to know
		  about how great it is
			227

Shrewsbury The Marches	■ Council tax low (band E £1,192) ■ History ■ Medieval buildings ■ Transport connections	■ Traffic congestion	233

East England

Fakenham East Anglia	■ Attractive town ■ Beautiful surrounding area ■ Near the sea ■ Cheaper than Holt	■ Lacks arts scene ■ Has a reputation for dullness	68

Frinton-on-Sea
East Anglia
	■ Select atmosphere
	■ Primarily residential and
	  retired
	■ Smart small shops
	■ Everything within walking
	  distance
	■ Peace and quiet
		■ Perhaps *too* select
		■ Terminally bored
		  youths
			71

Holt
East Anglia
	■ Health service above average
	■ Low crime
	■ Upmarket shops and galleries
	■ Pretty small town
		■ Filling up with ex-
		  Londoners
		■ Nearest serious arts
		  scene Norwich
			75

Hunstanton
The Wash
	■ Flat seafront
	■ Compact
	■ Miles of beaches
	■ Good for the less agile
	■ Fabulous walks
	■ Lively arts
		■ Very busy roads in
		  summer
		■ High percentage of
		  over 60s
			92

(Continued on following page)

Place	Good for	Less good for	Page

East England *(Continued)*

Place	Good for	Less good for	Page
King's Lynn The Wash	■ Annual arts festival ■ History ■ Attractive architecture ■ Beautiful surrounding area	■ Growing fast and developers are moving in	95
Mablethorpe Lincolnshire Fens and Wolds	■ Inexpensive eating places ■ Traditional seaside place ■ Fabulous sandy beach ■ Everywhere easily accessible for the disabled	■ Nearest hospital is 40 minutes away ■ Cold east winds in winter ■ Very quiet out of season ■ High proportion of transients ■ A bit run down	85
Skegness Lincolnshire Fens and Wolds	■ Compact town ■ Flat for miles ■ Great bus services ■ Big supermarkets ■ Short hospital waiting times	■ Whiplash wind off the North Sea ■ Very busy in summer ■ Caravan parks	88
Southend-on-Sea East Anglia	■ Majesty of the great tidal estuary of River Thames ■ Quiet walks towards Shoeburyness ■ London easily accessible ■ Lots to do for retired people	■ Largest town in Essex ■ Bingo halls along the seafront ■ Pretty low-lying ■ Drunken rowdies at night	77
Southwold East Anglia	■ Picture-book pretty ■ Time stands still (almost) ■ Cosmopolitan ■ Vibrant community of professionals, artisans and the retired ■ Marvellous walking from the town	■ Houses sell as fast as Glastonbury tickets	80
Spalding The Wash	■ Georgian architecture ■ Fascinating area ■ Friendly ■ Tulips and daffodils (fields of them) ■ Lots of space ■ Landscapes and big skies	■ Increased risk of flooding from global warming	97

South-east England

Herne Bay North Kent Coast	■ Quiet ■ Affordable ■ Improving facilities ■ Travel connections	■ Winds straight from the Arctic ■ Windfarm eyesore	158

Rye
Romney
Marshes
	■ History
	■ Pretty medieval walled town
	■ Seclusion
	■ Handy for Dover and
	  Folkestone
	■ Great for cycling, walking,
	  birdwatching
		■ Very expensive
		■ Lydd airport may
		  expand
		■ Sparse bus services
			161

South-west England

Bath Spa West Country	■ Elegant architecture ■ Sophisticated lifestyle ■ Massive arts scene ■ Cool shops	■ Mega tourism spot ■ Nightmare parking ■ Expensive	178

Dorchester
West Country
	■ Lively arts scene
	■ Transport connections
		■ Conservative with a
		  big 'C'
		■ Poundbury extension on
		  outskirts
			181

Exmouth West Country	■ Famous beach and views ■ Easy connection to nearby Exeter	■ Prevailing winds	185

Isle of Portland
West Country
	■ Beautiful seascapes
	■ Outdoor life
	■ Relatively cheap property
	■ Fairly undiscovered
	■ An island, but not an isolated
	  one
		■ Limited property comes
		  on to the market and is
		  snapped up for holiday
		  homes
		■ No big supermarkets
			187

Minehead
West Country
	■ Beautiful surrounding
	  countryside
	■ Slightly cheaper property than
	  the South Coast
		■ A bit off the main routes
		  (also an advantage?)
		■ Car essential
		■ Very quiet in winter
			191

(Continued on following page)

Place	Good for	Less good for	Page

South-west England *(Continued)*

Place	Good for	Less good for	Page
Poole West Country	■ Aquatic sports and sailing *par excellence* ■ One of the top retirement places in Britain ■ High level of care services for the elderly	■ The most expensive retirement place in Britain ■ Hilly	194
Roseland Peninsula Cornwall	■ Unique scenery ■ Water-based activities ■ Peaceful ■ Wonderful walking ■ Several pretty hamlets ■ Mild climate ■ Sociable and friendly area	■ Nearest large supermarket is 12 miles ■ Isolated	168
Salisbury West Country	■ Beautiful, timeless city ■ Culturally lively ■ Excellent transport links	■ Doesn't move with the times ■ Planners managed to do some damage to historic buildings in the 50s and 60s	197
Seaton West Country	■ Less crowded than many more popular resorts ■ Beautiful surrounding countryside and coast ■ Friendly ■ Long, flat seafront easily accessible for the less mobile	■ Less attractive seafront than many seaside places ■ Considered downmarket	199
Sidmouth West Country	■ Busy socially ■ Good amenities and arts scene ■ Sidmouth Folk Week every August	■ Expensive property ■ Reputation as hardcore oldie town ■ Too much traffic on the seafront	202
St Austell Cornwall	■ Largest town in Cornwall ■ Expanding ■ Town centre being modernised ■ Lots to do for over-50s ■ Local adult learning facilities excellent ■ Clean air	■ Flooded with visitors in summer ■ Aesthetic appeal lacking	171

Spalding The Wash	■ Georgian architecture ■ Fascinating area ■ Friendly ■ Tulips and daffodils (fields of them) ■ Lots of space ■ Landscapes and big skies	■ Increased risk of flooding from global warming	97
Swanage West Country	■ History ■ Beautiful, compact town ■ Fantastic location	■ Litter, traffic and public transport all need attention ■ Car essential	205
Torpoint Cornwall	■ Only one road into town ■ History and geography have kept it small ■ Spectacular wider surroundings ■ Frequent ferry to Plymouth	■ Opposite the industrial naval dockyards (eyesore) ■ Climate tends to be rainy	173
Torquay West Country	■ Balmy climate ■ Home to a national flagship hospital	■ Intimidating inebriates around harbour side	208
Weymouth West Country	■ Fantastic harbour area ■ Sailing paradise ■ Wonderful walking ■ Transport connections	■ Limited shopping ■ Limited arts scene ■ Not exciting enough for some people	210

South Coast

Bognor Regis South Coast and the New Forest	■ Lots of seafront retirement property ■ Good hospital in nearby Chichester ■ Cheaper than usual south coast property ■ In beautiful West Sussex	■ Poor shopping ■ Tatty seafront ■ Culturally dull	129
Bournemouth South Coast and the New Forest	■ Beaches ■ Beautiful walks ■ Everything you need near at hand ■ Lively (some say overly so) nightlife	■ Expensive ■ Very crowded in summer ■ Centre rowdy at night	132

(Continued on following page)

Place	Good for	Less good for	Page

South Coast *(Continued)*

Place	Good for	Less good for	Page
Chichester South Coast and the New Forest	■ Arts ■ History ■ Gentility and elegance ■ Computer literate seniors	■ Expensive ■ Third of residents are over 60 ■ Excessive traffic and parking problem	135
Christchurch South Coast and the New Forest	■ Strong identity ■ History ■ Mediterranean microclimate ■ Pleasant lifestyle ■ Retirement developments	■ In high crime area ■ Part of Bournemouth conurbation ■ 1 in 4 of the population is over 60	137
Eastbourne South Coast and the New Forest	■ Sunshine record ■ Beaches ■ Public gardens ■ Smart amenities ■ Safe (except at night)	■ Loutish drinkers	140
Isle of Wight South Coast and the New Forest	■ Congestion free roads ■ Best beaches in England	■ Roads in disrepair ■ Expensive/inconvenient getting on and off the island	142
The New Forest South Coast and the New Forest	■ History ■ Large animals roaming free ■ Commoners' rights ■ Outdoor activities ■ Transport connections	■ Rising older population ■ National Park status attracts trampling hordes ■ Expensive	146
Shoreham-by-Sea South Coast and the New Forest	■ Historic river estuary setting ■ Picturesque ■ Excellent climate ■ Conservation area ■ Traditional houseboat community	■ Surrounding area very built up ■ Fairly inactive economically ■ Not much property comes on the market	150
Worthing South Coast and the New Forest	■ Excellent bus and train services ■ Excellent medical facilities ■ Core development plan underway ■ Cheaper property than Brighton & Hove	■ May just be the town with highest number of oldies in Britain	152

Isles of Scilly

St Mary's	■ Beauty of landscape ■ Calmer pace of life ■ Climate is mild ■ Crime almost non-existent ■ Dinghy sailing and many other water and outdoor activities ■ Friendly people	■ Arts (but not artists) are very limited ■ Expensive property ■ Few properties on the market ■ Premium on everyday shopping ■ Fog ■ Hospital on island is limited ■ Isolated	101

North Wales

Llandudno North Wales Coast	■ Pretty town ■ Spectacular views ■ Fantastic Victorian promenade ■ Nice and flat for the less agile ■ Great walking nearby for the more agile	■ Beaches packed in summer ■ Unsophisticated	243
Moelfre Anglesey	■ Mild climate ■ On very beautiful island ■ Fantastic bird and nature watching ■ Empty beaches ■ Good connections to mainland ■ Walking ■ Wonderful community life for older folk	■ 75% over 65 years of age ■ Remote from most places	240
Rhyl North Wales Coast	■ Beautiful, wild surroundings ■ Cheaper property than most seaside places ■ Not remote ■ Two hospitals ■ Two airports within a hour's drive ■ Excellent road connections	■ Run down over the last ten years ■ Run down housing inhabited by unemployed and those with drug problems ■ Fallout from the Chernobyl nuclear disaster (1986) reached Rhyl ■ Too many charity shops and subject to car boot sale mania	246

(Continued on following page)

Place	Good for	Less good for	Page

South Wales

Place	Good for	Less good for	Page

Brecon
Brecon Beacons
	■ Fabulous surroundings
	■ Safety
	■ Sociable
	■ Theatre and arts
	■ Walking
	■ Clean air
		■ Late night brawling
		  outside pubs
		■ Predominantly older
		  population
		■ No pedestrian precinct/
		  too much traffic
		■ Small
			251

Abergavenny Brecon Beacons	■ Pretty town ■ Glorious surroundings ■ Public transport ■ Theatre	■ Mostly middle class ■ Drug problem in parts ■ Rain ■ Shopping	249
Swansea Swansea Bay	■ Arts events ■ Waterfront regeneration ■ Beaches ■ Gower Peninsula ■ Transport connections	■ High crime rate ■ High rainfall ■ Large, busy commercial city	254

Tenby and Saundersfoot
Pembrokeshire Coast
	■ Clean air
	■ Friendly people
	■ History and beautiful walled
	  town (Tenby)
	■ Pretty village (Saundersfoot)
	■ Sea clear enough to see your
	  feet in
	■ Fabulous beaches and
	  surroundings
		■ Cultural desert
		■ Inebriated stag and hen
		  weekenders (Tenby)
		■ Throngs in summer
		■ Fairly remote
		■ Bus services poor
			258

Central Wales

Place	Good for	Less good for	Page

Builth Wells
Upper Wye Valley
	■ Wide range of amenities
	■ Beautiful surroundings
	■ Community spirit
	■ Fishing mecca
	■ Safe and friendly
	■ Wonderful walking
		■ Car essential
		■ Expensive petrol
		■ Local community hospital
		  may be closing
		■ Rugby mad
		■ Small town where
		  everyone knows
		  everyone's business
			237

North Scotland

Shetland Shetland	■ Community spirit ■ Unpolluted ■ High standard of living and amenities ■ Longevity ■ Midnight fishing in summer	■ Alcohol abuse and associated violence on the rise ■ Nearest acute hospital is Aberdeen ■ Treeless ■ Winter makes you suicidal	274

East Scotland

Dunfermline Kingdom of Fife	■ Friendly people ■ Strong on community ■ Beautiful region ■ Big shops ■ Easy access to Edinburgh and many other interesting towns and cities ■ Great bus services	■ Bad driving and accidents	267
Perth Ancient County of Perth	■ History ■ Handsome architecture ■ Bustling ■ Compact ■ Amenities and shops ■ Beautiful surroundings ■ Great walking and golf ■ Less through traffic than many places	■ Historical flooding problems (may be resolved by new flood defences) ■ Cool summers	270

Central Scotland

Stirling The Lowlands	■ Attractive town and stunning castle ■ Scottish history in buckets ■ Fabulous surroundings including the Trossachs and Loch Lomond ■ Less than an hour from Edinburgh and Glasgow	■ Flooding. As recently as 2006 parts of the Riverside area of Stirling were underwater and inhabitants had to rescued by the fire brigade	263

Central northern England

YORKSHIRE DALES

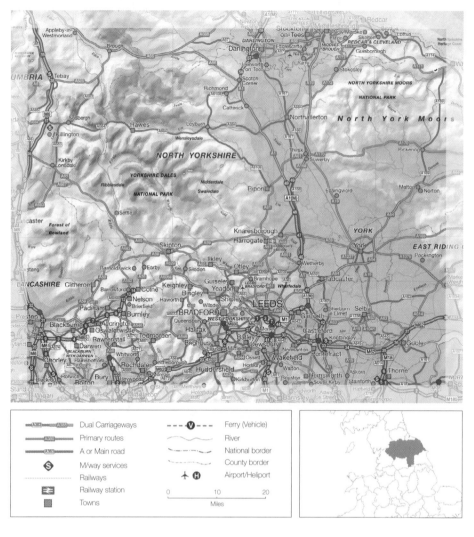

Dual Carriageways	Ferry (Vehicle)	
Primary routes	River	
A or Main road	National border	
M/way services	County border	
Railways	Airport/Heliport	
Railway station		
Towns	0 10 20	
	Miles	

The Yorkshire Dales refers to the area north of the Yorkshire towns Settle, Skipton, Ilkley, Otley and Harrogate and it is bordered on the west by the M6 between Tebay and Killington, and Scotch Corner and Knaresborough to the east. In some definitions it extends north into Teesdale. Those of a certain age will remember the television series *All Creatures Great and Small* about a vet, which was set in a fictional Yorkshire village and portrayed a rather folksy image of the Dales. The series may not have aged as well as the eternally beautiful scenery in which it was shot. Another more recent television series with a Dales backdrop is *Emmerdale*. The Dales' cinematic appeal extends to the big screen also. *Calendar Girls* is just one of several major films set in and around the area. The characteristic landscape of The Dales is formed by lush valleys with white limestone crests. The Dales include familiar names such as Swaledale, Nidderdale, Airedale, Wharfedale and Ribblesdale. The green swathes of the Dales are criss-crossed by drystone walls, which mark out interconnected fields and pastures. These are still grazed by local breeds of sheep, on whose backs the Yorkshire mills and cloth industry were once built. Shaped by elemental forces and manicured by man and beast, there is a geological fascination about the Dales. Beneath the surface, an underworld of giant cave chambers and subterranean rivers, weird forests of stalagmites and stalactites, waterfalls, and networks of passageways attract intrepid potholers and cavers from all over the world, while the surface attracts walkers and hikers.

Many areas of the Dales are protected areas of National Park and having all this natural beauty on your doorstep is a heady experience that tempts retirees to settle there. However, it is advisable to choose your spot to retire to very circumspectly, or pick one of the larger towns of the Dales such as Harrogate, rather than the villages. There may be a certain amount of animosity directed at those who are buying their dream retirement properties in the Dales and pricing local people out of the market, as journalist John Sheard found when he retired there. His article about *'offcumdens'* (the local word for incomers) appeared in the online internet gateway for the Dales, *daelnet* (www.daelnet. co.uk/news) from which this is extracted:

After some 25 years of Fleet Street stress, my York-born wife and I bought a cottage in a Yorkshire Dales village, which shall remain nameless. After the usual three days of removals, we were more or less tidied up and decided to celebrate by having Sunday lunch in the village pub. I had barely taken the top off my firstever village pint when a local lady came up to me and snarled that we 'offcumdens' were paying such ridiculous prices for property that we were forcing members of her family out. We had taken a huge drop in income to move to the Dales, we were working and not wealthy retirees, and we wanted to become part of the community. It never happened. We moved six miles away after just 18 months and, I am delighted to report, have lived happily ever after.

Harrogate

Harrogate is situated on the eastern edge of the Dales and together with Ripon is one of two main historic centres in the region. Harrogate's main claim to fame is the medicinal springs, which have been in use since their 'discovery' in 1571. The town became fashionable for taking the waters at the beginning of the 19th century. Harrogate is lively and affluent, with its bustling spa town atmosphere and café culture, enhanced by the Harrogate International Centre (www.harrogateinternationalcentre.co.uk), a world-class venue for conferences, exhibitions, events and entertainment. Harrogate's character is derived largely from its glory days as a fashionable spa town with gracious parks and huge hotels, many of them built in the early 20th century. In 2004, restoration of the original (1897) Turkish baths was completed. These are now the council run Turkish Baths and Health Spa where you can (in modern parlance) detoxify your system through the steam and hot rooms, and be relaxed by modern beauty treatments such as a chocolate wrap. Use of the Turkish Baths costs £13 for the recommended two and a half hours; a modest charge compared with privately run amenities in other spa towns. An economically thriving town, Harrogate is also the preferred home of those working in Leeds and Bradford, who can afford the higher-than-average property prices of this popular town.

Harrogate has a reputation for excellent shopping and has a staggering numbers of bars, cafés and restaurants. It also has a strong community safety partnership, which means it is considerably safer to be out at night than some other well-known towns. It also has a lower level of recorded social problems, but then it has fewer than average people in the 20–34 age group and has no college of higher education. Despite the lack of adult learning facilities, working people in the town have a higher than average level of qualifications, usually to at least National Vocational Qualification (NVQ) level and they are hardworking and prosperous.

My experience...

Bill Mallinson, aged 72, moved from Gloucester with his wife to Harrogate 12 years ago.

We were both born in Yorkshire in what is now a suburb of Leeds. We've lived in several places since then, but we always had in mind that when I reached retirement age, we would come back to Yorkshire and of all the places in Yorkshire, Harrogate seemed the most attractive. It's medium-sized, I think it's ideal for people retiring. I suppose it's a kind of nostalgia. We're Yorkshire people and we feel comfortable here. We knew Harrogate reasonably well and it's a place I used to visit on outings as a boy. So we knew it from that point of view, but not as a place to live. The town itself is a very pleasant town in a very beautiful setting. It's right on the edge of the Yorkshire Dales and just a short drive beyond that is the North Yorkshire Moors. The beautiful scenery is one of the reasons we moved here. We are quite keen walkers, but we're getting less keen as we get older. We still walk probably two or three miles a day. It takes about 35 minutes to walk from our house into the centre of town and sometimes we do that, sometimes we take the car part way. It's a beautiful town; one of the best parts is the area of big open space called 'The Stray', which makes a semi-circle round the town centre. It's 200 acres of open space, mostly grass with trees and flowers, which is there for people to enjoy; you can picnic on it, walk on it and it gives the town a very open, spacious feel as opposed to a lot of places where you feel hemmed in by buildings. Harrogate consists of two towns really: Harrogate and Knaresborough, which is nearly – but not quite – joined on.

Local transport services are very good around the town and, of course, free for us. Buses go every five minutes to Knaresborough and there is a bus service every 20 minutes to Leeds which is 15 miles away, and that is free as well. The train service isn't quite as good as you have to change at Leeds or York wherever you want to go. Leeds Bradford airport is good for European destinations, but we tend to do most of our flying from Manchester.

We find people very friendly in this area. We are both involved in U3A. I've found that it's a great benefit to retired people. In the town, there are lots of recreational facilities; we have a professional theatre and we have several amateur operatic and dramatic societies, a concert hall, choral society, two orchestras, and brass bands. As it's a tourist and conference town, there are lots of restaurants, cafés, coffee places, that sort of thing and eating out is relatively inexpensive as there is a lot of competition. As far as I'm concerned it's a well-run town and the Council is doing a good job, but it isn't like Eastbourne, there's a good mix of retired and locally employed people who commute to Leeds or Bradford and that's a positive thing.

Harrogate fact file

Access: Midway between ports of Hull and Liverpool. Leeds via M1 17 miles; York 21 miles; Manchester, 79 miles

Airports: Leeds–Bradford (www.lbia.co.uk), 15 miles; Manchester (www.manairport.co.uk), 85 miles

Average property price: Higher than the national average at £261,383 (predicted to go up by a third in the next five years)

Bus services: Transdev (01423 56061) (www.harrogateanddistrict.co.uk). Main operator of bus services in Harrogate and Knaresborough. Bus2Jet bus service to Leeds–Bradford airport.

Climate: Above-average sunshine hours per year and below average rainfall

Council: Harrogate Borough Council (01423 500600; www.harrogate.gov.uk)

Council tax: Band D £1,335.33; band E £1,632.07

Crime: Rated in the top third in the UK for low crime

Economic activity: In the top 6% of UK areas for economic activity

Ferries: P&O (www.poferries.com) Hull to Rotterdam and Zeebrugge

Hospital: Harrogate District Hospital (www.hdft.nhs.uk) has an excellent reputation for treatment of the over-50s, despite the high percentage of older people. Awarded Best Small Hospital Of The Year Award 2007 (Dr Foster Hospital Guide).

Percentage of people over 65: 17.4% (1.5% above national average)

Population: Approximately 69,000 (with surrounding district including Knaresborough 151,339)

Property prices: Flat, £181,739; Semi-detached, £268,842; Detached, £489,142

Railway station: Harrogate. Most trains to Harrogate involve changing at Leeds or York. There is a weekday service to London King's Cross via Leeds (3 hours 30 mins) or via York (2 hours 45 mins).

Residents' on-street parking permit: £15 per year (£25 for two years), 50% discount for over-60s

Specialised retirement property: Hollins Hall, Harrogate (01423 524115) provides assisted living in 71 upmarket new homes (from £243,000) built by Audley Court. Granby Gardens long-term leasehold luxury apartments (Four Seasons Healthcare).

East England

EAST ANGLIA

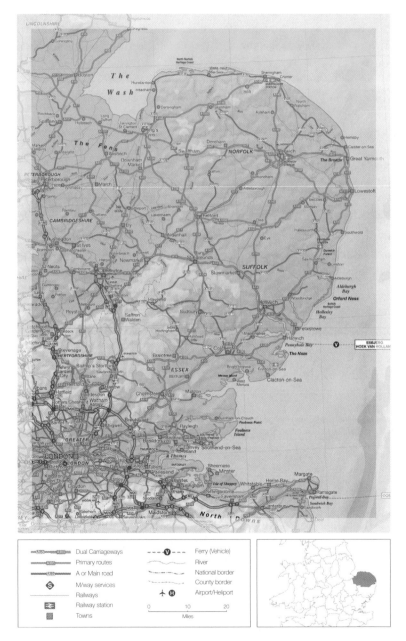

Dual Carriageways		--- **V** ---	Ferry (Vehicle)
Primary routes			River
A or Main road			National border
S	M/way services		County border
	Railways	**✈ H**	Airport/Heliport
≠	Railway station	0 10 20	
■	Towns	Miles	

The area known as East Anglia is the large bulbous area projecting out of the eastern side of England from the Humber to the Thames Estuary, which contains the counties of Norfolk, Suffolk and Essex. Its coasts, unlike those of the south-west of England, are exposed to the bracing effects of the Atlantic. As a report on East Anglia commissioned by Greenpeace for windfarms in 2002 put it: 'There is enough offshore wind energy in this one region alone to completely replace all of the UK's outdated and dangerous nuclear power stations.'

The inland county of Cambridgeshire is also traditionally in East Anglia, and sometimes Bedfordshire and Hertfordshire are included as well. East Anglia is named from the Anglo-Saxons (two tribes that intermingled) after invading the area from north-west Germany. Their kingdoms formed a loose federation of East Anglia and included North and Suth Folk (now Norfolk and Suffolk) in the AD400s. In the late AD800s the Danes took over the whole of East Anglia and the area beyond it as far as the East Midlands.

East Anglia is characterised by its attractive market towns such as Fakenham and Holt; seaside resorts including Cromer, Great Yarmouth, Southwold, Frinton-on-Sea and Walton-on-the-Naze; its flatness; the richness of the soil (particularly in Norfolk and Suffolk) and its low lying watery or ex-watery environments such as The Wash on the north Norfolk coast; the Norfolk and Suffolk Broads and the Fens which reach out from the Wash into Cambridgeshire. For many centuries it remained rural and isolated and dependent on agricultural production, with windmills a familiar sight. In many ways the level territory makes it an excellent retirement area with endless possibilities for gentle walking and cycling.

Large numbers of retirees and others are moving into the under-populated areas of East Anglia, particularly Norfolk, and helping to stimulate the area's economy, as well as pushing up house prices. Not all of this is regarded as progress by the indigenous population, who may seem as flinty as the soil that bred them, but incomers are present and arriving in sufficient numbers to make a social life among themselves.

Fakenham

Fakenham is a historic market town in the north of Norfolk, surrounded by heathland and quaintly named villages: Fulmodestone, Toftrees, Little Snoring, South Creake, Guist and Whissonsett among them. North Norfolk has been experiencing something of a property boom in the last decade; property prices there were some of the last in England to show major increases in value. The reason Norfolk real estate lagged behind the rises in other parts of the country is that north Norfolk is considered rather remote from civilisation. The railway may have arrived in 1848 but the line was axed in 1965 and Fakenham has been battling ever since to get a link to the mainline services at Norwich. Through the centuries the main industries of the town, including three mills, powered by the River Wesum, have been agricultural. Where sheep and cattle once grazed in small fields, hedgerows have been swept away to allow vast acreages of sugar beet and rapeseed to be planted.

Agriculture remains a large part of Norfolk life and Fakenham still carries a leisurely bucolic air, despite the fact that throughout the 19th and 20th centuries it had a small industrial revolution and became a centre of printing. Most of the printing works have been demolished or converted to other uses, and the only printing done in Fakenham these days is of the digital kind.

Light industry areas and superstore retail developments have led the traffic away to edge-of-town emporiums, and a section of narrow town centre streets, some with curiously isolated buildings, are now pedestrianised. There is a busy National Hunt racecourse (www.fakenhamracecourse.co.uk) on the outskirts, which you can walk to from the town centre. The town has regular furniture and antiques auctions and a farmers' market which sells specialist foods from the locality, including venison products from Holkham Hall, just north of Fakenham. A big attraction for those who have moved to Fakenham is the proximity of the sea. Fakenham is about 8 miles inland from the charming harbour of Wells-next-the-Sea, and accessible coastal resorts include Hunstanton (16.6 miles) and Cromer (20.4 miles). Even its devotees admit that Fakenham is not the liveliest of places, but the upside is that property tends to be cheaper than in trendier Holt, or places on the north Norfolk coast. This means that you share the same lovely countryside, but for less money. It is possible that Norfolk transport links will improve as demand grows for better links to London and the reinstatement of railway lines to boost the local economy, but this is a longer-term project and retirees may not want to wait.

My experience...

Brenda Gibson, a retired primary school teacher from Rutland, moved to Little Snoring, 2 miles outside Fakenham, 13 and a half years ago.

We used to live in Suffolk and know the East Anglia area well. We always said we'd retire to Norfolk or Suffolk because we had a holiday cottage and used to take our holidays in Norfolk, so there was a long-term plan to come to one or the other. Also my daughter lives in Aylsham, a nearby country town. Fakenham is an attractive place and as well as people who retire there, you get a lot of artists and writers who retreat to Norfolk. It's that kind of a place; somewhere to get away from the rat race, although Holt up the road is more sophisticated. For us it was the house that decided where we lived; its close to the sea, which is important to us, as to lot of

(Continued on following page)

(Continued)

people. Also, because Fakenham is considered less desirable than Holt or Burnham, properties here are about £50,000 cheaper so you get better value property for your money.

Even though we are only 2 miles outside Fakenham, we are in a village, so a car is essential. Very old people might have to give up driving which would make them isolated, so it would be better to buy in Fakenham. Public transport isn't wonderful here. From Fakenham you can get to Norwich. The shops are not great and I tend to shop in Holt but Fakenham does have a weekly market on Thursday and a farmers' market every fourth week. There is a cinema, which was recently reopened with private finance, a gym and fitness centre, drama club etc. We belong to the Ramblers [a walking organisation]; for that kind of thing it's the best. For hospitals you have to go to King's Lynn or Norwich; we're about 24 miles from either, which is a long round trip if you have to go for regular treatment.

Southwold Lighthouse, East Anglia

Fakenham fact file

Access: On the A148. King's Lynn, 22 miles; Cromer, 23 miles.

Airport: Norwich, 29 miles

Average property price: £241,800

Bus services: First (www.firstgroup.com/ukbus/eastanglia)

Climate: Tends to be sunnier and dryer than the western UK

Councils: Fakenham Town Council (www.fakenhamtowncouncil.org.uk); North Norfolk District Council (www.north-norfolk.gov.uk)

Council tax: Band D £1,319.90; band E £1,613.22

Crime: Average crime levels

Economic activity: North Norfolk has been targeted as a rural development area to help diversification towards high-quality businesses

Hospital: Queen Elizabeth Hospital, King's Lynn (www.qehkl.nhs.uk); Norfolk and Norwich University Hospital, Norwich (www.nnuh.nhs)

Percentage of people over 65: 24%. Average age of population of Fakenham is 45.

Population: 15,275

Property prices: Detached £263,592; semi-detached £174,953; terraced £154,894; flat £104,998

Railway station: Nearest is Sheringham (20 miles). The Bittern Line (www.bitternline. com) community branch railway runs between Norwich and Sheringham on the coast. Connects to London (Liverpool Street) via Norwich. Thus Sheringham to London takes approximately three hours.

Frinton-on-Sea

Frinton is on the Essex coast, south-east of Colchester on a large promontory, quite often referred to as the Tendring Peninsula, that lies between the Stour Estuary to the north and the estuary of the River Colne to the south-west. It is near Clacton-on-Sea, and the old Cinque Port of Brightlingsea is to the west. Frinton is within easy reach of the sailing port of Manningtree to the north and only four miles from Harwich for ferry sailings to the continent. Essex has 300 miles of low-lying coastline with sea views over mudflats, salt marshes, grazing marshes and sea walls; a coast that is easily eroded and ever shifting. Other seaside places near to Frinton-on-Sea are Jaywick, Great Holland, and West Mersea on Mersea Island. There are several thousand footpaths in the whole of Essex making it excellent walking country, without being too rugged for ageing limbs. By linking paths it is claimed that you can walk from the outskirts of London all the way to Harwich; and if that is a bit ambitious, you can settle for the walk from Frinton to Harwich.

Although separated from Clacton-on-Sea by a couple of miles, the resorts of Clacton and Frinton couldn't be more different in atmosphere and clientele. Clacton was a thriving resort in the 1920s and 1930s with dance halls and pier entertainments, but is now a fairly neglected seaside town that has become a haunt for 'chavs' on the razzle and for recovering (and not so recovering) addicts. Frinton was developed to be a select resort from about 1886 with broad, tree-lined avenues. As well as Victorian architecture, there are William Morris stained glass panels in Old St Mary Church and Edwardian and Art Deco buildings. Frinton together with its sister resort of Walton-on-the-Naze considers itself to be a tiny bastion of civilisation and its inhabitants have a fine-tuned sense of social and age-related hierarchy. A staggering 43.8% of the town's population is retired and anyone under 21 is regarded with suspicion. The town is divided by the Colchester to Walton-on-the-Naze railway and living inside the iconic (railway level crossing) gates is considered superior to living outside the gates, and adds another zero to the value of your house. Network Rail is planning an assault on the manned railway gates, to replace them with an automatic crossing. Locals claim that aged tearaways on mobility scooters will simply ignore the flashing lights with disastrous consequences. Frinton's famous draconian by-laws ban all commerce from the seafront as well as bicycles (but not mobility scooters) from the esplanade. A blow against genteel notoriety was achieved in 2000, when the first pub in Frinton's history, the Lock and Barrel (now with wi-fi), opened on Connaught Street in the Gates.

My experience...

Chris Perry, now 69, has lived in Frinton-on-Sea since 1998 after moving there from Bedford. He used to be a school bursar.

When you have five children, the places you can afford to go on holiday are limited. We found Frinton through one of my bosses and came here when my oldest son was 10 days old, and every summer after that. Slowly but surely the place grew on us. I became a member of the golf club and then eventually I got a bank loan and bought my wife a beach hut, followed later by a house. Frinton is sandwiched between Walton and Clacton – two lively, noisy towns, but then in between them is this jewel. To drive out from here is special because you have Constable country not far away. When it came time to retire, I probably knew as many people in Frinton as in Bedford. We did give Wales a cursory thought as I was brought up there, but Frinton had the edge without any question. It's everything we like: peace and quiet and the beaches are safe and magnificent for swimming.

I live just off the main shopping street, close to the off-licence and not far from the nearest restaurant. This was deliberate because part of the enjoyment of Frinton is being able to walk everywhere. You have all your daily needs in Frinton but for bigger shops we go five miles to bigger supermarkets. There is a bus service connecting Walton, Frinton and Clacton and other areas, but I tend not to use public transport. There is a wealth of good eating places within a 20-mile radius of Frinton and several well-supported churches of different denominations. I came here for a quiet retirement but find myself busier than I was before. I play golf and cricket and I'm chairman of a daycare centre, the only one in the area. My wife plays tennis with a local club.

Apart from the weather pattern being excellent, other good things are the great kindness in people, who do talk to you, especially if you're a dog walker. The local council's responsible dog policy means that there is one stretch of beach that dogs are not allowed to walk through. We have suffered a bit from bored youths who can't find anything to do in the evenings and we are coming to terms with the need for more policing to control the unruly element. Meanwhile an organisation called the Homelands Free Church is doing a superb job trying to provide the youths with activities through youth clubs.

Frinton-on-Sea fact file

Access: B1035 (and over the level crossing). Colchester, 17 miles; London, 79 miles.

Airport: Stansted, 65 miles

Average property price: £207,250

Bus services: First Eastern Counties Buses (www.firstgroup.com)

Climate: On Essex Sunshine Coast

Council: Essex County Council; Tendring District Council (www.tendringdc.gov.uk)

Council tax: Band D £1,366.57; band E 1,670.25

Crime: Low

Economic activity: The main business and commercial area is Connaught Street. Economic activity is low because of the residential nature of the area. A development plan for Walton is in the pipeline to attract mini-break trippers and conferences.

Ferries: From Harwich DFDS Seaways (www.dfds.co.uk) to Esbjerg (Denmark) and Cuxhaven (Germany). Stena Line (www.stenaline.co.uk) to the Hook of Holland.

Hospitals: Nearest A&E is Colchester General Hospital (01206 747474) run by Tendring Primary Care Trust

Percentage of people over 65: 26%

Population: 6,168

Property prices: Two-bedroom house £200,996; three bedrooms £217,559

Railway station: Frinton (reached from London Liverpool Street, via Colchester). Train services provided by One Railway (www.onerailway.com).

Residents' on-street parking permit: £20 per year

Specialised retirement property: Includes Frinton Lodge for the over-65s (www.homewise.co.uk) and retirement apartments such as those in Fourth Avenue marketed by Boydens (www.boydens.co.uk)

Holt

In 1821 William Cobbett wrote 'Holt is a little, old-fashioned, substantially built market town', a description that could easily be applied to the place today. With its boutiques, delicatessens, gift shops and celebrity shoppers, Holt is part of the area sometimes known as Norfolk's Chelsea, which includes a large chunk (453 sq km) of the coast, which is a designated Area of Outstanding Natural Beauty (AONB). It has salt marshes and creeks with superb sailing; there are excellent sailing facilities at Blakeney and Morston, just north-west of Holt. Nearby Cromer also has huge expanses of sandy beaches. Further west, Hunstanton and Wells-next-the-Sea have acres of pine forests where you can walk. The coast also contains such gems as Burnham Market (or 'Burnham Mark-up' as locals call it) with the premium prices that it and Cley-next-the-Sea, among other Norfolk places, now command. Norfolk locals have become quite adept at letting bidding wars develop over properties in this area, so that prices can go up an eye-popping 20% above the asking prices. In the coastal AONB, a staggering 15% of properties are second homes. Holt has mostly Georgian architecture, as a fire in 1708 destroyed most of the town meaning it was largely rebuilt. The shops are a draw, because they are individual and sell objects for discerning shoppers, such as antiques, bric-a-brac, galleries and antiquarian books. There are also expensive boutiques and several delicatessens, food shops and restaurants. Specialist shopping also extends to the coast. Sheringham is another vibrant shopping centre and you can get there from Holt via the North Norfolk Heritage Railway (www.nnrailway.co.uk).

Holt is in a county that is acquiring an increasing level of sophistication, with Michelin-starred as well as only slightly lesser restaurants proliferating. You can see why the area is becoming attractive, as it combines both a highly desirable lifestyle that is both civilised and up-to-date, but is far from the madding crowd and relatively unspoiled. You really need your own transport and an excellent guidance system, as the area is criss-crossed with rural routes linking small villages.

My experience...

Jane Harper, age 60, is the former picture editor of the Sunday Times Magazine, who moved to Holt from 'war-torn Hackney' in 2004.

Originally I had a holiday home in Stiffkey near Wells-next-the-Sea and took holidays there for about 15 years. I decided to move to Norfolk when I had problems with my parents; my father had Alzheimer's and my mother couldn't cope and I was travelling to Bexhill all the time to see to them. I bought a barn in Blakeney with my partner and lived at Stiffkey while the building work was being done. I moved my mother to Holt because I felt she needed to be somewhere she could walk to the shops. When I broke up with my partner, we sold the barn and with my half of the proceeds, all I could afford was a cottage in Holt.

Holt is fantastic. It's very touristy and has trendy cafés, bars, boutiques (where Camilla [Duchess of Cornwall] does her Christmas shopping) and a wonderful traditional department store called Larners. Lots of celebrities come here. Stephen Fry has a house in Norfolk and I've seen David Baddiel. Holt is really a little Georgian jewel. It has gone very upmarket. You couldn't get a cappuccino when I first moved here. Now you can get anything you want. Yet it still retains its 1950s feel, where the shopkeepers know you by name and let you pay next week. The only thing I miss is a busy arts scene. Holt has a cinema which shows mainstream blockbusters, but if you want anything art house or good theatre, you have to go to Norwich. I still practise photography and I belong to the Norfolk Camera Club, which meets in Holt Community Centre. I'm always out and about taking pictures and they are shown in local galleries; Holt has three galleries. The countryside is very pretty here and the Christmas lights in Holt, all white ones, make it look amazing. We have a bit of a parking problem as Holt, and Norfolk generally, get all-year tourism now. There are so many Londoners living here now that it's quite difficult to meet a real 'Norfolker'; hardly surprising I suppose when you see the price of property compared with their earnings.

Holt fact file

Access: A148 from Cromer and Wells-next-the-Sea. Norwich (B1149), 23 miles.

Airport: Norwich, 30 miles

Average property price: £199,319 (North Norfolk)

Bus services: Sanders Coaches and Local Bus Services (www.sanderscoaches.com/timetables.htm)

Climate: Drier and sunnier than west of England

Council: North Norfolk District Council (www.north-norfolk.gov.uk)

Council tax: Band D £1,371; band E £1,675

Crime: One of the lowest crime areas in the country

Economic activity: Just beginning a four-year North Norfolk Economic Development Plan to create greater economic diversity

Hospital: Nearest large hospital is Cromer; also Norfolk and Norwich, in Norwich (www.nnuh.nhs.uk)

Percentage of people over 65: Around 32% (North Norfolk)

Population: 99,000 (North Norfolk)

Property prices: Detached £254,961; semi-detached £166,052; terraced £152,169; flat £134,319

Railway stations: Nearest is Sheringham (6 miles) from where the Bittern Line, Community branch railway connects to Norwich. Norwich to London (Liverpool Street) approximately 1 hour 40 mins.

Specialised retirement property: Coming soon, McCarthy & Stone's Grove Lane, Holt retirement development of 43 one-bedroom and two-bedroom apartments close to the town centre (0800 521276)

Southend-on-Sea

Southend-on-Sea is the largest town in Essex and is situated on the north side of the Thames Estuary, so it is both an estuary-side and a seaside resort. Before sea bathing became all the rage it consisted of a fishing community tacked on the south end of Prittlewell. Nearby Leigh was an important naval harbour from the 16th century onwards. Both Prittlewell, which has a Norman church, and Leigh are now subsumed into greater Southend-on-Sea. The first mention of Southend as a bathing resort was in 1768 and the Royal Hotel was built in 1793. Meanwhile the place became popular for Regency notables and royalty in the early 19th century. It is easy to think of 'Sarfend' as it is fondly known, as a seaside resort for day trippers with its 'Golden Mile' of seafront arcades, bingo halls and other gaudy attractions. There is actually so much more to it, that once you have seen beyond its worst Blackpool-type fripperies you can find illuminations of another kind. For example, its beaches are not endless sandy miles like Bournemouth but the tidal edges of a great river, or as Joseph Conrad exquisitely puts it:

> We looked at that venerable stream not in the vivid flush of short day that comes and departs for ever, but in the august light of abiding memories. And indeed nothing is easier for a man ... than to evoke the great spirit of the past upon the lower reaches of the Thames.

For a quieter view of Southend, you can walk east along Thorpe Bay to Shoeburyness and gaze out uninterruptedly across the Atlantic. Southend has parks, good shopping, lots of restaurants and an annual Carnival and Air Show. Its famously long pier (1.34 miles), complete with train ride, is the town's icon.

There has been talk for some time of a major investment in Southend to change it into a world-class resort and to put the pier in the hands of private company, that would provide it with a luxurious refurbishment. Some regeneration has been carried out, such as the refurbishment of the Palace Hotel, so the plan has already progressed beyond the hot air stage. The umbrella organisation in charge of regeneration is Renaissance Southend.

Places to visit around Southend, such as Foulness Island and Canvey Island, are not of the rolling hills of Somerset or Yorkshire Dales variety, because they are flat and intersected with wandering waterways and inlets. Depending how seriously you take the predictions of an imminent sharp rise in sea levels from climate change, you may not choose to retire to Southend. If on the other hand you are not bothered, because it will probably be above water for your lifetime, then you will find that Southend has many affordable properties. It costs far less to buy here than in most seaside resorts in England. Convenience is optimal: apart from the shops in Southend, Basildon and Brentwood nearby, London is easily accessible for high-end culture and retail therapy. A recent survey showed that Southend-on-Sea is the safest large town in England, despite the fact that the High Street after dark is a place where loud-mouthed inebriates regularly fall into the gutter.

My experience...

Neville Peters, 76, moved to Southend (Leigh-on-Sea) with his wife from Redbridge in 1998. When she died, he found the U3A tremendously welcoming and inclusive.

It was a spur of the moment decision to move to Southend. We'd lived in the same house since we were married to the time I retired from being a company accountant in 1995/96. I wanted to carry on working after 66 but I was given a month's notice instead. On that very morning, I told my wife that we should move to Westcliff, which is the next suburb to Leigh; it's all part of Southend. I had a daughter down here and I've known the area practically all my life. Often as children our parents brought us here at weekends, and when my daughter had her first two children, my wife was down here every week. It was a joint decision to move here and it's a nice place to retire to. We decided on Leigh because two years earlier, a couple of close friends moved here. We looked at bungalows for months and eventually friends found this one for us. Sadly, after getting the bungalow all ready, my wife became ill and died 18 months ago. Friends of mine asked me to move to Westcliff, but I don't intend to move as I am happy here.

I use the buses; there's one every 15 minutes from just outside but it's inadequate for the evenings. The services are not profitable in the evening, so there aren't any after 8.20pm. I wouldn't want to walk around the town centre at night anyway, there's a lot of drunken rowdiness. Sadly, we lost the bandstand, which had to be dismantled because the cliff is subsiding. But on the positive side we have a couple of lovely theatres. There's a big political scandal dating from the time of the 2001 census which a lot of people in Southend didn't fill in. There are about half a million more people living here than the government thinks and the Council keep trying to get them to accept the larger figure as it affects the amount of money the government gives them, which currently is not enough.

There's a lot more to do in the Southend area than in many parts of Britain – for older and retired people it's unbelievable. Nobody needs to be lonely here. All my life, I've helped voluntary organisations. Here, I am chairman of a Jewish charity and I'm involved with the U3A. After my wife died, I went along to a U3A meeting, and they made me very welcome, much more than I expected. We met once a week and then they asked me to be on the committee and I suppose my life sort of revolves around it now. I've got it to become one of the biggest branches down here and we are opening a branch in Leigh with membership that is already snowballing. It keeps me going.

Southend-on-Sea fact file

Access: A130, A127 'Southend arterial road' and A13 from London (42 miles)

Average property price: £190,601

Airport: Stansted, 41 miles

Bus services: Arriva Southend (www.arriva.co.uk) and First Group

Climate: Fairly sheltered as the town's luxuriant cliff gardens show. Lowest average annual rainfall (517 mm) in the UK.

Council: Southend Borough Council (www.southend.gov.uk). Unitary Council of Southend-on-Sea (includes Parish of Leigh-on-Sea).

Council tax: Band D £1,120.14; E £1,369.06

Crime: Regarded as the safest large town in England

Economic activity: Currently in a programme to attract inward business investment and sites

Ferries: Ferry companies along the Medway change frequently with market forces and there is usually one plying between Southend and Gravesend

Hospital: Southend University Hospital (www.southend.nhs.uk). Has an A&E department.

Percentage of people over 65: 20%

Population: 176,000 (Council figure)

Property prices: Detached £317,201; semi-detached £213,112; terrace £173,641; flat £134,152

Railway stations: Served by two railway lines: C2C goes via Southend East and Southend Central from Fenchurch Street London to Shoeburyness (has its own unofficial passenger website (www.sarfend.co.uk/c2c/). One Great Eastern goes from London Liverpool Street to Southend Victoria.

Residents' on-street parking: £10 per year

Specialised retirement property: There are numerous retirement blocks of flats in Westcliff and overlooking Thorpe Bay. Double bedroom flats start from about £119,000. It is possible to buy non-retirement flats for about £20,000 less.

Southwold

Southwold is a picture-book, pretty English seaside town on the north Suffolk coast, with a 100ft-high (working) lighthouse, beach huts painted in rainbow colours, a pier and a row of seaward-glaring black cannons positioned on the cliff top. To the south-west are the River Blyth and Southwold Harbour, Walberswick and Dunwich forest, while nearest coastal neighbour to the north is Lowestoft (10 miles). They say that Southwold is changing, but remarkably slowly. Its exquisite cluster of 17th and 18th-century buildings has a mix of the retired, cosmopolitan incomers of younger ages, second homeowners and indigenous locals. For a retirement place it is unusually vibrant with a thriving mixed business community of professionals and artisans. The discovery of East Anglia by the Kensington brigade has meant local shops being squeezed by incoming ones aimed at cosmopolitan clientele.

Despite its undeniable charm, nearly half the pleasure of retiring to Southwold is the access it gives to the Suffolk coast, which is often lumped together with the Norfolk coast, when they are in fact quite different. Unlike the Norfolk coast, which is criss-crossed with access roads, in Suffolk there is no coast route, except the sea itself, to link the towns and villages, giving it a wilder feel. Typically, seaside-based towns and villages in Suffolk are the end of a single access road. This has helped the villages grow an individual identity and enabled them to maintain it for longer against the tide of the standardisation of everything. There is marvellous walking from the town itself. You can explore Walberswick (another gem), Dunwich and the Suffolk Coastland Heath, classified an Area of Outstanding Natural Beauty (AONB). In the winter (and the summer too, if you can bear to be indoors) you can enjoy classic films (old and new) at the volunteer-run, 66-seater cinema, modelled on an Edwardian picture house.

My experience...

Marianne Greening from Hertford, who is past retirement age, moved to Southwold in 2000 with her husband, having known the area for 20 years.

My husband and I came to Southwold with business connections and we knew the area well. We used to walk around, looking in the estate agents' windows until one day we saw an interesting looking house. We walked all over the town looking for it and then realised it was next door to the estate agent! We stayed an extra day in Southwold and six weeks after that we'd moved here. It wasn't planned, but I suppose we were getting a bit tired of Hertford, which had filled up with estate agents and wine bars and was no longer the small country town it was when we first moved there. Here, we can open our front door and see the sea and there is lots to do. There's good sailing and a golf club. There is a small cinema and clubs for art and classical music and lots of clubs for older people. I'm not really a clubbable person, but I did join the WI and after two years found that I was president.

The best thing we ever did was to get an allotment. The compactness of the town means that few houses have gardens and we found it a great way to meet local people. There's a reasonable bus service with reliable buses but because it's a rural area there are just not enough of them. I think some of them are coordinated

(Continued on following page)

(Continued)

with the local station at Darsham. On the other hand, the slight remoteness of Southwold is one of its charms.

The best things about living here are the wonderful beaches and the fact that Southwold has all the facilities a retired person needs, except perhaps large hospitals. There is a service called Rapid Responders, an emergency service that comes out for elderly people.. People are also very friendly here. I have people coming to see me from Hertford and they comment how genteel and polite drivers are here. We do get cold winds from the North Sea, but I think that's what's called bracing and we have a palm tree in our garden, so it can't be that bad. If you want Harvey Nichols and Selfridges, you are going to miss them here, but there are good clothes shops locally. People actually come to Southwold to buy nice clothes.

If you do want to retire here you have to be quick, as houses sell very quickly. A lot of houses never come on the market at all as they are passed on through local families.

Southwold fact file

Access: Ipswich, 35 miles; Norwich, 35 miles. Southwold is at the end of the A1095.

Average property price: 45% of property is sold is above £300,000

Airports: Norwich, 38 miles; Stansted, 87 miles

Bus services: To/from Beccles, Bungay, Halesworth, Ipswich, Lowestoft and Norwich

Climate: Bracing winds off the North Sea

Council: Southwold Town Council (01502 722576). Waveney District Council (www.waveney.gov.uk).

Council tax: Band D £1,307.95; band E £1,598.61

Crime: Low

Economic activity: Many small local businesses

Ferries: June to September there is a usually a rowboat ferry between Southwold and Walberswick

Hospitals: Ipswich (www.ipswichhospital.org.uk), Norwich (www.nnuh.nhs.uk)

Percentage of people over 65: 22% (Suffolk PCT area)

Property prices: Two-bedroom house £340,000 at time of press

Railway stations: Nearest is Darsham. Also Halesworth.

LINCOLNSHIRE FENS AND WOLDS

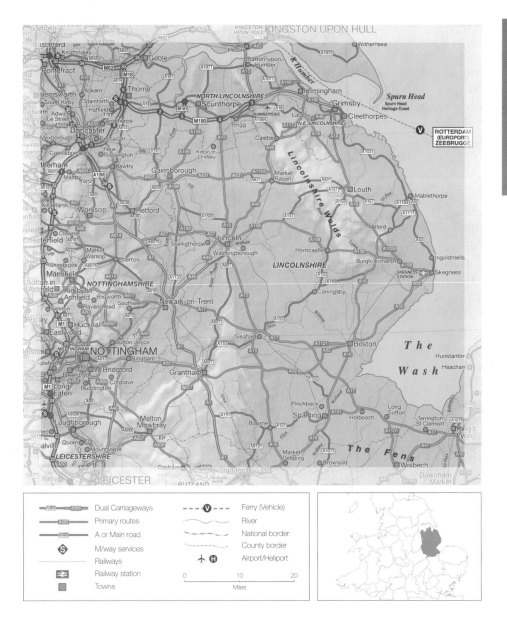

	Dual Carriageways		Ferry (Vehicle)
	Primary routes		River
	A or Main road		National border
	M/way services		County border
	Railways		Airport/Heliport
	Railway station		
	Towns		

0   10   20

Miles

At the time of the Domesday Book the whole of Lincolnshire was known as 'Lindsey'. Later, that name was used for the area around Lincoln when it was divided into three parts; the other two parts being named Holland (south-east Lincolnshire) and Kesteven (south-west Lincolnshire). Lincolnshire is the second largest county in England after Yorkshire, which it borders, but unlike that county, much of Lincolnshire is open and flat. In the 16th century much of the area was comprised of a vast inland expanse of marshes. The Lincolnshire Fens extend north-east of Boston and south to Long Sutton, with Spalding roughly in the middle. The Fens continue into north-east Cambridgeshire and Norfolk. The Lincolnshire coastal border of the Fens is The Wash (see below).

Originally, the vast Fens area was passable only by boat, and sometimes on foot, where firmer islands of higher ground permitted, and where communities gradually developed into towns and villages. In a process begun by the Romans, continued in the Middle Ages, and then completed on a grand scale in the 17th century by engineers, the alluvial soil of the marshes was gradually reclaimed through drainage. The resulting land became productive through agriculture and its own inherent richness. But drying the Fenland marshes caused them to shrink and then sink, and the lowered levels once again became flooded. The mechanical wizardry of the Industrial Revolution was brought to bear on the problem and through the 18th and 19th centuries, first steam power then diesel power and finally electric power drove the pumps and made the picturesque windmills which had preceded them obsolete. The maintenance of permanent drainage has thus imbued land ownership here, with a rather special significance, as solid land first had to be created before it could be worked on. The continuing problem of shrinkage and soil erosion means that the Fens are now in need of widespread conservation, perhaps by letting the land return to its natural state. The mass of minor roads and ditches make the Fens area easy to spot on a large-scale map as they form a distinctive grid pattern in ruler-straight lines. Today, the flat Fenland landscape, featureless at first glance, but full of charm on closer inspection, is characterised by wide horizons, fabulous skies at sunset, huge arable fields and fascinating towns and villages, of which Spalding is one.

The Lincolnshire Wolds is an inland area of north-east Lincolnshire, which reaches from Laceby and Caistor just south-west of Cleethorpes down to Spilsby and Burgh Le Marsh, west of Skegness. The B1225, which goes north to south from Caistor to Baumber (just north-west of Horncastle), follows the route of Caistor High Street, the Roman road. Other towns of the Wolds include Louth, Arlford, Market Rasen and Horncastle. The coastline east of the Wolds contains the town of Mablethorpe. Quite unlike the Fens, the Lincolnshire Wolds are an upland area of rolling chalk hills rising up to 500ft and plunging into wooded valleys and streams. The quintessential English poet of late Victorian times, Alfred Tennyson, was born and grew up here and felt its lasting inspiration.

There are great walks in the Wolds. You can follow the Bluestone Heath Road, an ancient drovers' route, which runs east west over the Wolds or the Viking Way, a long distance footpath that runs through the Wolds.

Mablethorpe

Mablethorpe is a traditional English seaside resort that has become a little run down in recent years. East Midlanders have been encouraged to holiday there by advertising campaigns promoting Mablethorpe and Skegness. They find Skegness easier to get to as it has a railway station, whereas Mablethorpe does not; although there is a bus service linking the two. Refurbishment and expansion money tends to pour into Skegness, so more people go there, thinking it is the better resort. Mablethorpe's best assets are its location and the fact that is has a worldwide reputation for being a friendly town. Mabo or Mabs, as it is affectionately known, has probably the best sandy beach in Lincolnshire (or perhaps anywhere else in England) extending for miles in either direction. It is one of the beaches most accessible to the disabled largely because the town and the beach are level. This makes it highly suitable for not-so-agile retired people, who might choose to live there for that reason; as they do in droves from Nottingham, Leicester, Sheffield and even London.

Mablethorpe's location is another asset: it is a good spot from which to branch out into the rest of Lincolnshire, particularly for those with their own transport. There are the Wolds (see description above) with excellent walking and fascinating towns. Boston, Grimsby and Louth are all within easy driving distance and a little further is Lincoln, with its fabulous cathedral that made do for Westminster Abbey in the feature film of *The Da Vinci Code*. That Mablethorpe inspires devoted loyalty in those who know it must also count as a big asset. Holidaymakers, who came there as children, now bring their own children to Mablethorpe, not just for a single holiday, but year after year. Those who can afford to are usually looking out for a place to buy there, often a mobile home, so they can keep on coming for holidays, and then eventually retire there. As a resort, it has a lot going for it in the traditional realm of seaside activities from donkey rides on the beach, spot amusements, a funfair, fish (fresh from Grimsby) and chips to die for, among them.

Out of season, things quiet down especially after the holiday parks close on the 31st October. However, there are still a number of events including an international tap dancing festival and sand racing, which keep the town alive through the winter. In September 2006 the first Mablethorpe Marathon was run and it is hoped it will become a regular event.

Mablethorpe may have a sea breeze that is bracing rather than balmy, and at present it lacks amenities such as a swimming pool or sports centre, and the seafront shops and arcades could do with a lick of paint, but the spirit of the place is alive and well and there are few places more friendly to retire to.

My experience...

Mr Broadhurst, now aged 69, moved to Mablethorpe in 1999 from Middlesex.

My wife had always wanted to live by the coast. When the pub opposite where we used to live changed into a nightclub that went on until 3am, it made our minds up for us. I looked on the website www.scoot.co.uk for estate agents in Mablethorpe and they sent us information on 14 properties in the Mablethorpe area and a little bit further afield. I didn't even know that Mablethorpe existed then. I knew about Skegness, but that's about all. We visited Mablethorpe and fell in love with it. We walked along the promenade, spent the day here and we just took to it. We stepped inside the bungalow where we are now living and we loved it and decided to buy it. Property prices were low at the time and that's another thing that prompted us.

We're about 10 minutes from the beach and we can walk into town and back to the peacefulness of where we live which is wonderful. Mablethorpe is very quiet in the winter, which is nice because you get lots of holidaymakers from March to October. There's everything to do here, if you get up and look for it. You need only go to the Tourist Information Centre and you'll see a list of clubs. I belong to the British Legion Club and found out before I came up here that there was a branch in the town. I'm also chairperson of the Old Age Pensioners Club and I belong to what they call the Remy Club, which is a venue for entertainment including comedians every Saturday night.

Mablethorpe has got a cinema and lots of cheap cafés and places to eat. You could eat out every day and it would still be cheaper than buying the meat joints to cook for yourself. There's a big Co-op here, but we could do with a big Tesco or Asda in the town. Tesco tried but it was blocked because it would have put the small shops out of business I think. Asda might be opening here. There's a bit of bad weather in the winter because we have the east winds and the shops start to close at 4pm, so it can turn into a bit of a ghost town, but we have the Remy and darts. People say, if you can put up with your first winter here, then you'll stay.

The only drawback is that the hospital is 40 minutes away and I don't drive, although I have friends who, if I needed them to, would drive me. National Express coaches come here and we can get to places, such as Lincoln and Nottingham. We have free bus passes, so we can get out and about. Getting to London by train takes five or six hours and if you miss a train you have to wait around for the next one. On the plus side, I'm much healthier since living here. The air is cleaner and my asthma has improved. We also like the friendliness here that you don't get in London, where people walk past you without speaking. If you go out here, people stop to say hello and chat for a bit.

Mablethorpe fact file

Access: A1104, A1031. Skegness, 18 miles.

Airports: Humberside Airport (www.humbersideairport.com), 30 miles

Average property price: £130,174

Bus services: Stagecoach (www.stagecoachbus.com). Also look at the range of routes at www.lincsinterconnect.com, eg Skegness–Chapel St Leonards–Mablethorpe. Book and ride service Call Connect Plus Bus (0845 234 3344).

Climate: Bracing

Council: East Lindsey District Council

Council tax: Band D 1,191.56; band E £1,456.35

Crime: Crime is more than double the average for the East Lindsey district in parts of Mablethorpe because the resort attracts a transient population

Economic activity: Area of rural deprivation

Ferries: Hull is nearest for Continental ferries to Rotterdam and Zeebrugge (www.poferries.com)

Hospitals: Nearest is Louth County Hospital (01507 600100). District General Hospital is in Lincoln (www.ulh.nhs.uk).

Percentage of people over 65: 26% in the area; approximately 40% of the population of Mablethorpe is elderly

Population: 6,800 (reaches 30,000 in high season; higher at weekends)

Property prices: It is estimated that there are 26,000 mobile homes on the coast between Skegness and Mablethorpe, which could provide a cheaper retirement alternative to bricks-and-mortar, although some will be more suitable than others for retired people.

Railway station: Waynefleet Road, Skegness

Specialised retirement property: New development of two and three-bedroom bungalows off Golf Road, Mablethorpe from £184,000 approximately (Willsons (0845 337 2038)

Skegness

Skegness is just off the south-eastern edge of the Lincolnshire Wolds, north of The Wash, almost opposite Hunstanton on the Norfolk (southern) side. Unlike Hunstanton, 'Skeggy' as it is familiarly known, faces east and gets the full whiplash of the wind off the North Sea, hence the famous slogan 'Skegness is so bracing'. Ingoldmells and Chapel St Leonards are the Lincolnshire resorts to the north, while to the south-west the East Fen spreads out flatly in a square patchwork formed from dykes and ditches. Long before Skegness became a seaside resort (some say Britain's favourite resort), it was a small port, which was washed away by a great storm in 1526. The traveller John Leland seeing 'Olde Skegnes' in the aftermath of this catastrophe, described the rebuilding 'a pore new thing... built by poor people deprived of all they possessed.' Even as late as 1850, Skegness was a town of barely 400 souls who earned a living from fishing or working on the land, although it had begun to be frequented by 'quality' people, in search of sea water cures for poor health. The arrival of the railway in 1873 brought the first crowds from the Midlands Industrial towns and from 1877 the town began to be developed as a resort. For the first time, many ordinary workers could save for a trip to Skegness, which for many meant just a day trip. Others would spend a week, but as there were no paid holidays for workers, this was not an affordable option for all. Skegness had its heyday in the 1920s and 1930s with the proliferation of boarding houses and seaside amusements: fairs, tea dances, the pier and of course, the beach. The Second World War heralded the end of an era. After the war, increased car ownership and regular mass transport, not to mention the package holiday, dulled the attraction of Skeggy for those who now found more exotic locations than Butlin's and Skegness could offer. There is still a Butlin's at Ingoldmells, revamped in a more modern guise.

Skegness is a very popular retirement spot; in one recent survey it was voted the number one place to retire in Britain. The reasons for this include the fact that Skegness feels safe at night and, unlike some seaside places it stays lively out of season.

My experience...

Jenny Letts, now 64, moved to a rented flat in Skegness in 2005, from the Belvoir foothills near Melton Mowbray. She was formerly an auxiliary nurse.

It wasn't always our intention to move on retiring, but we'd talked about it. We were out in the sticks in the Vale of Belvoir and we relied on our car to go anywhere. We were getting frustrated at not being able to do all the things that we wanted to, so we decided to move to Skegness. We used to come here for days out, as it wasn't too far to come, and it is flat so you can walk or cycle for miles. We've also got the beach and the sea nearby. Some of my stepchildren live around Nottingham so it's also not too far away for them to visit. We decided to rent a ground floor flat that's close to the town, about half a mile away. We also have some shops on the corner that are walking distance away, and buses on our doorstep; they're very regular and you can get off anywhere in the town.

Skegness is very compact with little shops, although it also has supermarkets, such as Tesco, Morrisons and Safeway. It has a very good library, a cinema, indoor bowling and the Embassy Theatre. The one thing I'd say about the area is that you can get a meal at any time of day, winter or summer. My husband and I are members of the U3A and there are lots of activities and groups within that – walking groups, language groups and so on. There really is something for everyone and no one need ever be at a loss. I go to aromatherapy, Chinese medicine and holistic therapies, but if I was on my own, I could be out all day and every night if I wanted to. Skegness does get busy in summer, but when you come to live in a seaside resort you expect it to be busy in the holiday season; it just means the locals go in at different times. Everyone was very friendly and helpful when we moved here. We had about seven months of exploring, looking in the library and tourist information centre, which are the areas to go to, to find out what is going on around you.

EAST ENGLAND

89

Skegness fact file

Access: A52. Lincoln, 43 miles.

Airports: Humberside, 30 miles; Nottingham-East Midlands, 93 miles; Stansted, 123 miles.

Average property price: £178,681

Bus services: Stagecoach (www.stagecoachbus.com); Interconnect (www.lincsinterconnect.com); dial a ride (0845 234 3344)

Climate: Bracing

Council: East Lindsey District Council

Council tax: Band D £1,191.56; band E £1,214

Crime: Despite an overall low crime rate, with so many caravans and chalets, break-ins can be a problem, although moves have been taken to reduce caravan crime since 2006

Economic activity: Considered an area of coastal deprivation with 40% of employment of a seasonal nature

Ferries: Nearest is Hull (67 miles) to Rotterdam and Zeebrugge with P&O (www.poferries.com)

Hospitals: Skegness Hospital (www.ulh.nhs.uk). Reputedly one of the shortest waiting times. When the Scarborough Ward of the Skegness Hospital was closed, local protesters came out on the streets and forced the PCT to re-open the ward in 2006 to maintain essential care for the elderly.

Percentage of people over 65: 22.3%

Population: About 19,000

Property prices: Detached £198,335; semi-detached £150,242; terraced £136,353; flat £116,000

Railway station: Skegness

THE WASH

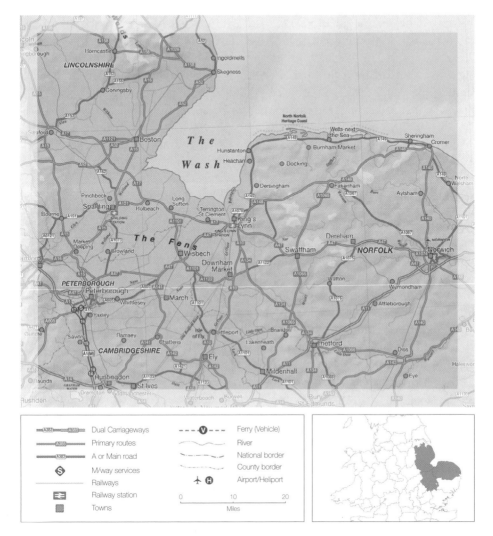

The Wash appears on maps as a giant, squarish bay on the east coast of England with five rivers debouching into it: the Steeping, Witham, Welland, Nene and Ouse. It is sometimes described incorrectly as an estuary. In fact, it is a large shallow bay with five estuaries running into it. It is partly on the Lincolnshire Coast and partly on the Norfolk coast. Over 10–12 millennia, the area of the giant bay has been progressively submerged by the rising sea level. It is an eerie thought that its seabed of peat and sediment, which is continuous with the reclaimed land of the Fens, conceals many ancient artefacts and the shipwrecks of many eras. The constantly shifting sediments of mud and sandbanks of The Wash, mean that these potentially revealing clues to the past will probably remain permanently inaccessible. The salt marshes which once provided a living in the days when salt was nearly as valuable as gold, are now a haven for all kinds of wildfowl. You can volunteer to be a Wash wader ringer, ringing migrating birds, or if your hobby is metal detecting, then the area around The Wash could provide you with endless retirement fun. You might even find King John's treasure. It fell from a baggage wagon in the 13th century and was sucked into quicksand, apparently never to be seen again. The spot at which it disappeared is believed to be along the Nene estuary and now about 6–10 miles inland. The Wash is associated with several conservation areas including The Wash and North Norfolk Coast European Marine Site, nature reserves and is an Area of Outstanding Natural Beauty (AONB).

Hunstanton

Hunstanton looks west across The Wash from the north Norfolk coast and is a small seaside resort of the traditional Victorian kind. Hunstanton has existed since before the Domesday Book, but the resort is largely the brainchild of local landowner Henry Styleman Le Strange. He set about creating the seaside bathing resort of Hunstanton St Edmund (as it was then known) in the mid-19th century. The first hotel, the Golden Lion opened in 1842. The railway arrived in 1862, and was taken away again just over a hundred years later, when the branch line from King's Lynn was axed. There was also a Victorian pier, but this was destroyed by a violent storm in 1978. You don't have to be a geologist to be fascinated by Hunstanton's famous striped cliffs comprising a thin layer of red chalk with a white layer of chalk above and brown sandstone (known as carstone) below. Many of the Victorian buildings in the town are built from carstone quarried at nearby Snettisham (4 miles), a nice walk from Hunstanton.

Mysterious things abound in Hunstanton. There is the archway of a ruined Norman chapel by the lighthouse (the latter now a holiday home). The old hall and ancestral home of the Le Stranges (now converted into flats) has a ghostly occupant, 'the lady in grey'. There is also a black ghost dog known as Old Shuck, who is said to run up and down the coast between Hunstanton and Cromer looking for its drowned master. In 1938 the sea around Hunstanton froze to a depth of about six feet forming ice floes more reminiscent of the Arctic, a very strange sight indeed for an English coastline. As for the sunsets, they are fabulous, and rare for the East Coast, they happen over the sea, because Hunstanton faces west. This also explains why the local name for Hunstanton is 'Sunny Hunny'.

Hunstanton is close to the villages of Dersingham (6 miles), Heacham, Docking and trendy Burnham Market and is 10 miles from the Royal Estate at Sandringham. It is an area that attracts thousands of caravanners. This is how some folk get to retire here, by buying a mobile home to take holidays in, and then living in it for most of the year when they retire. Along with other places in Norfolk, Hunstanton is suitable for the less agile, as it has a flat seafront and beach that goes on for miles when the tide is out. The area has some hills and some famous walks. The long distance footpath, Peddars Way, meets the Norfolk Coast Path just east of Hunstanton. The Princess Theatre (named after Diana) is a centre for amateur productions, touring shows and film shows. There is an active U3A and lots of local clubs in the town and surrounding area. Hunstanton is too small to rate as a shopping place, but the over-60s get free buses to Norwich and King's Lynn where there is more choice, especially for clothing.

My experience...

Norma Ham, aged 62, moved to Hunstanton from Hertfordshire in 2005, after retiring from being a speech and language therapist.

We always enjoyed visiting the coast and Hunstanton was the nicest bit that was within reasonable distance from Harpington, where we lived before we came here. Hunstanton had all the amenities we needed and was small enough to walk around. It's in lovely countryside and has lovely beaches but we are still within easy reach of King's Lynn. I am sure there are more beautiful spots, but what is the point if you are 10 miles from the nearest post office?

We bought a house on a new estate 10 minutes' walk from the seafront. There's a Sainsbury's opening across the road and also a main high street with local shops. There is also a combined theatre/cinema/music hall in Hunstanton and lots of nice cafés and restaurants with lots of good, locally grown food, which is very much a culture thing here. There is a railway station at King's Lynn and buses go there every half hour. The nearest hospital is also in King's Lynn; my husband had to use it recently and was very impressed with the fact that he didn't have to wait.

We're interested in local history and I am doing a course in this with the University of East Anglia. I joined the Norfolk Wildlife Trust and the National Trust and in summer there is a Historic Houses group I attend with the U3A.

Since moving here, I've found the best things are the sea and the easy access. All the things we moved up here for and everything we need are within a short drive and it is a beautiful part of the world. The roads do get very busy in summer as we're

(Continued on following page)

(Continued)

near a very popular area for second homes and there are all the daytrippers going by. There are also a heavy proportion of older people, which is why some people call it the 'Eastbourne of the east'. It would be better if there were a greater mix of ages.

Hunstanton fact file

Access: A149. King's Lynn, 16 miles; Norwich, 45 miles, London approximately 120 miles

Airports: Norwich, 59 miles; Stansted, 90 miles

Average property price: £245,144

Bus services: First Eastern Counties Hunstanton/King's Lynn service. Coast Hopper service Hunstanton/Wells-next-the-Sea/Sheringham.

Climate: Bracing, but snow and frost are rarities

Councils: Hunstanton Town Council (www.hunstantontowncouncil.org); King's Lynn and West Norfolk Borough Council (www.west-norfolk.gov.uk)

Council tax: Band D £1,326.39; band E £1,621.14

Crime: Lowest crime rate in West Norfolk

Economic activity: Quite high due to the high visitor penetration of north Norfolk generally

Ferries: Hull; Harwich, 65 miles

Hospital: Nearest is Queen Elizabeth's Hospital, King's Lynn (www.qehkl.nhs.uk)

Percentage of people over 65: Approximately 25% (West Norfolk)

Population: Just under 5,000

Property prices: Detached £321,622; semi-detached £252,253; terraced £181,658, flat £172,301

Railway station: King's Lynn. First Capital Connect service direct from King's Lynn and Downham Market via Ely and Cambridge to King's Cross London.

Specialised retirement property: Retirement development is being limited by the need to build developments to attract income-generating newcomers and businesses

King's Lynn

After Norwich, King's Lynn is arguably Norfolk's most famous town, tucked into the south-east corner of The Wash. It has a history as a port going back to the 12th century when it was known as 'Lin', meaning a tidal spread. Although King's Lynn now lies on the Great Ouse river, a millennium ago it sat on the edge of a tidal lake fed by two small rivers. The following excerpt on King's Lynn is from William Camden's Britannia, a chorography of Britain published (in Latin) in 1607:

> By reason of the safe haven which yieldeth most easy access, for the number also of merchants there dwelling and thither resorting, for the also fair and goodly houses, the wealth of the townsmen, it is doubtless the principal town of this shire except Norwich only.

In medieval times, King's Lynn was accepted into the Hanseatic League formed by German merchants from the Baltic, which gave the town access to European trade, and thereby a licence to prosper; it was as successful as Southampton. The league or 'Hanse' still exists today as historic link, which also provides a useful networking organisation.

The many fine buildings built by the merchants of Lynn's golden age surround the old port of Bishop's Lynn, as it was known prior to the Dissolution of the Monasteries. In Henry VIII's time, its name was changed to Lynn Regis, which finally became King's Lynn. The fine buildings are the merchants' lasting legacy to the town, and a big tourist attraction helping to increase prosperity today. Such buildings include the St George's Medieval Guildhall and the magnificent Customs House built in 1683. Historically important Lynn folk include George Vancouver, the explorer and sailor. Horatio Nelson, later a lord and admiral, was born near Lynn at Burnham Thorpe (just outside Burnham Market). King's Lynn has its dollop of culture in the King's Lynn Festival of the Arts, which has been held since 1951 and attracts big names from the world of arts.

King's Lynn is probably one of the most attractive small towns in England at the edge of both The Wash and the North Norfolk coastal Area of Outstanding Natural Beauty (ANOB). It is great walking country; for instance the route from King's Lynn to Snettisham (14.6 miles), although it will never challenge your uphill skills. There are many other small towns in the vicinity, including Downham Market (12 miles), Dersingham (10 miles) and Wisbech (14 miles), so you are never at a loss for an outing or somewhere to visit. The Sandringham estate is also a big attraction.

My experience...

Margaret Fisher, now 73, moved with her husband to King's Lynn from Sidcup in 1998.

We had initially decided to move to Horsham while my husband was still working for Shell, because you can commute to London from there. But while we were in the process of organising that my husband had a heart attack and was not able to do anything at all. So we waited until that was sorted out, only to find that there weren't many houses on the market, which left us in limbo. We were on our way to see some friends in Lincolnshire and decided to drop in and see King's Lynn on the way. Although we had been there before and stayed in Hunstanton, I'd never shopped there before and it made a real impression: I liked the open space and that it's near the coast without being on it. We looked in some estate agents and spotted a house that met all the things I wanted: it had an open fireplace, south-facing garden and lots of other things and I could see what we could do with it. We made the decision so quickly that most people thought we had lost our marbles.

We moved into the house, which is five miles from the centre of King's Lynn and 10 minutes' walk from a supermarket and a parade of shops. I admit I wept my last few nights in Sidcup because I was leaving a garden that was 90ft long, for a much smaller one, but I know that gardening becomes harder work as you get older. Since moving, we've found the surrounding area of King's Lynn marvellous for walking: you're spoilt for choice. There are also lots of clubs that do pensioners' meals and lunches at a reasonable price, and we are not too far from Norwich, where there is an excellent theatre with West End shows. The bus service here is excellent and the hospital is only 15–20 minutes' drive away. There's also a railway service that takes you straight to London in an hour and 40 minutes, and we get free bus rides not just around Norfolk, but into the Lincoln area. We joined the U3A last year, but I haven't joined any clubs. I do china painting and I'm involved with art and family history.

The best thing for me is the open space. We get spectacular sunsets. The pace of life is slower and when I first came I thought people didn't have that get up and go that I was used to. They've certainly got beyond their resentment of incomers, but I think that a lot of people weren't that open to change. King's Lynn is growing fast: I think people are slowly accepting the changes.

King's Lynn fact file

Access: via A47, A10, A134, A149, A148, A1078. Peterborough, 36 miles.

Average property price: £176,530

Airports: Norwich, 45 miles; Stansted, 78 miles

Bus services: Norfolk Green (www.norfolkgreen.co.uk) operates throughout West Norfolk as far as Spalding, March, Cromer and Norwich

Climate: Seems to have its own milder microclimate

Council: Borough Council of King's Lynn and West Norfolk (www.west-norfolk.gov.uk)

Council tax: Band D £1,358; band E £1,660

Crime: Town centre crime and criminal activity around car parks and shopping centres has been reduced through installation of CCTV

Economic activity: Main centre for the area so quite economically active, especially tourism

Ferries: Harwich. The Dutch Flyer (www.dutchflyer.co.uk) is a ferry/rail ticket.

Hospital: Queen Elizabeth's Hospital, King's Lynn, district general hospital (www.qehkl.nhs.uk)

Percentage of people over 65: 25%

Population: Approximately 33,000.

Property prices: Detached £222,478; semi-detached £153,665; terraced £131,321; flat £108,760

Railway station: King's Lynn direct line to London King's Cross and London Liverpool Street (via Cambridge)

Specialised retirement developments: Bryant Homes have two developments (not specifically for retirees): Abbey Grove near King's Lynn and Kings Reach on the outskirts. There is also a new mobile home park for the retired and semi-retired over-50s at Shouldham, 5 miles from King's Lynn.

Spalding

The market town of Spalding is the main town of the South Holland district of Lincolnshire near the border with Cambridgeshire, midway between Boston and Peterborough, and just inland from the north-western corner of The Wash. It is one of those towns surrounded by villages with graphically bucolic names including Cowbit, Whaplode, Hop Poole, Tongue End and Twenty to name a few. Spalding is very much 'The Heart of the Fens', that fascinating area of reclaimed land that once ran with cattle, horses and the sheep whose wool made the district rich in the Middle Ages. No longer do 20,000 geese reared on the Lincolnshire Fens, feet dipped in tar to toughen them, get driven to Nottingham

Goose Fair in time to be eaten on the feast of Michaelmas. And how did the good burghers of the time show their appreciation for the Lord's great bounty? They built the magnificent churches, with which the area of Lincolnshire is dotted. Spalding was originally a trading place by the river Welland, which is still a prominent feature of the town today, providing shady walks along its banks within the town.

By the 16th century Spalding was described as 'a handsome town' and in 1566 Mary Queen of Scots stayed in the White Hart Inn, which still exists. On the edge of town is the most ancient building in Spalding, the medieval Ayscoughfee Hall, built in the 1430s and architecturally tampered with in subsequent centuries. The town continued to grow throughout the 17th and 18th centuries and contains many fine Georgian buildings, some of which conceal older interiors. In recent times the land has been converted to arable farming and horticulture. It is said that more flowers are grown in South Holland, Lincolnshire, than in Holland in the Netherlands. Each spring vast acres of tulips and daffodils are grown for the floral trade and are celebrated in the Spalding Flower Parade (www. flowerparade.org), which has been held since 1958.

My experience...

James Gibbs moved with his wife to Spalding from Solihull in 2001. He retired from the water industry, although he worked 10 years after that for a charity as their finance officer.

We wanted to find a property that we liked. It wouldn't have mattered where in the country it was, but we came to Spalding first because we had seen that property prices were incredibly low in this area. I've also got knee problems and the fact that the area is flat was a consideration. We spoke to some developers about coming to see some of their developments in the area and they arranged to collect us from our hotel when we came here. In the event, nothing they offered us appealed to us, but we liked what we saw of the area and had spotted a bungalow for sale in an estate agent's window and were delighted to find we could afford it. We are actually in Holbeach about 5 miles outside Spalding and 10 minutes' walk from the bank and shops. The important thing for us has always been the house we lived in and the immediate surroundings rather than the broader picture and this bungalow ticked all the boxes. Having said that, this landscape grows on you and the sky has magnificent sunsets.

When we first moved in we weren't particularly interested in local clubs although we have established ourselves in some now. We were more interested in the countryside. We are not too far from the coast on The Wash, and you can walk there or in The Wolds. Although the opportunities for eating out are rather more limited than we were used to in Solihull, we are more than compensated by the pace of life and the friendliness of local people. People who work in the shops are very friendly and if you are looking for something and they haven't got what you are looking for, they will tell you another shop that might have what you want. They go the extra mile to help you. You don't get that in bigger places.

Spalding fact file

Access: A16. Reasonable connections to the A1/M1. Peterborough, 18 miles.

Average property price: £126,456

Airport: East Midlands, 66 miles

Bus services: Call Connect (www.lincsinterconnect.com); dial a ride (0845 234 3344); Cavalier buses (01406 362518); Norfolk Green buses (01553 776980)

Climate: Low summer rainfall. With global climate change more winter rains and possible increased risk of flooding.

Council: Southend Borough Council (www.southend.gov.uk)

Council tax: Band D £1,284.61; band E £1,570.08

Crime: Town centre drunk and disorderliness but other types of crime fairly low

Economic activity: High employment levels reflect the economic buoyancy produced by horticulture and agriculture, but wages are low

Ferries: Nearest international ferry routes Hull

Hospitals: Johnson Community Hospital (has minor injuries unit); Welland Hospital (services for the elderly) both come under United Lincolnshire Hospitals (www.ulh.nhs.uk)

Percentage of people over 65: 25%

Population: 20,000

Property prices: Detached £168,875; semi-detached £146,333; terrace £112,333; flat £96,625

Railway station: Spalding. Connection via Peterborough to London King's Cross. Peterborough to London approximately 55 mins.

Specialised retirement property: McCarthy & Stone forthcoming development Swallows Court (0800 521276); Jelson Homes mixed type new development Flinders Park, close to Spalding (not specifically for retirement). Prices from £142,950 to £214,950.

Isles of Scilly

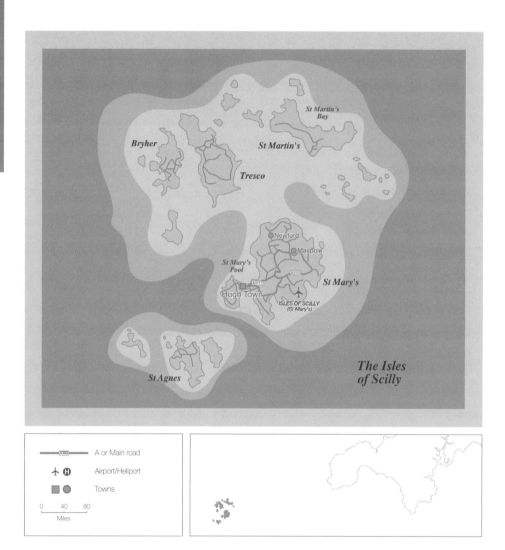

A or Main road		
Airport/Heliport		
Towns		

0   40   80
Miles

If there was some part of the British Isles where there was no traffic congestion and the main form of wheeled transport was the bicycle; where the climate was mild enough to allow tropical plants to grow; where the relationship between people and the land is still strong; and where you don't need to lock your front door because crime hardly exists, would you retire there? Oh, and if you can only get to and from by helicopter or plane (20+ minutes), or boat (2.4 choppy hours over the Atlantic), would you still want to retire there? It has been calculated that 40% of visitors to the Isles of Scilly return year after year, and evidently, the inconveniences and lack of a West End style arts scene or sophisticated shopping do not deter the new breed of retirees from making their holiday more permanent.

Scilly (after the Unitary Authority), the Scillies or Scilly Isles, but more correctly, Isles of Scilly, are an archipelago 28 miles off Land's End and they are included in the list of assets of the Duchy of Cornwall (www.princeofwales. gov.uk). Geologically, they are indeed part of Cornwall, having been formed at the same time and from the same granite found at Land's End. Before sea levels rose at the end of the last ice age, the four largest islands formed a single one. Only five of the hundreds of islands are inhabited: Bryher, St Agnes, St Martin's, St Mary's and Tresco. Tiny St Mary's is the main island and offers a port for ferries from Penzance. Many of the hundreds of 'islands' are no more than rocks, making for some exciting sailing, although the most popular local seafaring sport is gig racing. Gigs are pilot rowing boats that once guided boats into harbour before their use was given over wholly to recreation.

The total Scillies population of 2,000 humans is greatly outnumbered by seabirds, a fact that results in a deluge of excited twitchers, hellbent on spotting a rarity. They descend on the Scillies every October around the time of seasonal migrations. For those of the feather-loving fraternity, the publication *The Birds of the Isles of Scilly* by Peter Robinson (Christopher Helm Publishers 2003) is a must-have publication priced at £45, but possibly less if available second-hand on www.amazon.co.uk. Other popular pastimes are walking, dinghy sailing, fishing, wreck diving and gardening. Before tourism, the ill-wind profit from wrecks and small-scale agriculture helped the islanders to subsist, and more of the islands, such as Samson off Bryher, were inhabited by farming communities. Early spring flowers, such as daffodils and narcissi, have been grown as a crop by on the islands since the late 19th century, when the first consignment was sent up to London.

St Mary's

St Mary's island is 2.5 miles by 1.75 miles and is the home of three-quarters of the Isles of Scilly population. As it is such an unusually small and isolated retirement place, a description of it inevitably includes a shopping list of facilities and the word 'unique'. It has 9 miles of road and a circular bus service that operates from Easter to October. There are also taxis on the island. Islanders tend to keep small cars for getting around and although a car may be practical, it is not essential. Hugh Town, on a promontory of St Mary's, is the capital of the Scillies, and the former fortification has been converted into a hotel. Hugh Town has a town hall, health centre, churches of the mainstream persuasions, several public houses, cafés and restaurants, post office, banks and all the essentials of basic daily life. Despite being a diminutive area, the island manages to conjure up a variety of landscape including heath, marsh and woodland, as well as vestiges of neolithic habitation, burial, rocky coves and when the tide is out, white beaches. The coast is very indented giving rise to a surprising number of footpaths. If you retired to St Mary's you would probably have to be a keen dinghy sailor so that you could make the most of sailing possibilities around the archipelago. Sailors often comment that the weather at sea can be better than on the mainland, although fog can be a problem. When all is bright and clear, the sea is a near translucent blue and at very low tides it is possible to walk between some of the islands.

The main problem for anyone who wishes to retire to Scilly is that there are few properties on the market at any time and they have rocketed in price. An estate agent from the island reckoned that as many as 40% of houses on Scilly are bought as second homes. To answer the inevitable question about what is it like retiring to an island so small that you can see all of it in a day, it is probably best to hear from someone who has done just that.

My experience...

Maureen Shaw, aged 62, moved to St Mary's from Nottingham in 1997. She was a nursing assistant and her husband was a hospital manager.

We decided we wanted to move down south, when my husband, who is older than me, retired. We wanted a quieter pace of life compared with Nottingham. We'd been coming to the Scillies for nearly a decade and we really loved it, but never thought we would be able to afford to move here. We thought we'd move to Cornwall, but when we started looking, we couldn't find anywhere that we liked as much as Scilly. The people here are so friendly and the scenery is stunning, very beautiful. It's like stepping back in time a bit; hardly any crime or violence and people don't lock their doors, because it's safe.

We more or less sold everything we had to buy a flat here. When we moved, things weren't quite as expensive as they are now, but they were expensive. We decided on St Mary's because there weren't many places on the market when we were looking; there were about four properties, so not a good deal of choice. We are well-located for amenities; it's a very small island and nobody is far away. In Nottingham, you had to drive everywhere; here you just jump on your bike or walk. Everything you need is a stone's throw away. There's quite a lot going on for older people: whist drives, bridge club, dancing, WI ... I'm a member of the WI and I also help at the library. I didn't do much research into clubs and things before moving here and I had always thought the WI was rather stuffy, until I joined it and made a lot of friends and now I think it's such fun.

Although there are lots of cafés dotted all over the place they are seasonal and closed for winter. People who live here actually like the winter because everything calms down. There's no cinema. We've got a local hospital, but for anything major, you have to be flown to the mainland.

The best thing about St Mary's is its beauty. It's so stunning and I have never grown tired of it and I never take it for granted. Also the safety; I know I'll never be mugged or attacked, people look out for you and the community aspect is lovely. I'm not saying there aren't drawbacks, like the fog and the expense of travel to the mainland; it is very expensive even for residents. For us, the solution is to have the family to stay with us several times a year, which keeps us all happy. The cost of living is also expensive and it has shot up since we moved here. We knew it would always be a bit more expensive because everything has to be imported, but we have only one supermarket, Co-op, and it's about 6% more than the mainland. Despite these things, I can truthfully say that I've been walking round for 10 years with a big smile on my face.

St Mary's, Isle of Scilly

St Mary's fact file

Access: British International Helicopters (www.islesofscillyhelicopters.com) from Penzance; Skybus plane from Land's End or Newquay; also flights from Bristol and other UK regional airports. Boat (see ferries below).

Average property price: £200,000 (Cornwall and Isles of Scilly)

Airport: St Mary's in the, south of the Island

Bus services: Circular bus in summer on St Mary's

Climate: The Isles of Scilly are in the path of the Gulf Stream, responsible for their famously mild climate

Council: Council of the Isles of Scilly (www.scilly.gov.uk). Smallest unitary authority in the UK.

Council tax: Band D £1,027.57; band E £1,255.92

Crime: Almost non-existent

Economic activity: Based on the islands' assets: early spring flowers, fishing and tourism activities

Ferries: Scillonian to and from Penzance (www.ios-travel.co.uk)

Hospital: St Mary's on the Isles has minor injuries unit (www.cornwall.nhs.uk). Mainland hospital depending on treatment required; nearest is Penzance.

Percentage of people over 65: Approximately 22%

Population: Approximately 2,000

Property prices: Properties on market at time of survey include one-bedroom flat with harbour view £205,000; three-bedroom flat with harbour view from £400,000; small, semi-detached modern house from £350,000

Railway station: Nearest on the mainland is Penzance

Specialised retirement property: Very limited; sheltered accommodation only

North-east England

NORTH YORK MOORS

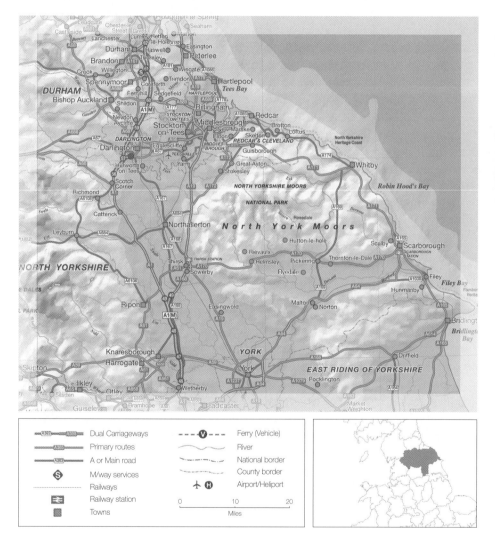

Dual Carriageways		Ferry (Vehicle)	
Primary routes		River	
A or Main road		National border	
M/way services		County border	
Railways		Airport/Heliport	
Railway station	0	10	20
Towns		Miles	

The North York Moors reach north of a line made by the A170, which runs west from Scarborough on the coast, through Pickering, Kirkbymoorside and Helmsley. The area north of this line, up to the A171, which skirts around the northern edge of the Moors from Whitby, through Redcar and Cleveland before joining the A172, continues the route around the north-western edge of the Moors and contains the towns and villages of the Moors including Helmsley, Ryedale, Hutton-le-Hole and Rievaulx Abbey. The Moors themselves and their stunningly varied landscape include Rosedale, Pickering Moor, the forests around Scarborough and the Cleveland Hills. As well as Scarborough, the eastern coastal edge of the Moors contains the popular resorts of Whitby and Filey. Most of the Moors area falls within The North York Moors National Park (www.visitnorthyorkshiremoors.co.uk), which is fabulous walking country. There is any number of walks to choose from, such as from Rosedale following the course of the defunct Rosedale railway, or the Cleveland National Trail. The website www.nym.cam.co.uk gives you a taste of what to expect. It shows photographs of the scenery along various walks; or you may prefer to wait, and see the real thing, for the first time when you explore the area with a view to retiring there. To the south of the North York Moors are the gentler slopes of the Yorkshire Wolds.

Scarborough

Best known as a seaside resort, Scarborough is in Yorkshire on the east coast. To the south of it are the resorts of Filey and Bridlington and to the north is Whitby. Scarborough embraces areas north and south of a prominent headland giving it not one, but two, magnificent bays, which are among its plentiful assets; these also include 383 acres of landscaped green spaces and parks. The origin of the town, like many on the east coast, was as a Viking stronghold. Long before it was a seaside resort, Scarborough was a market town that had grown from a fortified town with a castle, and it continued about its business throughout the Middle Ages and for centuries afterwards. 'Are you going to Scarborough Fair?' asks the well-known song. Scarborough's fair was originated by royal charter in 1253. Simon and Garfunkel's popular version of the song made the town more widely known abroad, and probably boosted the incoming tourist trade from the United States from the 1970s onwards. The last siege of the castle took place during the English Civil War, but not before spa water had been discovered flowing into the sea in 1626. The Restoration period saw the publication of a book by a Hull doctor, detailing the curative properties of the spa's waters. In 1679 the first visitors were reported to be in Scarborough for the purpose of 'sporting in Neptune's bosom' (in other words, sea bathing). Scarborough, with the best of both worlds, spa water and seawater, has never looked back, expanding in capacity and keeping its reputation for quality throughout the 18th century. The Victorians brought the gentrified Georgian town up-to-date by linking it to the railways in 1845, and opening a new Spa Hall in 1858, thereby inviting the prospect of mass tourism. Scarborough still attracted the nobility of Europe, the 'wobblier' of whom could be seen swathed against chills, being trundled along in bath chairs down the gently sloping paths of the spa gardens by their strong-armed servants. It might seem a little unfair to mention that the cliffs of Scarborough do have an alarming propensity for subsidence as this is a problem with many coastal areas, which have, like Scarborough, seen the loss of a few structures over the centuries. It should certainly not deter anyone eyeing up Scarborough as a possible place for retirement.

My experience...

Dennis Shaw aged 70, a retired scientist, moved to Scarborough from Northamptonshire in 2006 with his partner Marianne Cooper, a former teacher of the same age.

I had never been to Scarborough until I came up here with Marianne to visit some of her family, just over five years ago, and I was very taken with it. There's a wonderful seafront and you've got the cliffs and there is plenty of walking. It's also a lively town. In late 2005, when we were walking along the seafront, I suggested that we move here and she was enthusiastic because her grandchildren live here. The fact that we had links to the place meant that if we had any questions about the area, her son could help us out. Marianne had seen a beautiful cottage for sale in her son's village and asked him to arrange a viewing. Now we live in a good location about 4 miles from the centre of Scarborough. We've got a good Spar less than a mile away and an excellent bus service round the corner with fairly regular buses up to Scarborough, where there is an excellent train service. The only downside to travel is that we are a long way from an international airport.

Scarborough is good for day-to-day shopping, but Marianne thinks it would be good to have another department store. York isn't too far, though, if you want anything special. Then there's the Stephen Joseph Theatre, which is quite special, as well as the old Spa Theatre on the seafront. The whole town has a Victorian feel to it and it is unspoiled. We have never encountered a traffic jam at this end, not even in rush hour – not until you get to York. We weren't new to the U3A when we moved, but it's flourishing here. There are over 350 members, which is good for a small town. There are lots of groups and societies. We're keen on walking and there are lots of walking groups and we also belong to two bridge clubs and a recorded

(Continued on following page)

(Continued)

music society outside the U3A. Everyone is very friendly here. For Marianne the best thing is the scenery. Whenever we go for drives, she never fails to gasp at it. There are many lovely villages as well as countryside, lots of National Trust places to visit, and nice pubs and places to eat. The best thing for me is the climate; surprisingly it is drier than it was in the Midlands, and certainly milder than we expected.

For us the only major problem was finding an NHS dentist. Eventually we got on an NHS list 10 months after applying. We tried private dentists but there wasn't one we could go to here. In the end, we had to drive about 15 miles out of Scarborough.

Scarborough fact file

Access: A64 Scarborough to Whitby Road; A161 Scarborough to Filey. York, 45 miles. Harrogate, 50 miles.

Average property price: £166,109

Airports: Humberside, 62 miles; Leeds–Bradford, 75 miles. There is also a train service to Manchester Airport (change at York).

Bus services: Scarborough & District Motor Services (www.eyms.co.uk/scarborough.htm)

Climate: Winters can be very cold and heavy snows came to Scarborough and the North York Moors in February 2006

Councils: Scarborough Borough Council and North Yorkshire County Council

Council tax: Band D £1,331.52; band E £1,627.41

Crime: High level of car crime

Economic activity: Scarborough is in the throes of transforming itself into a forward-looking town by the sea as opposed to just a classic seaside resort

Ferries: Hull (approximately 60 miles) to Zeebrugge and Rotterdam

Hospital: Scarborough Hospital (www.scarborough.nhs.uk)

Percentage of people over 65: 17.4%

Population: 106,692

Property prices: Detached £243,157; semi-detached £157,327; £150,358; flat £125,840

Railway station: Scarborough

Residents' on-street parking permit: £15 per year (free for over-60s)

THE EASTERN SCOTTISH BORDERS AND NORTHUMBERLAND COAST

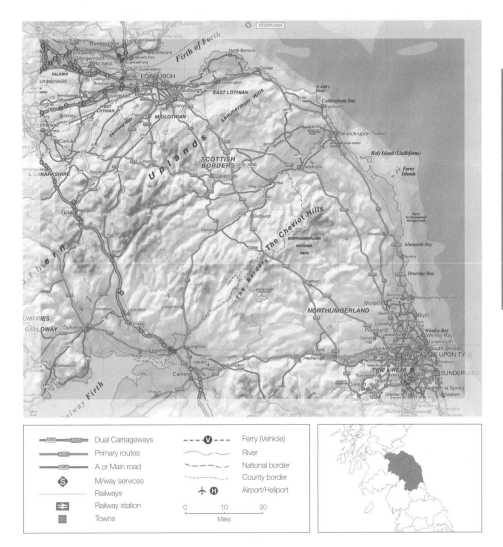

Dual Carriageways		Ferry (Vehicle)		
Primary routes		River		
A or Main road		National border		
M/way services		County border		
Railways		Airport/Heliport		
Railway station		0 10 20		
Towns		Miles		

The great length of the River Tweed has long been a natural border between Scotland and England. At the river's mouth, on the eastern coast, is the well-known border town of Berwick-upon-Tweed, the most northerly town in England, and also of the Northumberland coast. The latter is designated an Area of Outstanding Natural Beauty (AONB) which stretches 80 miles from Berwick in the north to Newcastle-upon-Tyne in the south. It incorporates the Holy Island of Lindisfarne, a place of mysticism and pilgrimage, and the Farne Islands, famous for seabirds of so many different kinds that it makes birdwatchers dizzy. Devoted twitchers may, however, find themselves being dive-bombed by alarmed birds during the nesting season. Further along the Scottish border, and just inside it, is Coldstream, another famous 'border toon', with a name many people know from the regiment of Guards based there and named after the town. Berwick-upon-Tweed is linked to Edinburgh via the A1, which partly hugs the coast, but mostly veers inland before arriving at Edinburgh on the Firth of Forth.

Berwick-upon-Tweed

To many Scots, Berwick-upon-Tweed is 'Scotland's lost limb'. To quote Alexander Eddington's *Castles and Historic Homes of the Border* (Oliver & Boyd 1949) on Berwick's change of fortunes:

> Berwick, by the middle of the 13th century, was considered a second Alexandria, so extensive was its commerce; in 1296, Edward I killed thousands in Berwick, (thus) the greatest merchant city in Scotland sank into a small seaport.

After Edward's annexation of Berwick, the town changed hands between England and Scotland 13 times before ending up 'English' in 1482. Today, Berwick is a town that is either schizophrenic, or has managed to combine the interests of both sides of the border. Berwick's popular theatre draws its clientele from both Scotland and England, energy is supplied by both English and Scottish companies, and Scottish customs such as Burns Night are celebrated in Berwick, which simultaneously flies the flag of St George. To solve the problem of which citizens in Berwick are Scots and which are English, the neutral term 'Berwicker' (pronounced bericker) is useful. Things weren't always so equable. By the end of the 16th century, Berwick's massive defences were falling into disrepair and the town became increasingly dependent on supplies from Scotland. Border officials were so alarmed that Berwick might be turning Scottish by stealth, that they expelled all Scots from the town and dismissed English soldiers married to Scottish wives. It might be churlish to point out that Berwick was part of the Kingdom of Northumbria until the battle of Carham in 1018, when Malcolm II of Scotland declared the River Tweed to be the boundary of his kingdom, thus placing Berwick in Scotland. While Berwick is on the north side of the river mouth, two other smaller settlements on the south side make up the bounds of Berwick-upon-Tweed area today. Five years ago, property in Berwick was a steal but has rocketed since, thanks to an interest in second homes in the town. Berwick is in a fascinating area, especially the castles, coastal nature reserves and English and Scottish history. There is fabulous rugged walking, salmon fishing and the startlingly wild, mystical and beautiful county of Northumberland, Newcastle-upon-Tyne and the Scottish capital all within easy reach.

NORTH-EAST ENGLAND

Seagull infestation of Berwick has reached crisis point, even making the minutes of the local council's meeting in late 2006, 'This council recognises the public concern about the large seagull population in Berwick-upon-Tweed.'

Terrorised citizens can call the council's seagull helpline (01289 301734). Perhaps it's time to do the remake of Hitchcock's *The Birds* for the local budding film festival?

My experience...

John Bamford, aged 71, moved to Berwick from Salisbury in 1999, together with his wife. He is a retired senior lecturer in technical teaching.

My wife is from this area and knew it well. In fact, for years she had owned a house up here that was used as a family home, and if you like, it was also a holiday home, so it was always our intention to move up here on retirement. We had visited the region many times because we love the walking. It's a slower pace of life here than in the south, where we'd come from. There's a terrific amount of local history up here and far less traffic and background noise. There are also fewer people and life isn't as frantic, plus you have got marvellous fresh air.

We bought a house 100 yards from the sea. It's next door to a village shop and a 20-minute walk into Berwick centre, where there are pubs, a post office and a market twice a week. We did join the Ramblers before we came and found out about local societies and clubs and things. We belong to a club called the Berwick Naturalists and a local historical society, which has monthly lectures on aspects of the area's history. Berwick has shops and a Morrisons and Somerfield; there are no big supermarkets like Tesco. The thing we miss, though, is theatre and cinema; Berwick has neither. There is an arts centre, which shows films during the small local film festival and has visiting theatre groups. For serious arts, though, you need to go to Edinburgh or Newcastle for the cinema. Late night transport isn't too good and trains don't run at night, so you've got to go to matinées.

A lot of people have to leave Berwick to get jobs and they nearly always return when they retire. Many people retire this way – back to their roots – and you do notice the high retired population. However, as a seaside resort we get visitors in the summer, so there's a change in the population. We have found that people here are very friendly. I've also found the weather isn't as bad as one expects; we've had 52 dry Sundays in a row, which makes walking very enjoyable, and the winters are getting milder. On the practical side, finding plumbers and carpenters here isn't nearly as easy as in the south, but if you do your research you will find one in the end.

NORTH-EAST ENGLAND

Berwick-on-Tweed fact file

Access: On the A1 and almost equidistant between Edinburgh (57 miles) and Newcastle (53 miles)

Average property price: £149,856

Airports: Newcastle, 60 miles; Edinburgh, 65 miles

Bus services: Buses to/from Edinburgh, Newcastle and border towns. Service providers include First Group (www.firstgroup.co.uk).

Climate: Dryer and milder than you might expect. The eastern side of England/ Scotland gets far less rain than the western side.

Council: Berwick-upon-Tweed Borough Council (www.berwick-upon-tweed.gov.uk)

Council tax: Band D £1,339.46; band E £1,637.12

Crime: One of the safest areas in England and Wales

Economic activity: Among the lowest in England. Tourism, including salmon fishing, is important.

Ferries: Newcastle to Holland and Norway (www.dfds.co.uk)

Hospital: Berwick Infirmary (small); nearest large Hospital is Wansbeck General on the outskirts of Ashington (60 miles) (www.northumbria.nhs.uk)

Percentage of people over 65: 22.5%

Population: Approximately 26,000

Property prices: Detached £231,312; semi-detached £128,639; terraced £139,017; flat £112,819

Railway station: Berwick-upon-Tweed served by the East Coast Line that runs north-south

Residents' on-street parking permit: £75 per year

North-west England

THE LAKE DISTRICT

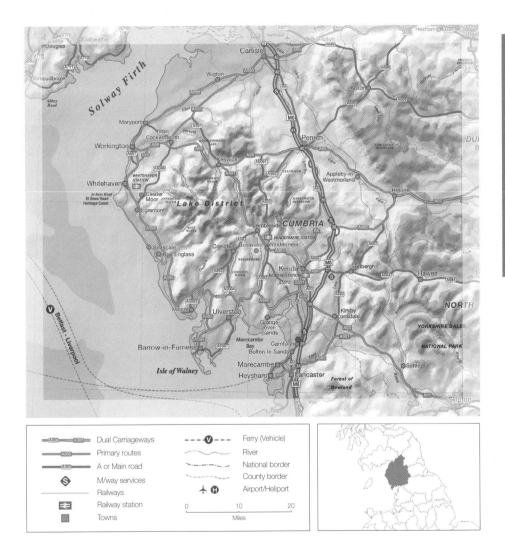

	Dual Carriageways		Ferry (Vehicle)
	Primary routes		River
	A or Main road		National border
	M/way services		County border
	Railways		Airport/Heliport
	Railway station		
	Towns		

0   10   20
Miles

The county of Cumbria contains England's largest national park, the Lake District (www.lake-district.gov.uk), bounded on its western side by the A595 and on its eastern side by the M6. 'The Lakes', as the area is familiarly called, embraces stunning landscapes of fells and dales and over a dozen lakes, the largest being Windermere, Ullswater and Derwent Water, and the coast including Ravenglass and Saltcoats. Westward towns of the Lake District include Cockermouth and Broughton-in-Furness, with Kendal and Penrith on its eastern edge. Just south of the Lake District, and thus the southern coast of Cumbria, are the areas of Duddon Sands and Morecambe Bay, which have come to be known in tourist-speak as the Lake District Peninsula. Retiring in the Lake District would provide you with a lifetime of walking opportunities and a chance to explore the Lakes and coastal region to your heart's content, since it would probably give you a very healthy constitution. Some idea of the walking potential can be gathered from John Dawson's Lake District Walks (www.lakedistrictwalks. com), although there are many published guides on the subject. Since walking in the Lake District has been popular since Victorian times, there is a treasure trove of classic guidebooks that can be tracked down through antiquarian bookshops, at jumble sales or via websites. The best-known guides in recent times are by Alfred Wainwright, whose handwritten guides, illustrated with his own drawings, are mostly, but not entirely out of print. If you should ever tire of the Lake District, visiting the Isle of Man is another possibility; it lies south-west off Barrow-in-Furness on the Lake District Peninsula and ferries go there from Heysham on the eastern side of Morecambe Bay. You can also hop on a ferry from the Isle of Man to Ireland.

The Lake District is also sheep country and is scattered with picturesque hamlets and farms. Second and holiday homes are nearly as numerous as sheep flocks and it would seem many people picture themselves eventually retiring to a house in the Lake District; cotton wool mists and the wet of winter notwithstanding. It is just as well to bear in mind that the Lake District is a supreme example of the law of cause and effect: the Lakes are there for a reason. The area has 200 wet days and 20 days of snow a year on average; so rain is the norm and waterproof gear is not only *de rigueur* but essential. Since there are hundreds of holiday cottages to rent in the Lake District having a try-out period would not be a problem.

Kendal

Kendal is on the south-western edge of the Lake District on the River Kent and is a few miles from the sea at Milnthorpe and Grange-over-Sands. Lake Windermere is just on the doorstep and just west of Windermere is the smaller lake of Coniston Water. The other lakes are an hour or two away by car. Kendal has been a prosperous town several times in its history from the 1400s to the late 19th century, as can be seen from its size and substantial buildings. These include the Holy Trinity church, one of the largest parish churches in England, which could be mistaken for a cathedral. Kendal was a wool-processing town powered by several mills on the river Kent. In more recent times, it was the home of K Shoes, whose factories closed in 2003 creating a local unemployment problem.

Up to the Second World War, the Lancaster Canal helped to feed industry in Kendal. When the canal fell into disuse, the Lancaster to Kendal section was eventually filled in; a sad end to an historic canal built in 1812. There is hope that the restoration group campaigning to get the Kendal canal link restored might eventually achieve their aim, not least because it would enhance tourism prospects in the Kendal area by linking into the national canal network. However, the scheme needs a huge amount of money, and certainly more than the £60m quoted. In fact, architectural vandalism in the name of progress seems to have hit Kendal particularly hard and robbed it of many architectural gems, demolished for the sake of roads and modern developments. Many of the buildings of note that have survived the 1950s demolition blitz date from the 1600s, and there is also the ruined Norman castle. However, Kendal has many good points, including excellent transport connections, reasonable shopping, friendly people and not least, the wonderful watery scenery of lakes and coasts immortalised by Alfred Wainwright (see above) in his guides to the Lakeland fells. He lived in Kendal from 1941, until his death in 1991.

Farmhouse in the Lake District

NORTH-WEST ENGLAND

My experience...

Jenny Ottewell, aged 67, moved to Kendal on her own in 2005 from St Albans, after retiring from teaching and working abroad for many years.

I didn't actually choose Kendal initially. I was looking for a house with certain characteristics in an area I could afford, and I wanted it to be accessible for people to visit or for me to travel. I had an open map and it gradually narrowed down to this area, which I had a bit of an association with from childhood holidays and visits. Kendal is a medium-sized town and there are plenty of people and activities, plus it's very easy to access the Lake District.

I stayed with a friend and arranged some places to visit, then, on my way to the church, I saw this particular house and, after seeing it, I cancelled all the other house-viewing appointments. I moved in almost immediately and it was a miracle to me that I could afford such a place; but houses are less expensive here than in the south-east. I'm 10 minutes' walk from the shops and I can walk along the river to supermarkets. Everything is within walking distance and there are town buses that go around town if you are less mobile. Within Kendal itself there's a branch line that goes to Manchester Airport and we are also near the famous West Coast Line. Kendal has a leisure centre, which has concerts, and a town hall, art gallery, museum and a theatre/cinema in a converted former brewery. The shops are more varied here than in St Albans because Kendal is a bit on its own, so it needs to have local and high street name shops.

When I came to Kendal, I had no contacts at all within the town. The first contact was with the church, but then I wanted to meet people outside the church, so I looked around for other activities and now I paint through the U3A, which I joined. I also volunteer in a drop-in centre for the homeless and a cancer charity. Since moving here I've found it a very friendly place. I feel welcome and have friends here without knowing everything about everybody. People here have been made very angry at the government trying to withdraw services, such as hospitals, or a reduction in train services and these are things that unite the community; there's a very good community spirit. Some people complain a bit about the rain, but it doesn't bother me.

Kendal fact file

Access: 6 miles along the A684 west from junction 37 of the M6. Fed also by the A591, A684 and the A6. Windermere, 9 miles; Keswick, 30 miles.

Average property price: £177,000

Airport: Manchester, 95 miles

Bus services: The principal operator is Stagecoach. Publishes twice yearly free publication Cumbria and Lakesrider timetable of buses, trains and lake ferries throughout Cumbria.

Climate: A lot of rain

Councils: Kendal Town Council (www.kendaltowncouncil.gov.uk); South Lakeland District Council (www.southlakeland.gov.uk)

Council tax: Band D £1,424,67; band E £1,741.26

Crime: Alcohol-related town crime, petty vandalism and graffiti

Economic activity: Agriculture and industry in decline. Kendal is looking at regeneration plans.

Ferries: For Lake ferries info see 'Bus services' above

Hospital: Westmorland General Hospital in Kendal (www.mbpct.nhs.uk). Coronary care unit currently under threat of closure.

Percentage of people over 65: Approximately 20%

Population: 28,000

Property prices: Terrace £157,000; semi-detached three-bedroomed house £186,000

Railway station: Kendal is on the branch line from Oxenholme to Windermere. There are direct services from Oxenholme up to Scotland and down to London and the South Coast.

Residents' on-street parking permit: Currently free

Whitehaven

Whitehaven is a Georgian town on the west coast of Cumbria, on the edge of the Lake District. To the north is Workington and to the south is the Sellafield site, which reprocesses spent nuclear fuel rods and other fissionable material, that has to be stored hermetically for thousands of years. It is also near the Victorian resort of Seascale. Satellite villages around Whitehaven are Egremont, St Bees, Cleator Moor and Frizington. One of Whitehaven's many claims to fame is that it was the first planned town since medieval times. It grew prosperous on the back of mining (coal and iron ore) and shipping interests. The many fine houses are a testament to the wealth of the merchants and sea captains who made their homes there – 250 buildings in the town are listed and nearly all of them are 18th century. The last coal mine closed in 1986 and there is a monument to the human face of mining in the Beacon area. Whitehaven's special relationship with America is even closer than Tony Blair's: Mildred Gale, the grandmother of George Washington, the first US president, is buried there. Whitehaven harbour was the only place in Britain to be attacked by American ships during the American war for independence in 1778. Throughout the 1700s Whitehaven was one of England's most important ports, exporting coal and importing tobacco, rum and other cargo, including shameful human ones. Whitehaven's grid pattern is reputedly the template for the most famous planned town of all, New York City. Whitehaven's main industries went into terminal decline from the 1950s. Despite its obvious attractions, including a fine harbour and solid architecture, the town remained a neglected and depressed area until the 1990s when a phased regeneration programme was carried out. The town now has a sparkling and orderly appearance, a new marina and all the amenities, including new doctor's surgeries and a sports centre, which are deemed requirements for an excellent quality of life. Tourism is very important to the town and events including an annual Maritime Festival, which brings tall ships into the harbour, and the fact that the town is the Gateway to the Lakes, guarantee to attract tourists. Whitehaven is also the start of the C2C (coast to coast) cycle route, which goes from Whitehaven to Sunderland and also the Reivers route Whitehaven to Tynemouth. The nearest sandy beach is at St Bees, four miles to the south. Nice bars and restaurants also help to make life pleasant, but above all it is the history and interest of the place itself that make Whitehaven an attractive place to retire. It has received two accolades that are tributes to its regeneration of recent years. In a survey by the Sunday Times, it was voted one of the top 10 seaside places in Britain. In October 2007 it became the first place in Britain to have the analogue television signal switched off and replaced with a digital one, thus bringing it firmly into the 21st century and bolstering its place in the history books.

My experience...

Claire Francois, aged 77, moved from Bromley to Egremont, on the outskirts of Whitehaven, in November 2006.

Although I had a very full life and lots of friends in London, I had family up here and after three years of them trying to persuade me to move up here I decided to look around. I thought I'd probably look for a retirement flat, but they don't appear to exist up here. I looked in Cockermouth, but found it dreary. My friends found a three-bedroom bungalow with a large garden on the outskirts of Whitehaven that I liked. Having made up my mind, I was very positive about making a life here and even though I didn't choose Whitehaven I love its natural beauty and wonderful views. I love that it's open; when you walk out of your door you see hills, and at the back of my house are open fields.

Before moving, I made a point of finding out what there is to do and my main focus was the U3A, because I knew that I would meet people with similar interests. I joined and everyone was very kind to me; it was absolutely wonderful. I think that the U3A is the very best place to meet people when you are older. I haven't had a chance to join any of the other groups yet, but I have started to make tentative plans for a music group. There's also a Sunday luncheon club, which visits different places and gives me a chance to find out about what the area has to offer – and it's much cheaper than London.

I'm five minutes from local shops, which is handy, although compared with London they are a bit disappointing. There are several supermarkets including Tesco, Morrisons, Netto and Iceland, all a short drive away. There are a couple of cinemas in Whitehaven and a charming small local theatre/cinema. The health services are brilliant, I have seen the doctor and chiropodist and there's a very good emergency health clinic in the village where I live. The best thing about retiring here is the friendliness of the people. I didn't know anyone when I moved into this close of 16 bungalows and I got welcome cards and Christmas cards from everybody. I've also found that if you want something done and you phone up and arrange a time, they come when they say they will. I do miss London theatre, ballet, Covent Garden and London Transport. Here there are lots of buses, but the distances are further. I would say you definitely need a car here.

NORTH-WEST ENGLAND

Whitehaven fact file

Access: Via M6 to Penrith (junction 40) then west on A66. Keswick, 26 miles; Cockermouth, 13.5 miles

Average property price: £139,803

Airports: Newcastle and Leeds-Bradford are closer (93 miles and 130 miles), but Manchester is easiest as there is a rail link from Manchester Airport to Whitehaven (by car it takes 2 hour 30 mins)

Bus services: Twice-yearly free bus timetable published in conjunction with Stagecoach which gives all bus, train and ferry services in Cumbria (01228 606705) or go to www.cumbria.gov.uk/roads-transport/publictransport/busserv/timetables/default.asp

Climate: Can be wild, wet and stormy

Council: Copeland Borough Council (www.copelandbc.gov.uk)

Council tax: Band D £1,091; band E £1,247

Crime: Vandalism and petty crime quite high

Economic activity: Regenerated town in a deprived area

Ferries: Liverpool (to Ireland and the Isle of Man)

Hospital: A&E at West Cumberland Hospital (01946 693181). Also Cumberland Infirmary in Carlisle opened in 2000 (www.ncumbria.nhs.uk).

Percentage of people over 65: Approximately 22%

Population: 35,000

Property prices: Detached £200,138; semi-detached £124,520; terrace 120,752; flat £96,475

Railway station: Whitehaven. West Coast trains go to Carlisle, then regional train from Carlisle to Whitehaven.

Specialised retirement property: Not specifically for retirement, but plentiful supply of town flats from about £85,000 (one-bedroom).

MERSEYSIDE

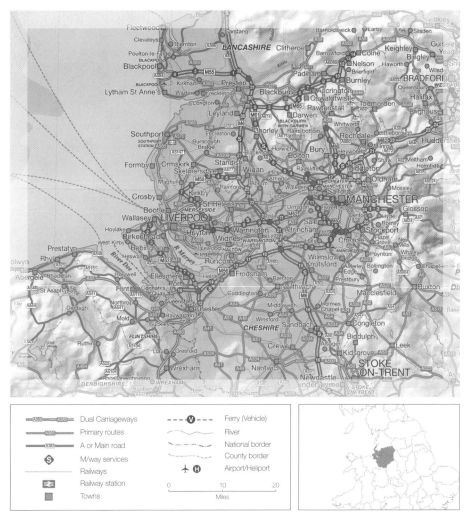

Dual Carriageways	Ferry (Vehicle)	
Primary routes	River	
A or Main road	National border	
M/way services	County border	
Railways	Airport/Heliport	
Railway station		
Towns	0 10 20	
	Miles	

There is a tendency to think of Merseyside as the Liverpool city region. Much of what has taken place on the great inlet of the River Mersey seems to have been dominated by this once great port, as it served the vast manufacturing hinterland of north-eastern Britain, facilitating the trade of the British Empire on a global scale. Between 1824 and 1860 docking capacity in Liverpool was doubled. Liverpool is now seventh in the league of importance of British ports, having once been the second busiest. The most recent dock to be built was finished in 1974, but with the decline of British manufacturing and the rise of technology, changes in world trading, and competition from other ports, Liverpool was in terminal decline, with the old industries no longer able to support the large population of Merseyside (now around 1.5 million). In recent times Merseyside has been subjected to the first phase (completed 2007) of a massive 'regeneration and rejuvenation' programme focused on the Merseyside Waterfront Regional Park, which includes 83.8 miles of the Merseyside coastline. This has seen many of the old docks converted to new purposes including tourism and heritage, shopping, housing and business. Liverpool's other attractions include more than 2,000 Georgian listed buildings, renowned art galleries such as Tate Liverpool and Lady Lever, and the hectic nightlife has seen the city centre become an appealing place to live and work. The transformation of Liverpool into an entertaining and cultural hotspot will be paraded in 2008 when Liverpool will be the European Capital of Culture that year.

Merseyside does expand further than Liverpool and its adjacent areas of Bootle and Garston. It embraces the south bank of the Mersey formed by the Wirral peninsula, where the port areas of Wallasey, Birkenhead and Ellesmere are located. From Merseyside there is easy access to Chester and North Wales. There are also regular ferries from Liverpool to Dublin or Belfast with P&O Irish Sea Ferries and Norfolkline Irish Sea Ferries, while Steam Packet ferries service Liverpool to Douglas Isle of Man. Liverpool's John Lennon Airport is south-east of Liverpool.

Southport

In 1792, when the first hotel opened at 'South-port', on the junction of what are now Duke Street and Lord Street in Southport, Liverpool to, the south, was already England's second largest port. North of Liverpool were some hamlets: Birkdale (now famous for its golf course) and Churchtown (mentioned in the Domesday Book); the area just south of Churchtown was known as South Hawes. These and other villages, Ainsdale, Birkdale, Churchtown and Hillside, have been subsumed into the Southport area. Two hundred years ago, the sea also reached much further inland making a tidal estuary that proved a safe haven for local boats. Within 10 years of its creation, Southport had a population of about 2,000 and before the advent of the railways visitors came by canal as well as by road. By the mid-19th century railways had linked Southport to both Liverpool and Manchester bringing workers from the Lancashire mill towns in much larger numbers than their more genteel predecessors. The Victorian heyday had arrived in all its glory of seaside amusements, parks and gardens, rows of villas and a pier (still standing). The best-known street is Lord Street, a mile-long avenue with Victorian shop frontages, considered a prime area for shopping and dining.

Southport has become a retirement hotspot for several reasons: the place itself is sophisticated, with tremendous facilities and ambience along with the fact that it is flat, so decreasing agility doesn't mean decreased mobility. In fact the town has just enlarged its shopmobility scheme. Transport connections are good and there is plentiful sheltered housing. One-bedroom retirement flats are preposterously easy to find.

My experience...

Dame Helen Nelson, who is now 67, moved alone from Upholland near Wigan to Southport in 2001, having retired from recruitment consultancy. She is widowed.

We used to live about 20 miles away and I'd been to Southport as a visitor and was quite impressed. You go out on this high street and you are immediately impressed by its classiness; it's not your run-of-the-mill place. I was planning to move from where I was living because I was in a large house with five bedrooms and, for a widow, the maintenance was horrendous. Southport was one of the places I considered along with Preston and Wigan and it had advantages over the other places because it has many contrasts. In summer there's the beach and lots of summertime activities and in the winter there are lots of alternatives that I find interesting to do. We've beautiful botanic gardens with a great little café, the arts centre and two theatres. There are also pubs with music evenings and there's lots of jazz played here, which I love.

I noticed that the housing costs here are considerably more expensive than where we were, but I think when you balance it out with what the town has to offer, it is good value. I bought a flat a mile from the town centre, close to the beach and I'm very happy with the decision I made. I've joined a few music groups and the U3A as well as a history group, dancing group, folk singing group; I'm never in! For me, it's the best thing since moving here: the ability to continue to be really active, which I have been all my life. There's such a variety of activities and all tastes are catered for.

I'm a mile and a half from the hospital, which used to have a bad reputation, but has been turned around. I had a bad accident and had to stay there for over a month and it was quite good. I had no problems. I also have quite bad arthritis and when I have a really bad day, I can go and get an electric shopmobility scooter from the local scheme. This helps me get out and about and do my shopping and keep my independence.

There has definitely been some resentment of incomers, but I've found the longer I'm here, the more I am accepted. I think that if you're seen as an outsider who's going to try and change things, then you will be resented, whereas if you are prepared to join in with what's already here then you will be made much more welcome.

Southport fact file

Access: A565; nearest Motorway M58 (10 miles). Liverpool approximately 17 miles.

Average property price: £185,000

Airport: Liverpool John Lennon, 27 miles

Bus services: Many run by Arriva Merseyside. See also www.merseytravel.gov.uk or telephone 0870 608 2608.

Climate: Reported frequency in storm events and increased winter rainfall over the past few winters

Council: Sefton Council (www.sefton.gov.uk)

Council tax: Band D £1,341.66; band E £1,639.80

Crime: High crime area

Economic activity: Increasing economic activity in the town and on the seafront

Ferries: Liverpool to Ireland and Isle of Man

Hospitals: Two large hospitals, Southport & Formby District General Hospital and Ormskirk and District General Hospital (www.southportandormskirk.nhs.uk)

Percentage of people over 65: Approximately 16%

Population: 90,000

Property prices: Detached £350,000; semi-detached £202,000; terrace £196,000; flat £146,000. Large amount of semi-detached property popular with families and thousands of flats and apartments.

Railway station: Southport

Residents' on-street parking permit: £20 per year

Specialised retirement property: Rosewood, Cambridge Road, Churchtown development for over-60s. Lots of flats in town may be suitable for the retired although not specifically designed for them.

WELSH BORDERS

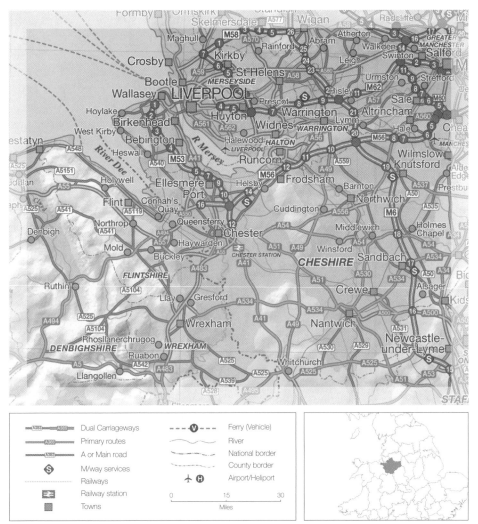

Legend	
Dual Carriageways	Ferry (Vehicle)
Primary routes	River
A or Main road	National border
M/way services	County border
Railways	Airport/Heliport
Railway station	
Towns	0 15 30
	Miles

The Welsh border counties of England reach from Merseyside in the north to the River Severn in the south and are, north to south: Cheshire, Shropshire and Herefordshire and the north-western part of Gloucestershire. Border towns in England include Chester, Oswestry, Knighton, Hay-on-Wye and Coleford. The Welsh borders conjure up a pleasing picture of hills, marches and lush deep river valleys. The chain of strategically placed castles and fortifications were built from the time of the Norman Conquest of England to the 14th century when the Normans were forced to hem the fiery Welsh in, and there was a lot of hard fighting on both sides. Nowadays, the Welsh borders are a place to find peace and quiet, and fine touring country, with hills, valleys wide rivers, notably the Wye and Dee.

Chester

Historically, Chester, on the River Dee in Cheshire, is a strategic Welsh border town in Welsh border country, with a complete encirclement of city walls. It was also an important town in Roman Britain 2,000 years ago, as its fully excavated, grand, two-tier amphitheatre reveals. The Romans called it *Deva* (the 'v' is pronounced as a 'w') although *castra*, the Latin for a military camp is the derivation of the name Chester. In the industrial 19th century, Chester was part of the Merseyside hinterland with connections to Ellesmere Port. In our consumerist times, Chester is a place for leisure driven by affluence. It provides a pretty backdrop full of historic buildings, including the cathedral and castle, expensive restaurants and bars. It is an easily reached honeypot from the West Midlands and the conurbations of Liverpool and Manchester, and it has become an increasingly prosperous place from its tourism, financial services and retail therapy. This is not surprising as Chester lies at the heart of the wealthy county of Cheshire. Chester makes an appealing alternative to the increasingly crowded south-east of England, as it is surrounded by beautiful countryside with the Pennines to the east and south-east and the Welsh hills and Welsh coast to the west and north-west. It also has excellent transport connections by road, rail and air and a great little racecourse, which claims to be the oldest in England. There is an easy cycle route along the old railway freight route from Chester to Connah's Quay.

My experience...

Roger Fielding, now 67, moved to Chester with a partner from Bishop's Stortford. He was formerly involved in the oil/gas business.

When I retired, we had an open map, so it came down to what our interests are. We like walking, especially hill walking, and found ourselves gravitating northwards. The south-east was getting too busy for us, but we didn't want to go too far north, so we sort of decided on Shrewsbury, but failed to find the right kind of property there. My daughter had been to Chester and suggested that we try there and it sort of struck a chord. We've got hills and nice walking here and there's a theatre and others in Mold and Liverpool, so we've got as much choice here as we used to have in Bishop's Stortford. We concentrated our research into the area on clubs and societies, rather than on the town itself, and we went to the library, read up about it and asked people what there was here. As well as walking, we're into Scottish dancing and there are at least two clubs in Chester. We also play bridge and there's the Diva Bridge Club and an active U3A here that we are both members of. You have to make an effort to go out and do things as nobody is going to come knocking on your door.

We moved into our house within seven months. We're now 20 minutes' walk from the centre of Chester and there are some locals shops 10 minutes' walk away. There's also a bus stop a few minutes away, but there are only two buses a morning so you have to plan ahead. Train services from Chester are very good; Chester to Crewe takes 20 minutes.

There are old buildings in Chester, so it's got a lot of character. The centre is compact and you can walk round it and there are retail parks nearby. We noticed that people here are a bit more friendly and open than in the south-east, and they seem more relaxed. Chester is big enough to be a bit cosmopolitan compared to some places. Some areas of the city are noisy and undesirable but we tend to stay clear of those. I'd say we're very content to be here.

Chester fact file

Access: M53, M56, A41, A51, A55. Liverpool, 27.5 miles.

Average property price: £216,450

Airports: Liverpool John Lennon, 25 miles; Manchester, 34 miles along M56

Bus services: First Chester & Wirral (www.firstgroup.com) provides direct link to Liverpool and routes radiating from Chester city centre

Climate: West coast has higher rainfall than east coast

Council: Chester City Council (www.chester.gov.uk)

Council tax: Band D £1,361; band E £1,663

Crime: Many residents feel the city is intimidating at night and Chester attracts a lot of homeless people

Economic activity: Very affluent area

Ferries: from Liverpool to Belfast, Dublin and the Isle of Man

Hospitals: Countess of Chester, large NHS hospital, 3 miles from city centre (www.coch.org)

Percentage of people over 65: Approximately 21%

Population: 120,600

Property prices: Detached £320,541, semi-detached £201,583; terraced £158,802; flat £145,334

Railway station: Chester. From Crewe, direct connections to London.

Residents' on-street parking permit: £60 per year

The South Coast including the New Forest

THE SOUTH COAST AND THE NEW FOREST

	Dual Carriageways		Ferry (Vehicle)
	Primary routes		River
	A or Main road		National border
	M/way services		County border
	Railways		Airport/Heliport
	Railway station		
	Towns		

0   10   20

Miles

Just as the ponies of the New Forest know exactly which spot to congregate in for a cooling breeze in summer, retired people know the place to congregate where the winter climate is the mildest in the UK. For some, the South Coast is the place to retire. The South Coast of England includes the southern edge of the New Forest around Barton-on-Sea and Milford-on-Sea, and the Isle of Wight. It has many of the most popular retirement towns, including Chichester, Christchurch, Bournemouth and Eastbourne, and the seaside towns of West Sussex from Bognor Regis to Brighton & Hove. The South Coast's very built up sections and ribbon coastal development means some towns form virtual conurbations: Poole–Bournemouth–Christchurch at the western end of the South Coast, and Worthing–Shoreham-by-Sea–Brighton & Hove in West Sussex, towards the east. East of Brighton & Hove is the appropriately named Eastbourne. Between Eastbourne and Folkestone is the atmospheric (some might say 'empty and desolate') landscape of Romney Marshes (see south-east England section from p156). The western end of the lengthy South Coast is convenient for the West Country. In the middle of the South Coast the Isle of Wight is pitched opposite the city ports of Southampton and Portsmouth, which are also jumping-off points for ferries to the Continent. The eastern end of the South Coast is very convenient for London, Brighton and the Channel Tunnel entrance at Folkestone as well as ferries from Folkestone and Dover to France. The main problem facing many people looking for a retirement location here, is that the most sought-after places on the South Coast have also become some of the most expensive both for property purchase and the cost of living. Brighton is casually known as 'London on Sea', with property prices to match. However, it is still worth looking for specialist retirement property. For example, an apartment in a Bournemouth retirement complex was for sale at £180,000 in 2007, while Worthing, a stone's throw from Brighton, but still much cheaper, is well worth a look.

Bognor Regis

Sickly and near death, George V reputedly retorted 'bugger Bognor' when his physician suggested a visit there would be good for his health. Formerly the high and haughty, and latterly the less exalted, have found Bognor Regis, a seaside resort in West Sussex, approximately halfway between Portsmouth and Brighton, a more attractive prospect than the name or the royal alliteration might suggest. In 1275 it was recorded as the hamlet of Buggenore. At the end of 1785, Bognor was a development project in the mind of an aristocratic entrepreneur, who aimed to cash in on the new craze for the use of seawater as a cure for glandular diseases. The town expanded until nowadays it embraces five, mostly urban parishes with no separation between them – from Middleton-on-Sea in the east, through Felpham, Bognor Regis, Aldwick, Pagham in the west, and Bersted to the north.

Bognor has had the vote of retirees since strings of bungalows were built along its coast in the 1960s and 1970s. It also has a higher-than-average number of singles in their 20s living in small rented apartments. For decades the local

Butlin's, which opened in the 1960s, employed northerners who worked a season and then hung around louche and unemployed in Bognor through the winter. These days, Butlin's are plucking their workforce from Eastern Europe including Poland and other countries that are now in the EU. Bognor town centre has been described as 'a bit depressed', even by those who love the resort. However, this may be about to change. A local development plan is afoot for 700 new dwellings to be built immediately to the north of Felpham on the edge of Bognor Regis. There is also a £100 million project to regenerate the town centre, including new shops, restaurants and office space, with a cinema, theatre and new apartments. Local people fear that the sudden additional population will put an insupportable strain on the schools and primary healthcare facilities of the area, not to mention the roads, which are notoriously congested. There is a well-run NHS general hospital for the area in Chichester (St Richards; www.rwst.org.uk). Nonetheless, waiting times for hip operations are from six months to a year and those with the means tend to have their hip operations carried out in a local private hospital.

Property prices in Bognor used to be lower than nearby Chichester but with prices rising everywhere along the coast, those in Bognor have doubled in the desirable areas in the last six years. Property is still more affordable than some other South Coast towns and the number of retirement developments there is growing. Retirement flats are often more reasonably priced than other properties, so now may be the time to buy your retirement property there.

My experience...

Mr and Mrs Hollingsworth, now aged 81 and 70, spent most of their lives in South Africa, but planned ahead for their return to the UK for retirement by buying a house in Bognor.

We bought a house in Bognor Regis in 1992 when we had family living nearby. We looked around and found this house, which we used as a holiday home for 10 years and rented it out when we went back to South Africa. We'd do six months in England and six months over there. We looked around a bit in other places on the South Coast, because the climate down here is better than cold and windy Suffolk or Norfolk where we were born. Coming from South Africa, climate was really important actually, and we wanted the best possible. Property is very expensive here compared with South Africa but it was really about finding a suitable property. This one had been on the market six months and was for sale fully furnished. This was ideal for us, as we wanted to use it as a holiday home. We moved here permanently in 2002. Bognor is very convenient for lots of places of interest: Arundel, Chichester, Littlehampton, Portsmouth, Brighton and Southampton are all within easy distance and Gatwick is also very convenient. The transport system is fantastic and we have free bus passes. Medical care is very good here, and St Richard's Hospital is just down the road in Chichester. We've found lots of new opportunities here; we belong to Middleton Sports Club and play a lot of bowls matches, which means we travel around and meet people. We do lots of walking and have made so many friends it's unbelievable.

Bognor Regis fact file

Access: Via A259 from Chichester; long overdue improvements needed. Chichester, 7 miles.

Average property price: £192,000

Airports: Southampton, 38.5 miles; Gatwick, 54 miles. Also train service.

Bus services: 15+ local bus services

Climate: Highest recorded hours of sunshine in Britain

Councils: Bognor Regis Town Council (www.bognorregis.gov.uk) and Arun District Council (www.arun.gov.uk)

Council tax: Band D £1,310.46; band E 1,601.67

Crime: Lower rates for most crime categories than the national average. Violence against a person is near the national average.

Economic activity: Low to medium

Ferries: Portsmouth to Isle of Wight, Channel Islands, France and Spain

Hospitals: Local hospital is the Memorial Hospital Bognor Regis. Nearest large hospital with A&E is Chichester St Richard (www.rwst.org.uk). Long wait for hip operations due to the higher than average number of older people.

Main local newspaper: *Bognor Regis Observer* (www.bognortoday.co.uk)

Percentage of people over 65: 10% of the population of Bognor is over 75. Approximately 29% are retirees in the Arun district as a whole.

Population: 22,000 Bognor (60,000 total in the five parishes that make up Bognor Regis)

Property prices: One-bedroom retirement apartments from about £80,000. There is a wide choice of retirement developments. There is a considerable difference in prices between the most expensive areas and the cheapest areas. In some areas prices have doubled in the last six years but are still well below those of nearby Chichester. Retirement developments have reasonable prices.

Railway station: Bognor Regis. Direct line to Brighton and London.

Residents' on-street parking permit: £30 first resident's permit; then £60 per year

Specialised retirement property: Lots, including Victoria Place, Regis Gate, Buckingham Court (Middleton) and Claremont Court. Several care homes in the area have been rebuilt as warden-managed retirement complexes.

THE SOUTH COAST INCLUDING THE NEW FOREST

Bournemouth

Bournemouth is in Dorset, west of the New Forest and Southampton and north-west of the Isle of Wight. It sits between Poole and Christchurch. Two hundred years ago, where Bournemouth now stands, was an expanse of heath used for cattle grazing. Between 1837 and 1840 some holiday villas and a hotel were built and a village with a population of 695 grew up around them. The seaside holiday location of Bournemouth expanded throughout the 19th century, gradually absorbing the surrounding villages of Boscombe, Southbourne and Pokesdown, until the population of the combined conglomeration reached 59,000 in 1901.

Today, Bournemouth is the traditional ideal of a seaside holiday and retirement town on the South Coast – or is it? The truth is, Bournemouth is about as far from being an old person's ghetto as a popular retirement place can get. It has had quite a turnaround in style over the last decade and there is less of a feel of 'God's waiting room' and more 'wake up and smell the coffee' about this thriving resort. It may never become hip and alternative like Brighton, but the adjectives 'chic', 'cool' and 'cosmopolitan' now frequently prefix a mention of the place. It has a university, arts institute (www.aib.ac.uk) and a college of further education (www.thecollege.co.uk). When UK student holidays begin, the language schools fill with thousands of foreign students on English courses. The type of over-50s who are attracted to Bournemouth are the livelier sort, with the energy to enjoy the activities on offer, including beautiful coastal walks and a branch of the University of the Third Age (see p43). However, while appreciating the fact that Bournemouth is full of life, the more staid citizens view Bournemouth's edgy nightlife, fuelled by 30 nightclubs and a rising number of restaurants and bars, with concern. Some parts of town have become no-go areas after dark, as Alan Kellner, a retired banker explains:

> People we know of the same age as us and older won't go into the centre of Bournemouth of an evening. They are intimidated by the crowds of young kids drinking. But we don't go much into the centre; we don't really need to except for the occasional cinema visit. There is plenty to do around where we are. I don't think this problem is peculiar to Bournemouth though.

Furthermore, Bournemouth no longer relies on tourism for its continuing prosperity. These days it is also a mini-centre for financial services, building societies and insurance companies, but beneath the acquired sophistication, Bournemouth is still the splendid seaside resort of character. There are 12km of Blue Flag sandy beaches, a traditional pier and thousands of acres of parks and gardens. No wonder it attracts people of all ages. Even when the peak season is over, there is more to do than you might expect in an out-of-season resort, and nearby is rural Dorset with friendly locals used to seeing and dealing with retired incomers. The drawbacks, if any, are the sheer volume of visitors in summer and the high cost of living.

My experience...

Alan Kneller made a joint decision with his wife to retire to Bournemouth, where they moved in 1997.

We had always lived in Essex but visited Bournemouth many times during our married life and loved it. Compared with Essex, it's cleaner, tidier, and a bit slower, which suited us. We always had an idea in the back of our minds that it might be a nice place to retire to. One day we simply realised we had no mortgage on the house we were living in and everyone was saying 'now's a good time to buy'. There were cheap mortgages a-plenty, so we thought we'd come down to Bournemouth for a look. We didn't do any research and we had no friends or family in the area, so it was a bit of a gamble, but we found something we liked. We are not in the town itself though. The area is considered Boscombe East or Littledale, depending on your source of information.

When we were looking around, we were staying in a hotel and the proprietors found out that we were on a mission for property. They offered us advice including what areas to avoid. The house we bought is the first one the agent showed us. We looked at others but these just made us realise how good the first one was. It's a bungalow. We didn't want a flat, but otherwise were interested in all types of housing; this just happened to be the one we fancied most. When we bought the house in 1992 we were both still working. We had the property for five years before moving in permanently. Before that, we used it as a weekend retreat. We have everything we need on hand; shops, hospital, the sea, the countryside and the town, which is lively. We're both members of the U3A; I'd never heard of it before I joined, but it's excellent. I am also chairman of the computer club – I saw a notice in the library about people over-50 who have computers and would they be interested in meeting up; that's more or less how the club started.

THE SOUTH COAST

INCLUDING THE NEW FOREST

Bournemouth fact file

Access: From London via M3 and M27 (one and a half hours). Southampton, 34 miles.

Average property price: £211,066

Airports: Bournemouth International Airport (www.flybournemouth.com) at Hurn near Christchurch. Airport bus takes 15 minutes and is free for over-60s.

Bus services: Transdev Yellow Buses (www.yellowbuses.co.uk) is the main operator for all routes across the area and to Poole and Christchurch

Climate: Sunny Bournemouth, need one say more?

Council: Bournemouth Borough Council (www.bournemouth.gov.uk)

Council tax: Band D £1,285.26; band E 1,570.87

Crime: Second highest crime rate among in the south-west of England, especially in violence against a person, 25 per 1,000 (national average 16.5%). Theft from cars is also above national average.

Economic activity: Not dependent on tourism alone; foreign students and finance industries also make important contributions to the town's prosperity

Ferries: Poole (5 miles) to the Continent and Channel Islands with Brittany Ferries (www.brittany-ferries.co.uk). Lymington to Yarmouth (www.isle-of-wight-ferries.com).

Hospital: Royal Bournemouth and Christchurch Hospital and NHS Foundation Trust (www.rbh.org.uk). Royal Bournemouth Hospital has low waiting times.

Percentage of people over 65: Nearly 26%

Population: 163,500

Property prices: Detached £286,096; semi-detached £197,634; terraced £185,224; flat £167,145

Railway stations: Bournemouth and Pokesdown. On Weymouth to Waterloo line (97 minutes).

Residents' on-street parking permit: £50 per year

Specialised retirement property: 20+ developments including Brompton Court, Viscount Court and Andbourne Court

Chichester

The small cathedral city of Chichester in West Sussex was founded in the first century AD by the Romans. The Roman road of Stane Street runs like a ruler through the city centre on its way to London. Remains of Roman life in Chichester have revealed that the grandest houses had mosaics, glass windows, mural painted walls and underfloor heating, public baths for socialising and an amphitheatre for 'entertainments' such as animal baiting and gladiator fights. Chichester has also been an ecclesiastical centre for 900 years, so the cliché 'steeped in history' is apt; you can very nearly see it oozing from the Roman city walls, most of which are still standing. The city also has a wealth of Georgian architecture, from a period when the old town was largely rebuilt, which gives it an elegant and genteel air. Historically, it is connected to Chichester harbour by the Chichester canal, currently undergoing restoration under the management of the Chichester Ship Canal Trust. The harbour area comprises a series of saltwater channels with a delicate ecosystem popular for boating, fishing, and birdwatching.

Chichester has a reputation for being affluent, with a high number of professionals, both working and retired. But the city also has a social conscience and there is a centre for asylum seekers and a day centre and shelter for the homeless. The recent closure of the Grayling Well Psychiatric Hospital has left a lot of people with problems with need for outside support. The former Bishop Otter teacher training college is now Chichester University with a campus in Chichester and another one in Bognor Regis. There is a thriving local computer group (www.betaplus.org.uk), which is open to all, but attracts many retirees. It shares knowledge about computer expertise and has regular (real as opposed to virtual) meetings, lectures and visits, all with a computer angle. Recent statistics show that 33% of Chichester's population is aged 60+, an increase of 10% in 10 years. Chichester has been home to the annual Chichester Festival since 1962, when the Festival Theatre opened and it has remained at the centre of the festival events. One thing Chichester residents have noticed is the huge increase in city traffic over the last decade. Finding somewhere to park is a huge problem.

Chichester's surroundings are as attractive as the city. Fishbourne, the fabulous Roman Palace is just outside the city. Bognor Regis is five and half miles to the south-east, while Goodwood Racecourse is two miles to the north. For Romanists there are additional extensive remains near Pulborough, while for nature lovers there is the South Downs and the Arundel Wildlife and Wetlands centre. A stone's throw away are several pretty seaside places including Selsey and West Wittering. The historic cathedral city of Arundel is 10 miles to the east. Chichester's status as a much sought-after neighbourhood is reflected in its property prices, which are way above average both for West Sussex and the south-east of England. So although Chichester rates near the top of any chart for one of the best places to retire in England, its dazzling charms are only available to those with ample financial resources.

My experience...

Barbara Child Hopkins, now in her 60s, moved from Henley-on-Thames to just outside Chichester in 2004 with her husband, a former engineer.

We were down in the area and saw some houses being built and quite liked the look of them. Although we never thought to live here permanently, we found Chichester to be a very nice city – a reasonable size without being too large. It has a fascinating history and lots going for all sorts of people. My daughter worked in this area, which is what brought us down here first of all. We came for weekends and had a vague idea of what there is to do.

We live in Aldsworth, a hamlet of 19 houses with a mixture of ages, just outside Chichester, between the city and Emsworth. Where we live feels remote, which was initially very appealing to us as we'd never lived in the countryside and we thought we'd like it. We planned to stay a maximum of five years. There are buses in Emsworth and Chichester but no bus stop here, so you have to drive.

Chichester is an old city, Roman originally and has a history. We belong to the Friends of Chichester Theatre and the Friends of Chichester Cathedral where there are talks and things and we also belong to a local gardeners' group, although that's not in Chichester, but Emsworth. For us, the downside is that where we are living is not very sociable. I was a little surprised that there was not more of a community spirit; nobody seems to want to know anyone else, even though in our village people are mostly incomers. Chichester and Emsworth are very popular spots for retirement. Sadly, I find that Chichester is gradually losing its individuality. It's becoming like so many other cities that are clones of each other. The big supermarkets are culprits, pushing out the smaller businesses. Emsworth still has individual shops, which are very nice, but the last independent butcher's has gone in Chichester, which is a shame.

Chichester has a very good hospital that my husband has used; it has a very good reputation. I like that Chichester is clean and, I would say, relatively safe. There's a lot happening all the time such as events around the theatre and cathedral. There's a big flower festival every other year that I have done a couple of arrangements for, and walks, because you have the Chichester canals. I also like that Chichester is pedestrianised and easy to walk around. Then of course there's sailing and horse racing not too far away.

Chichester fact file

Access: A27 and A259. Bognor Regis, 7 miles.

Average property price: £323,964 Chichester; £250,791 in West Sussex as a whole

Airports: Southampton, 22 miles; Gatwick, 45 miles

Bus services: Stagecoach South (www.stagecoachbus.com/south) and Emsworth and District (www.emsworthanddistrict.co.uk) are the two main companies. Approximately 40 local routes including Portsmouth, Winchester, Worthing, Midhurst, Bognor and Brighton.

Climate: Favourable microclimate similar to the Isle of Wight. Often better than inland.

Councils: Chichester City Council (www.chichestercity.gov.uk); Chichester District Council (www.chichester.gov.uk); West Sussex County Council (www.westsussex. gov.uk)

Council tax: Band D £1,260.06; band E £1,551.07

Crime: Lower than the Sussex average, but violent crime in Chichester has been increasing according to annual statistics

Economic activity: Consistent with activity for West Sussex

Hospitals: Chichester St Richard (www.rwst.org.uk)

Percentage of people over 65: 33%

Population: Approximately 26,000

Property prices: Detached house £465,129; terraced house £232,018; semi-detached £244,892; flat/maisonette £167,622

Residents' on-street parking permit: £125 (£150 for a second permit)

Specialised retirement property: Churchill Retirement new site (0800 458 1856)

Christchurch

The attractive medieval town of Christchurch lies between the New Forest and Bournemouth on the Dorset coast, where the rivers Stour and Avon intermingle at their exit to the sea. For centuries, the town did not expand much beyond its medieval walls, until the urban sprawl of Bournemouth crept up to its edges, linking it to a large conurbation (Bournemouth plus Christchurch has a population of 250,000). Nevertheless, Christchurch has kept an independent identity and its borough council is one of the UK's smallest in terms of population and area. Another distinguishing characteristic is that it has the highest number of retirees as a percentage of its population of any town in the UK. This might indicate a place of economic torpor but there are many very active businesses in the area. This is a far cry from the 17th and 18th centuries when times were lean and the main source of income for whole communities was smuggling. The entrance to Christchurch harbour (known as 'The Run') proved too narrow for revenue cutters to pursue their quarry home, and the local population made sure it did not stay that way. Christchurch's popular tourist attractions and amenities include a ruined castle and priory, several sandy beaches stretching from Mudeford Sandbank round to Highcliffe Beach (the only shingle beach), and the Two Rivers Meet Leisure and Fitness Centre, which has some activities for the over-50s. The town also has a very active U3A (www.christchurchu3a.org. uk). The website www.dorset-newforest.com/sporting_activities lists a dizzying array of walking, fishing, sailing, and golfing possibilities, and useful links for these activities in the area.

There is no doubt that Christchurch offers a very pleasant lifestyle for the over-50s. Although property is not cheap, there are many retirement developments where prices start at just under £100,000 for a one-bedroom apartment, although many more stylish apartments will cost more than that. The main drawback is that Dorset itself has higher than average levels of criminal damage and theft in the annual crime statistics. Coastal protection measures to prevent erosion have been built into the Highcliffe area.

My experience...

Rodney Robinson, now aged 66, and his wife moved to Christchurch from Denham in Buckinghamshire in 2004.

Up to when we moved here, I had lived in Denham all my life, but it was getting to be part of London. We were just inside the M25 and under a flight path, which made it very noisy, and we wanted to move somewhere quieter. We started to look for somewhere in Devon and Somerset and as far as Cornwall, but my parents were still living in Denham and the West Country seemed too far away. We popped down to Christchurch for the day and we both decided how much we liked it; it's very genteel. The area is getting very built up, but there is a large estate of privately owned land between Christchurch and the New Forest. This acts as a green buffer and it's unlikely to be sold for development in the near future. We bought a bungalow here on the east side of Christchurch. We are 400m from the sea and one and a half miles from the New Forest.

I am an outdoor person and spend my time sailing and walking, and my wife plays golf. This area is fantastic for all of those. There is a golf course in Christchurch at Highcliffe, and two more nearby including the championship course at Barton-on-Sea. I volunteer with the Christchurch Borough Council Countryside Services. There are about 50 of us volunteers, from all walks of life, who work under the supervision of qualified foresters and naturalists. You can work for a couple of hours or spend the day; it's very sociable. We do things like bramble cutting and tree planting and we are returning the countryside to its natural state. I like to think of it as caring for our communal garden. There is an organisation in Christchurch called Greystones, which organises lots of activities for senior citizens and is run by them; everything from art to dancing. The interests of older people are very well catered for in Christchurch.

The downside is traffic congestion, especially in summer. There is a terrible bottleneck around Lyndhurst and traffic gets clogged up in Christchurch. However, buses are excellent and also the taxis. You can commute to London from Christchurch thanks to very good train services via Southampton.

Christchurch is a beautiful place, even though the area itself is built up, the town has kept its charm. The famous Priory, our local church, is spectacular and you can walk or cycle everywhere and if you want to go to Bournemouth for a change you can nip on to a bus.

Christchurch fact file

Access: Roads A35 and B3073. Bournemouth, 6 miles.

Average property price: £234,272

Airports: Bournemouth, 3.5 miles; Southampton, 33.4 miles

Bus services: Wilts & Dorset (www.wdbus.co.uk). Excellent local services but not many buses later in the evening.

Climate: The microclimate supports mediterranean plants such as oleanders and myrtle

Council: Christchurch Borough Council (www.dorsetforyou.com). One of the smallest boroughs in the country in terms of population and area.

Council tax: Band D £999.99; band E £1,222.21

Crime Rate: Main crime activity in Dorset area is criminal damage, followed by theft

Economic activity: Very active economically; over 1,300 local businesses

Ferries: Condor Ferries (www.condorferries.co.uk) from Weymouth and Poole to the Channel Islands and St Malo

Hospital: Royal Bournemouth Hospital (www.rbch.nhs.uk), 17.4 weeks' wait for a hip replacement

Percentage of people over 65: 33%.

Population: 45,000

Property prices: Detached house £300,000; semi-detached £212,145; terraced £201,210; flat £169,500; retirement flats from about £100,000

Railway station: Christchurch. Service to London.

Residents' on-street parking permit: £25 per year (£60 in one or two streets)

Specialised retirement property: Lots including Regency Crescent, many flats and bungalows suitable for retirees

Eastbourne

Eastbourne is at the eastern end of the South Downs in East Sussex. East Sussex extends beyond Crowborough to the north. The seed that sprouted Eastbourne was a spillover of royalty from nearby Brighton, which the Prince Regent made fashionable at the beginning of the 19th century. This made the area around the hamlets of Bourne (Old Town), Southbourne, Meads and Seahouses, the four original villages that make up modern Eastbourne, popular. These villages were subsumed into Eastbourne from the mid-19th century, when the new craze of seaside bathing promoted Eastbourne's transformation into a fashionable watering place that could be reached by train from London. In recent decades it has had to find new ways to supplement the income that it has lost to the inexhaustible appetite for foreign travel. These include a regular influx of foreign students of English who arrive from Easter onwards. The city of Brighton and Hove as well as the Channel port of Newhaven lie to the west, while Bexhill, Hastings and Rye on the Kentish coast, are to the east. Eastbourne's landmark white cliffs at Beachy Head lie three miles to the south-west. The magnificent views from them are to die for, literally, since they have a reputation as a jumping-off point for those seeking eternal oblivion.

This sombre note does not, however, reflect the place as a whole – Eastbourne's credentials as a retirement place are impeccable. It has one of the best sunshine records in the UK (more sunshine and less rain than Cornwall); 4.8 miles of sea promenade, and four miles of beaches; 13 acres of public gardens; considerably cheaper property than Brighton; smart amenities and a safer ambience than many seaside places (except at night when the pubs turn out). While the 2001 census revealed that a quarter of its inhabitants are over 65, it has developed appeal to a younger clientele. To call Eastbourne a 'boomtown' is an exaggeration, but regeneration has produced trendy areas such as 'Little Chelsea', which have attracted younger property buyers and families, especially those who want to move out of London and who have passed over nearby Brighton as too expensive. Recreational attractions are top notch including three private golf courses, and lawn tennis. The Ladies Tennis Championship, a prestige event that is held as a precursor to Wimbledon, is a popular spectacle. There are good transport links along the coast and to London. Europe is a ferry ride away via Newhaven (about half way between Brighton & Hove, and Eastbourne), or 50 miles east down the A259 is the Channel Tunnel at Folkestone. Such convenient links, clean air, and café society developments of trendy bar and restaurant areas have given the town a younger feel. However, Eastbourne suffers the usual ills of drunken loutishness around the drinking spots and crime rates are high (especially violence against a person) but you can usually avoid the places where these things tend to occur regularly. Nevertheless, Eastbourne has much to recommend it and is a serious contender in any chart of the best places to retire in Britain.

My experience...

Don Groves is from Hampshire and is quite content with his decision to move to Eastbourne – although it was initially prompted by family illness rather than a retirement plan. He now lives in a retirement complex.

I moved to Eastbourne about 10 years ago to look after my sick brother. I knew the area quite well and liked being by the sea. I moved into a retirement complex in the Old Town, fairly central, in 2000. Residents have their own apartments and keys. I decided to move there because it provided me with everything I needed. Before that, I was renting an apartment because I was not sure if I would stay; I just wanted to be near my brother. After he died I could see that rentals were going up and I realised I would need to buy somewhere; that's what prompted me to move into a retirement complex. I am glad I bought when I did as rents have gone up since. I can see Waitrose from my window and there are many well-serviced bus routes. Moving to Eastbourne has given me the opportunity to join U3A, which is very enjoyable. There are lots of things nearby: it's 20 miles to Brighton and there's Glyndebourne if you're into that kind of thing. I also really enjoy walking, and the walking opportunities are good here and the countryside is lovely. Eastbourne is full of retired people ... but then, why would I mind that?

The promenade at Eastbourne

THE SOUTH COAST INCLUDING THE NEW FOREST

Eastbourne fact file

Access: A259, A27 and A22. Hastings, 17 miles.

Average property price: £190,812 (compare with Brighton & Hove £243,648), 46.5 miles

Airports: Gatwick, 46.5 miles (50 minutes' direct rail link from Eastbourne)

Bus services: Eastbourne Buses (www.eastbournebuses.co.uk). Sussex Countycard gives free travel throughout East and West Sussex (including Brighton & Hove) for over-60s.

Climate: Sunniest place in Britain (joint with Weymouth, Bognor, and Bournemouth)

Council: Eastbourne Borough Council (www.eastbourne.gov.uk)

Council tax: Band D £1,388.95; band E £1,697.61

Crime: High level of violence against a person (27 per 1,000). National average 16.5%.

Economic activity: Fairly active

Ferries: Newhaven (12 miles west) to Dieppe

Hospital: Eastbourne District General Hospital (01323 417400; www.esh.nhs.uk). 70% of patients wait fewer than three months for their operations.

Local newspaper: *Eastbourne Herald* (www.eastbournetoday.co.uk)

Percentage of people over 65: 26.9%

Population: 106,000

Property prices: Detached £314,127; semi-detached £194,559; terrace £181,197; flat £152,528

Railway station: Eastbourne. Eastbourne to London Victoria, 90 mins

Residents' on-street parking permit: £25 per year (and there is a waiting list). Permit zone is only in an area around the town centre.

Specialised retirement property: Many retirement developments consisting of blocks of purpose built flats including Cheriton Court, Fairfield Lodge, Granville Court and Ruxley Court.

Isle of Wight

The diamond-shaped Isle of Wight is set just off the South Coast in the English Channel. The narrow water dividing it from the mainland is the Solent (the busiest shipping lane in British waters), and the water between Ryde and Portsmouth is known as Spithead. Much about the Isle of Wight seems to shriek Victoriana. In fact, the future Queen Victoria first visited the Island for holidays in 1831, at a time when most of the population (then around 25,000) was involved with smuggling. In 1845 Queen Victoria acquired the Osborne Estate and by 1851 Osborne House, summer residence of the Queen, had been built near Cowes. The first America's Cup yacht race had been held in the same year. The most popular seaside towns then and now are: Cowes, Shanklin, Ventnor, Ryde and Sandown, all on the eastern side of the Island. Newport, the main administration centre, is inland south of Cowes while the island's only westerly resort, Totland, has a shingle beach and a bay for boats. The Needles rock formation is nearby at the western extremity of the island. In size the island is smaller (just) than Rutland, the smallest county on the English mainland, and is 22.5 miles across and 13.5 miles from north to south. Until recent times, most people contemplating places on the South Coast for a retirement spot, viewed the Isle of Wight only as a great place for holidays and a source of extra amenities (eight golf courses, dedicated cycle routes) on their doorstep, rather than somewhere they'd like to retire to. However 'the times they are a-changin'' as Bob Dylan sang at the original (and now revived) Isle of Wight Festival in 1970. Is it really possible that the island's 1950s time warp feel is receding faster than an Arctic glacier? Well, it might be – roads are still quieter, less congested and speed-freak free, compared with the mainland, but there is a universal grumpiness about the state of some of them. The island's population is increasing, with incomers buying up property to retire to and developers such as Barratt Homes (Marlborough Park, Ryde; 01983 618769) and Kings Oak (Carisbrooke Grange, Newport; www.kingsoakhomes.co.uk) have built new 'tasteful' estates of pristine properties. However, such estates are not specifically aimed at retirees, who might prefer one of the island's detached bungalows with fabulous views. These don't come cheap – a three-bedroom bungalow in Totland recently sold for £320,000. Those now moving to the island include commuters who work in Southampton, Portsmouth and London (two hours away). Fortunately, at least half the island is designated an Area of Outstanding Natural Beauty, (mostly segments in the south and west) which means that development is very strictly controlled. Although the countryside is great and wild flowers grow in more abundance than in the pesticide-sprayed countryside on the mainland, most people would agree that the beaches along the island's 60-mile coastline are the Isle of Wight's greatest natural asset. Two stretches of the coast are designated Heritage Coast – the Tennyson Down (St Lawrence to Totland Bay in the south) and Hamstead on the Solent (wooded estuaries and the bay of Thorness).

Despite its numerous attractions, living on an island necessitates some inconvenience. You have to make a ferry expedition every time you need to visit the mainland (day return trip for foot passenger from £13, with car from £29). When native islanders have a different word for anyone not from the islands (in this case 'overners') it usually means they have to be persuaded to treat them as 'caulkheads' (islanders born and bred). Around 98.7% of the resident population is white, well above the national average of 92%. Potential problems include the fact that by 2020 the number of over-65s on the island will be 28% of the population. This presents a challenge in terms of social care for those with age-related frailties, which rural isolation and poor road infrastructure on the island could exacerbate. The cost of living tends to be higher than on the mainland because of the extra transport costs.

My experience...

Mrs Rayner, a widow and formerly a school cook, moved to Niton, near Ventnor from Maidstone, 10 years ago when she was 59, to be near her family:

My son and his family moved to the Isle of Wight a few years before I did and I used to visit them every school holidays. I liked it so much and wanted to see more of my grandchildren and I thought that if I could, I'd move here. When my husband was alive, we'd moved from Bramley to Kent hoping to do semi-retirement, but then he died and I had to go back to work. I actually left my job just before my retirement was due because the opportunity for a house came up on the Island. I needed a bungalow because I have a problem with mobility. Niton is a very friendly little village. We have a butcher, post office (which we're fighting to keep), family grocer, bookshop, library – everything you need and there's an hourly bus service to Newport. I like the slower pace on the Isle of Wight. In fact, when I go to the mainland now, I find it bewildering. We have speeded up a bit over here, but nowhere near as much as the mainland. The climate is lovely too; it's much warmer here. I'm on what seems to be the Mediterranean side.

It's not cheap to live on the Island. We pay more for everything and the trip across the water is especially dear. They do have cheap day trips and special offers, but never at holiday times. I've not found any resentment of incomers here and I've some really good island friends – a couple of them born and bred here and never been off the island. Rarely does anyone local walk straight past you without a greeting. My neighbour came to call when I first arrived and invited me to join in a few things and be introduced to people. Our village hall is used nearly every single day ... I belong to an art group, a weaving club and I run the Wednesday Club.... you can keep very, very busy. It's a very friendly little village.

Isle of Wight fact file

Access: Lymington, Portsmouth and Southampton and then ferry/hovercraft/ catamaran

Average property price: £206,929

Airport: Southampton International (www.southamptonairport.com)

Bus services: Southern Vectis (www.islandbuses.com)

Climate: Mild enough to grow garlic (and export it to France) and lavender. The climate of the Island has long been recognised as beneficial. The Royal National Hospital at Ventnor (pulled down 30 years ago) was originally built to treat consumptives. The weather has its own website, www.isleofwightweather.co.uk.

Council: Isle of Wight Unitary Authority (01983 821000; www.iwight.com)

Crime: Crime statistics on the IOW show a small fall in burglary and theft from motor vehicles. Violent crime is quite high, as is vandalism in some areas.

Economic activity: Mainly services industry and agriculture, especially all year salad ingredients such as lettuce and tomatoes, grown in polytunnels

Ferries: Portsmouth to Fishbourne/Ryde and Lymington to Yarmouth (Wightlink, www.wightlink.co.uk); Southampton to Cowes (Red Funnel, www.redfunnel.co.uk); Hovercraft Southsea and Ryde (Hovertravel)

Hospital: St Mary's Hospital, Newport (www.iow.nhs.uk) has an A&E department but many other treatments are provided on the mainland such as at St Mary's Hospital in Portsmouth, which has a bad reputation for MRSA

Local newspaper: *Isle of Wight Press* (www.iwcp.co.uk)

Percentage of people over 65: 26%

Population: 132,731 (2001 Census); 138,231 (2006)

Property prices: Detached £293,880; semi-detached £179,755; terrace £159,271; flat £130,860

Railway stations: Portsmouth and Southampton on the mainland. Island train service from Ryde Pier to Shanklin (www.islandline.co.uk).

Residents' on-street parking permit: £80 per year

Specialised retirement property: Not much, but many coastal bungalows and apartments suitable for retirement

THE SOUTH COAST

INCLUDING THE NEW FOREST

The New Forest

The ancient New Forest goes back 900 years and covers approximately 90,000 acres, reaching 25km north from the South Coast, between Christchurch and Southampton Water up into Hampshire; it also spills over into Dorset and Wiltshire. It is 30km across at its widest point. Embedded in this area of rugged heathland, woods, boggy bits and natural forest lawns are picturesque towns and villages, most notably: Ashurst, Boldre, Beaulieu, Bramshaw, Brockenhurst, Burley, Cadnam, Fritham, Fordingbridge, Hythe, Ibsley, Lyndhurst, Lymington, Minstead, Nomansland, Ringwood and Sway. The New Forest has a tradition as a recreation area, starting in Norman times when William the Conqueror acquired it as a hunting preserve. In our now egalitarian times, walkers, cyclists, picnickers, horse riders and retirees, among others, enjoy its tranquility, pubs, very varied wildlife (from fallow deer to lizards), and its free-roaming large animals – the New Forest ponies and commoners' cattle. The commoners of the New Forest have ancient grazing rights and other rights to do with collecting wood, peat, and clay. A few hundred commoners are still exercising these rights today supervised by Agisters, who are the officers of the Court of Verderers (commoners). Details of these arcane rights, and who can claim them, can be obtained on the local government website www.hants.gov.uk and from the Forestry Commission in Lyndhurst (023 8028 3141). The website www.dorset-newforest.com/sporting_activities lists a dizzying array of walking, fishing, sailing, and golfing possibilities and useful links in the area.

The New Forest's status as one of the nation's treasures was confirmed when, in 2005, it became the UK's newest and smallest national park. This move was received with mixed feelings by the 'foresters' who fear a disproportionate rise in visitors attracted by its enhanced celebrity status. Some of the families who live in this area have ancestral roots in the New Forest going back centuries, as the recurring surnames on local tombstones attest. It is common sense to suggest that mass trampling over ancient commoners' territories could be detrimental to the delicately balanced environment. The popularity of the area with incoming retirees means that, as elsewhere, property prices have risen above what younger locals can now afford. The proportion of older people in the New Forest is rising partly because younger people are moving elsewhere, and partly because the area has obvious attractions (including friendly village communities) to those wanting to retire.

The New Forest has double the number of 'independent elders' (over 25% of the population) compared with all other areas of Hampshire. Around 36% of the population of Barton-on-Sea, overlooking the Solent, are retired. Other towns on the 60km coast of the New Forest with a high proportion (23%–30%) of retired people include Milford, Becton, New Milton, Hythe and Lymington. Around 19% of pensioners living in the New Forest are designated 'prosperous', which is double the percentage for Hampshire as a whole.

My experience...

Sheila Hayden (see also below) found it very easy to make friends when she and her husband moved to Bransgore.

When you are working, of course, you don't really have time to belong to anything so when we came here, I joined quite a few things because I wanted to get to know more people. We had a couple of friends in Burley, which is four miles across the heath from here, before we moved. We'd met them when we used to come here on holiday, but we didn't know anyone in Bransgore. I joined things in Burley as well. An awful lot goes on in both villages. If you joined everything, you'd probably be out every night. My husband joins in all the things I get involved with. He participates in them with me if I need help.

Thatched pub in the New Forest

THE SOUTH COAST INCLUDING THE NEW FOREST

My experience...

Sheila Hayden, aged 69, and her husband, who took early retirement, moved from Rickmansworth to Bransgore, on the Hampshire/Dorset border at the edge of the New Forest between Ringwood and Christchurch. She explains why they chose the New Forest and what they think about it.

We used to visit the New Forest quite a bit and it sort of evolved from there. My husband 'discovered' it when he was working for IBM and they held seminars there. He retired when he was 54, and for some years before that, we had been thinking it would be a great place to retire to. We are not great coastal people, although it's nice to have it near. We like walking, preferably when the weather is right. It's very wet and muddy here in winter; that's why it's nice to be near the coast as an alternative. We were both in our mid-50s – quite young – when we retired and the main thing was to find a village that had everything we needed close by – banks, shops, and so on – because you have to think there will probably come a time when you can no longer drive, so we did our research as far as daily needs are concerned. This location is wonderful for shops; they're five to 10 minutes' walk away. Sadly the banks (we had two) have gone, so we use the local post office for our banking. I did miss the big shops when we first moved here; you know, popping into a store at lunchtime to buy a birthday present; that kind of thing. We go to Ringwood and Christchurch which are OK, but the nearest decent shopping centre is Southampton. We are still young enough to enjoy driving, but I know people who get around the area quite easily on buses; there are services to both Ringwood and Christchurch from Bransgore. The New Forest has quite an aged population, so it's good there's a brand new hospital just opened in Lymington. The old one closed and was rebuilt.

One thing I have noticed is that the villages vary, in that some of them have a lot of holiday homes. This causes a certain amount of resentment, not least because the holiday people don't contribute to village life. Luckily, Bransgore has few holiday homes. I think it makes a difference to how well you settle in, although we are still regarded as newcomers after 15 years. If you are willing to move in and participate, you will be accepted.

New Forest fact file

Access: Junction 1 off the M27. Main roads A35, A337, A31 run through it.

Average property price: £279,538

Airports: Southampton International (www.southamptonairport.com); Bournemouth International (www.flybournemouth.com)

Bus services: Wilts & Dorset (www.wdbus.co.uk) serves Ringwood, Lymington and the New Forest area

Climate: Oceanic, mild wet winters and warm, wet summers

Council: New Forest District Council (023 8028 5000; www.nfdc.gov.uk)

Crime: Considered to be one of the safest places to live in the UK. Theft from motor vehicles is high.

Economic activity: 80.3% of the population of the New Forest is economically active (83% for Hampshire as a whole). The biggest single commercial activity is real estate.

Ferries: From Portsmouth WightLink (www.wightlink.co.uk) to Isle of Wight; Brittany Ferries (www.brittany-ferries.com) to France and P&O Ferries (www.poferries.com) to northern Spain

Hospitals: New Forest Primary Care Trust became part of the larger Hampshire Primary Care Trust in 2006. Includes South Hants Southampton hospital and the Royal Bournemouth (nearest A&E departments). The new Lymington New Forest Hospital opened in January 2007 and has an MIU (minor injuries unit). For fuller details of medical facilities in the area see www.hampshirepct.nhs.uk.

Percentage of people over 65: 25%

Population: Approximately 170,000. 49.4% of the population of the New Forest is aged 44 and above.

Property prices: Detached £364,173; semi-detached £237,872 terrace £199,627; flat £170,810

Railway stations: Ashurst, Beaulieu Road, Brockenhurst, Sway. Served by South West Trains and Virgin Trains.

Specialised retirement property: Penny Farthing Homes (www.pennyfarthinghomes.co.uk) is a developer with many smaller high-end apartments (mostly two and three bedrooms) and groups of houses (up to five bedrooms) in New Forest places including Barton-on-Sea, New Milton, Brockenhurst and Lymington. Prices start at about £272,500. Cheaper option is Sandy Balls Holiday Centre (01425 653042) (www.sandy-balls.co.uk) residential park homes for retirement (£199,000–£210,000).

Shoreham-by-Sea

The small provincial town of Shoreham sits on the West Sussex coastal plain, at the edge of the South Downs, between the city of Brighton & Hove and the resort of Worthing. It is joined to these two places by a coastal ribbon of urban development. It is part of the council district of Adur, which takes its name from the River Adur, which enters the sea east of Shoreham. The river estuary provides a setting that gives Shoreham its unique character. The harbour has been subject to silting since medieval times and a permanent static entrance was not constructed until 1821. At one time the estuary of the Adur ran straight north–south, but by a process known as 'littoral drift', the coastline has altered continuously over the centuries, moving the river exit east. Shoreham Harbour has been the lifeblood of Shoreham, having been a centre of shipbuilding and a busy commercial and ferry port (for France and the Channel Islands). However, since the 1970s its importance has dwindled, and it cannot compete with other, larger ports, such as Newhaven. Shoreham beach is a shingle spit about three miles in length, separated from the town by the River Adur. In the early 20th century, film studios were constructed on Shoreham beach and a permanent film community lived there, attracted by the perfect climate for outdoor filming. According to the Prospect Film Company in 1920, 'The air is wonderfully clear, and quite free from fogs … and clean light may be obtained, probably unrivalled in England.'

Economically Shoreham, compared with the wider south-east area, is characterised by low productivity, lower skill profile and lower knowledge-based sectors and a relatively low rate of business start-ups and high tech businesses. In rural and east Worthing and Shoreham 60.7% of people aged 16–74 are categorised economically inactive. Those who worry about their health might also bear in mind that although cancer is the biggest single killer in the Adur district there are no cancer treatment centres in West Sussex.

Those thinking of retiring to Shoreham should note that the area is very built up. Further new properties such as the Ropetackle Waterfront development, built on a derelict site at the west end of the High Street and now sold out, are unlikely to occur, as much of the town is a conservation area. The Ropetackle development includes 180 dwellings, which were snapped up by people wanting to invest in property, or those who cannot afford Brighton property prices. Not much older housing becomes available as Shoreham is a small town and people tend to stay a lifetime. If you are lucky enough to buy a retirement home there, you will benefit from the excellent transport links, particularly from Shoreham station direct to London (Victoria) every hour and the service to Gatwick Airport. There are a couple of apartment blocks for those of retirement age and there are also a couple of brownfield sites towards Brighton, which developers have got their eye on. You could consider Shoreham's other dwellings – river houseboats. There has been a tradition of these in Shoreham since just after the

Second World War. A deal made in the 1980s between the council and the river boaters means that moorings can be bought freehold for about £20,000 plus the cost of a boat (£50,000–£90,000). Local estate agents handle sales. There are certain peculiarities that need to be mastered for a successful retirement on a houseboat, the website www.livingonboats.co.uk has a lot of essential information. Philip Simons, a local author, recently published a book *Retired on the River* about living on a Shoreham houseboat; more details at www. canaljunction.com.

My experience...

Mrs Goode, a retired matron, now 82 and originally from London, moved to Shoreham.

I moved to Shoreham to be near my family. I was initially thinking of Brighton and Worthing, but decided I really liked Shoreham when I was visiting my family here. It was close to the sea and had some lovely little shops. It went through a bad patch after a big Tesco and Marks & Spencer opened nearby and put some local shops out of business. But the local community rallied and there are local shops and charity shops in the town again. I moved into a flat; it's in a great location a few minutes walk from the sea. I've always lived in a flat, as they are lower maintenance than houses. The travel links aren't that bad, although ideally, you need a car. There is no theatre or cinema in Shoreham, but there are good train services to Brighton and London. I didn't really think about whether there would be any clubs when I moved here, but now I'm a member of the U3A and I love it. I got into it from joining a French conversation club, which was one of the groups organised by the U3A.

Shoreham is a clean area and I also noticed when I moved here that people are very friendly. The only bad thing is that we have a lot of traffic. Shoreham is near the Brighton bypass, the A27 and the roundabout leading to the A259, as well as rush-hour traffic being bad. When there's a traffic jam it causes a bottleneck.

Shoreham fact file

Access: A259 and A27. Brighton, 6 miles.

Average property price: £216,122

Airport: Gatwick, 34 miles (35 minutes by train)

Bus services: Compass West Sussex and Surrey bus services (www.compass-travel.co.uk); Brighton & Hove Bus (www.buses.co.uk); Stagecoach South (www.stagecoachbus.com) further afield to Portsmouth, Eastbourne and Chichester. Bus travel is free throughout Sussex for the over-60s.

Climate: Typical south coast

Councils: Adur District Council (www.adur.gov.uk); Shoreham Parish Council (www.shorehamparishcouncil.gov.uk)

Council tax: Band D £1,357.18; band E £1,658.79

Crime: Burglary is down by more than 50% compared with 10 years ago, but anti-social behaviour is a problem. Generally, Shoreham is a low crime area.

Economic activity: Lower than average compared with the south-east

Ferries: 32km to nearest at Newhaven (for Dieppe, France).

Hospital: Southlands Hospital, Shoreham. In late 2006 all the local primary care trusts were merged into one, West Sussex Primary Care Trust (www.westsussexpct.nhs.uk). It remains to be seen how well this works, but some services such as cancer treatment are lacking in the area.

Local newspaper: *Shoreham Herald* (www.shorehamtoday.co.uk)

Percentage of people over 65: 22%

Population: 31,385 (Shoreham plus Southwick)

Property prices: Semi-detached £184,950; terrace £190,000, two-bedroom apartment £199,950, houseboat £70,000

Railway station: Shoreham. Fast services to London and Gatwick.

Residents' on-street parking permit: Permits not required at present

Specialised retirement property: St Paul's Lodge (www.churchillretirement.co.uk), 42 one and two-bedroom apartments £164,950–£274,950; Homehaven Court (apartments), for over-65s £118,500–£157,950 (www.homewise.co.uk)

Worthing

Worthing in West Sussex, 12 miles from Brighton and just west of Shoreham-by-Sea expanded from a sleepy fishing village into a seaside resort, initially for the wealthy, during the 19th century. The esplanade was built in 1821 when

George IV, who was on the throne, made the South Coast, and in particular Brighton, fashionable for its sea-related health benefits (and in his case hedonism as well). Throughout Queen Victoria's reign, Worthing, like the other South Coast resorts experienced a heyday. The pier opened in 1862 and its tribulations, including storm damage (1913), fire (1933) and Second World War damage (1940), have made it a symbol of the town's ability to renew itself. By the 1960s Worthing was moving to a new beat far wilder than the genteel elegance of bandstands, bustles and Oscar Wilde characters, when it became a top venue for bands of a different kind such as The Who. When the taste for cheap sunshine holidays abroad took off in the 1970s and 1980s, Worthing settled back into its faded chintz armchair and became the face of retirement Britain and a town of Methuselahs.

A chart-topping 45% of the population of the borough of Worthing is of pension age, and it has more than three times the average number of over-85s. However, since 2000, Worthing has been seen as a ripe candidate for regeneration. It has become an alternative to overpriced Brighton and Hove, for both companies and younger property buyers. Younger people have been moving to Worthing and local schools are doing well in the league tables. A core development plan for Worthing has brought changes to the city centre and along the five miles of seafront, offering a range of amenities for beach recreation as well as beachside entertainment and restaurants. A local housing company, Worthing Homes, has built properties all over the town, many of them offered under a shared ownership scheme which benefits people who cannot afford to buy a property on their own. Such properties are not normally aimed at the retired but there is no upper age limit for them. However, as you might expect, Worthing has more than its fair share of dedicated retirement flats and developments compared with other towns. There is no sign of it losing its popularity with the older folk who seem to thrive there.

Worthing has much going for it as a retirement place. It is an integral part of the West Sussex coastal strip that stretches from Bognor Regis to Brighton and hence there are good bus and train services. West Sussex is a very picturesque and desirable place to live. Littlehampton is eight miles to the west and it is only a couple of miles in either direction to Lancing, Ferring and Goring-by-Sea, all but conjoined to Worthing through urban sprawl. So while much has stayed the same about Worthing, much has been happening about town, including the arrival of large companies and the arrival of smart young executives who are buying up property, especially apartments. Until recently, Worthing had some of the cheapest property on the South Coast and still does (just). It has excellent GP services and a large general hospital with an A&E department and a private hospital attached. Perhaps now is the time to snap something up so that you can enjoy retirement in a seaside area with an excellent range of activities and amenities to offer.

My experience...

Thomas Kearny, who is 76 years old, moved to Worthing from Ireland with his wife in 1991. He is not only a longtime admirer of Worthing's charms, but also highlights its considerable advantages for older people.

We always liked Worthing; we'd been here a couple of times and fell in love with the place. It was always warmer here than anywhere else we went and the cost of everything is much cheaper than in Ireland. There wasn't much choice involved. We looked at a few other places, but not very hard; Worthing was really it. We're actually in Goring-by-Sea about two miles from the centre. You can walk from Goring along the seafront and promenade for about three miles. The contour of the land is flat, ideal for elderly people. My wife loves the shopping facilities. Normally we use the buses to go to the town centre (10 minutes), or to Eastbourne, Bognor Regis and Littlehampton – all free for the over-60s. We lived in a rural part of Ireland with non-existent bus services, so we think the buses are fantastic. We use our car to drive around a bit and for visiting garden centres.

We had no problem finding a place to buy. There are masses of estate agents. Our bungalow was pinpointed by friends from the Catholic Church across the road. The thing about the Catholic community is that when they know you are on the way, they start looking out properties in their parish for you. There are lots of churches of different denominations and church communities attached to every parish here. Elderly people need not feel lonely or confined because you are living in these communities and there is something to do every night.

There are lots of retirement clubs; ours has upwards of 80 members. Activities are very good and it's a famous place for ballroom and sequence dancing. You can get 100 people in each evening. It's very important when you are over 70 to keep active; that's what the Council and most of our clubs harp on about. Keep active? Believe me, we have no choice! The facilities for the elderly are wonderful because Worthing has the biggest proportion of retired people in the land; libraries, community buses, doctors' surgeries, lots of retirement campuses and retirement homes. It's a very friendly place, very welcoming. The only concern is that there are plans to build lots of new homes around here and we have such lovely wide open spaces, it would be a shame to spoil them.

Worthing fact file

Access: A259. Main east-west road A27 runs just north of the town. Brighton, 11 miles.

Average property price: £203,240

Airports: Gatwick, about 24 miles

Bus services: Stagecoach (www.stagecoachbus.com); Brighton & Hove (www.buses.co.uk); Compass Buses (www.compass-travel.co.uk). Free buses to local Holmbush shopping centre.

Climate: So mild that Worthing used to supply London society with hothouse grapes, flowers and early fruit and vegetables in the late 19th century

Council: Worthing Borough Council (www.worthing.gov.uk)

Council tax: Band D £1,303.38; band E £1,593.02

Crime: Environmental crime (including graffiti and fly tipping) are regular local problems

Economic activity: Mini boom with big name company offices in town and a new local business park

Ferries: To The Continent from Portsmouth and Southampton

Hospital: Worthing Hospital (www.worthinghospital.nhs.uk) is a large hospital providing acute clinical services including A&E. Waiting times for a hip replacement are six months minimum. A private hospital (Downlands Suite) is attached to the main hospital.

Local newspapers: *Worthing Herald* (www.worthingtoday.co.uk); *West Sussex Gazette* (www.westsussextoday.co.uk)

Percentage of people over 65: 45%

Population: Approximately £100,000

Property prices: Detached £308,541; semi-detached £226,080; terrace £187,570; flat £143,372

Railway station: West Worthing. London (Victoria) in 75 minutes. Served by South West Trains and First Great Western.

Residents' on-street parking permit: £15 (£25 for the centre) per year

Specialised retirement property: Lots including 52 flats at Bakers Court (020 8868 900), Belmaine Court (75 flats) and The Cloisters both run by Raglan Homes (0845 070 772); The Courtyard (37 flats) run by Grange Management (www.grangemanagement.com)

THE SOUTH COAST

INCLUDING THE NEW FOREST

South-east England

NORTH-EAST KENT AND THE ROMNEY MARSHES

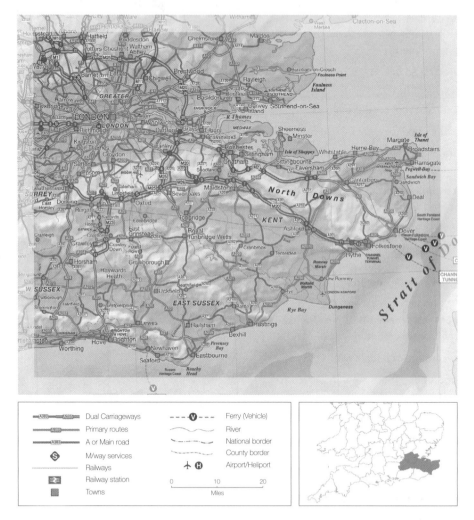

Dual Carriageways			Ferry (Vehicle)	
Primary routes			River	
A or Main road			National border	
M/way services			County border	
Railways			Airport/Heliport	
Railway station		0 10 20	
Towns		Miles	

The county of Kent in south-east England was the first part of Britain to be invaded by Julius Caesar in 55BC, when he landed on the shores of Cantium (Kent). The area continued to be the backdrop to some of the other most momentous developments in English and British History. These include 1066 and the invasion by William the Conqueror; the Thames Estuary becoming the source of the port of London's growth and maritime industry; the founding of

Canterbury, which became famous for pilgrimages (the tourism of its day) and martyrs' remains. One of Kent's iconic landmarks, the White Cliffs of Dover, became a symbol of 'welcome home' for ships' passengers and soldiers returning from war. For several centuries Kent was 'the garden of England' particularly for hops, vineyards and fruit orchards, supplying London and places further afield. The north-eastern part of the county reaches from the southern edge of the vast Thames estuary, eastwards past the Isle of Sheppey, to the north Kent seaside resorts of Whitstable and Herne Bay, towards the Isle of Thanet (not a real island, but a peninsula), the ports of Margate and Ramsgate and the seaside resort Broadstairs. Following the coast southwards, you reach Dover, Folkestone and Hythe. West of Hythe, towards East Sussex, are the Romney Marshes, one of the more mysterious and fascinating areas of England.

The climate of Kent differs considerably from the 'tropical' South Coast, or the warmer south-west of England. Unlike these, Kent is subject to more extremes of weather, hot and cold. Historically, it has more than a few records for the highest summer temperature, the worst drought, and the coldest, snowiest winter. On the coast, extreme tides sweep across open beaches and horrendous sea fogs can descend for days. On the plus side, north-facing resorts along the east coast, such as Herne Bay and Whitstable, backed by the Kent Downs, can reach record spring and autumn temperatures. Of more concern than the effect climate change and global warming could have on the levels of the Thames Estuary in the future, is the immediate problem that most of Kent still has a hosepipe ban. This dates from 2005 and at the time of press is under review. The replenishment of water reserves has improved since the ban was imposed.

The Romney Marshes comprise 100 square miles of flat land that has been called 'a gift from the sea'. The coastal stretch of the Marshes reaches from the Kent–East Sussex border to Hythe. It was formed from the alluvial deposits washed down by the River Rother. First sandy islands were formed and then areas of solid land. Until Saxon times, most of the marsh was waterlogged, but over time it was drained for agriculture, and prodigious bounty resulted from its rich and fertile soil. Quite a large part of the marshes lies below sea level and it is protected by sea defences and walls. The ancient cliff that formed the coastline 10,000 years ago at the end of the last Ice Age provides a hilly backdrop to the Marshes. Despite continuous habitation for many centuries, the Marshes have never been more than thinly populated. There are eight, so-called 'lost villages', ruins of houses and churches, whose medieval inhabitants undoubtedly perished from the plague or one or other type of waterborne disease. There are about a dozen picturesque small villages surviving today which have a long watery history, punctuated by dastardly deeds. For much of the 17th, 18th and 19th centuries smuggling was organised by ruthless local gangs, probably based in Rye and Lydd. The perpetrators were romanticised to the hilt, in the *Dr Syn* books by Russell Thorndike. A nefarious past only adds to the spirit of this mysterious and often desolate place characterised by wide horizons, a fascinating ecosystem, wildlife and a higher-than-average accumulation of folklore and superstition woven about its features. There are a surprising number of churches, including the 800-year-old one at Old Romney with its crusader's tomb. Romney Marsh inspires artists and writers through its landscapes and oddities. The Marshes are officially protected areas for bird and wildlife, Dungeness nuclear power stations (one obsolete, one functioning) notwithstanding. There is a gallows humour about the jest that the local eatery serves excellent 'fission chips'.

Herne Bay

Herne Bay is a Victorian seaside town on the north-east coast of Kent adjacent to trendy Whitstable, and eight miles from the historic city of Canterbury. Like many seaside towns, it grew out of Victorian speculators cashing in on the boom in seaside holidays. Herne Bay is named from the original village of Herne, now 1.8 miles back from the seafront. Pleasure steamers plied the Thames Estuary bringing thousands of visitors to Whitstable, Herne Bay and Margate. Later the railway added to Herne Bay's customer base. The last steamer docked at Herne Bay in 1963. The original pier was built in 1837 for the disembarkation of steamer passengers. It was a great attraction and an admired feat of engineering, until corrosion and storm damage finally truncated it in the 1970s. There is a local organisation (www.hernebaypier.com) that ambitiously aims to raise the £12 million needed to rebuild the pier with private funding. Herne Bay went into decline about the same time as package holidays abroad took off, and like other abandoned British seaside resorts, it assumed the air of 'God's waiting room': looking sad and derelict with an increasing elderly population. That was until about 10 years ago, when local government began to pull up its socks, turn its attention and funds away from Canterbury, and focus on the reinvention of Herne Bay. It has smartened up the seafront, pedestrianised the shopping area, improved housing, built up sea defences, created a new harbour and improved recreational and sporting facilities. There are further plans to make the town centre more user-friendly. Families have moved to Herne Bay from London and demand for places at local schools is now exceeding supply. However, despite an injection of cash and young blood, Herne is still a quiet place, and it is still somewhere you can retire to. Perhaps now is the time to do so. It has lots of independent shops and affordable property; far cheaper than nearby Whitstable or the south-east in general. In 2007 a restored five-bedroom Victorian villa was on sale for £300,000, although many well-appointed bungalows can cost that and more. Herne Bay has numerous streets of red-brick Victoria villas and a rising number of specialised retirement developments with flats from about £99,000. Those who live there find it friendly, congenial and convenient for other interesting places, and for connections abroad. Ferries go to Ostend from nearby Ramsgate, Dover and Folkestone are not far, and there are holiday charter flights from the local airport, Kent International. London is accessible by train and road, the countryside, particularly the Kent Downs is nearby as is Canterbury, which is the nearest big town and main shopping centre. Perhaps Herne Bay lives up to its Victorian advertising slogan: 'Herne Bay – The Healthiest Spot in England' as it provides an unstressed lifestyle. The only blot on the seascape is the recently built wind farm of 30 lighthouse-size turrets topped with windmills located eight and a half miles off Herne Bay and Whitstable and clearly visible from the shoreline. But just think, they are supplying you with electricity and they are guilt and carbon emission-free. This windfarm is a smallholding, however, compared with the 271 London Array wind turbines shortly to be built 12 miles off the coast of nearby Margate.

My experience...

Maureen Ryan, aged 69, worked in the National Health Service and retired to Herne Bay from Brentford in 2004. She explains how luck and local knowledge helped her get there.

I've never been married and I moved here on my own. I knew Herne Bay from visiting my sister in Whitstable, where she's been living for 40 years. We moved our elderly mother from Aylesbury to be near my sister. I used to come here a lot at weekends and take mum out in the car to Herne Bay because it has a nice seafront that she loved to visit. I just couldn't wait to leave Brentford as my home there was not very nice. Herne Bay was the obvious choice really, but I didn't actually know that I would end up here. I had to go through the Housing Trust that I am with and I could have been offered a place at any of their properties in Kent. I got a letter saying I was on the list for Herne Bay for the sheltered accommodation flat I am now in. It's a block of 55 apartments and there is a very nice communal lounge downstairs, which is a sociable place to meet, play Scrabble and chat. The rent covers all costs including electricity and cleaning of communal areas. I couldn't have chosen better, even if the choice had been mine to make. I thought I was a bit young for sheltered housing, but this was all they could offer and it has worked out very well. Living costs here are cheaper; the council tax is less.

There are more individual shops here rather than big supermarkets, the sea is three minutes' walk away. Canterbury is half an hour away on the bus. There are lots of clubs and I am driving more. Driving in Brentford and the surrounding area was getting worse and worse. Here you can be in the middle of the countryside in 15 minutes. It's all here, everything you could possibly want. The only thing I miss is going to concerts at the Albert Hall, but I have managed to go to them from here a couple of times.

SOUTH-EAST ENGLAND

Herne Bay fact file

Access: M2 from London to junction 7. A299 (the Thanet Way), London, 65 miles.

Average property price: £176,511

Airports: Kent International Airport (www.kentinternationalairport-manston.com), 13 miles. Flights to Spain and Portugal (www.kentescapes.com); flights to Norfolk, Virginia, USA (www.cosmos.co.uk). Gatwick, 72 miles.

Bus services: Stagecoach East Kent (www.stagecoachbus.com/eastkent)

Climate: Reputation for sunshine and fresh, clean air said to come from the Arctic with nothing in between except the North Sea; so no soft south coast breezes

Council: Canterbury City Council (www.canterbury.gov.uk)

Council tax: Band D £1,267.11; band E £1,548.69

Crime: Rise in nuisance from teenage drinking on the streets; petty vandalism. Slightly higher than national average for violence against a person.

Economic activity: Considered an area of low economic activity but the Herne Bay regeneration plan has two aims: to make the town a more attractive and lively place for residents and visitors (especially weekenders), and to promote business growth.

Ferries: Transeuropa (www.transeuropaferries.co.uk) Ramsgate to Ostend (Belgium); Dover (25 miles) and Folkestone (29 miles) to France (P&O, Hoverspeed, Norfolk Line, Speedferries).

Hospitals: New health trust East Kent Coastal Primary Care Trust formed in 2006 (www.ekht.nhs.uk). Queen Victoria Memorial Hospital Herne Bay, small local hospital. Nearest A&E and large hospital Kent and Canterbury Hospital. Long waiting times for orthopaedic surgery.

Percentage of people over 65: Approximately 16.2%

Population: 31,335

Property prices: One-bedroom flat £122,000; two-bedroom house £195,086; 3-bedroom house £227,000; beach hut £8,000

Railway station: Herne Bay. 10 minutes' walk to the seafront. Trains to London Victoria and London Charing Cross.

Specialised retirement property: An increasing number including Oakland Court (01227 40122 warden); Cavendish Court (01227 457648; www.orbit.org.uk)

Rye

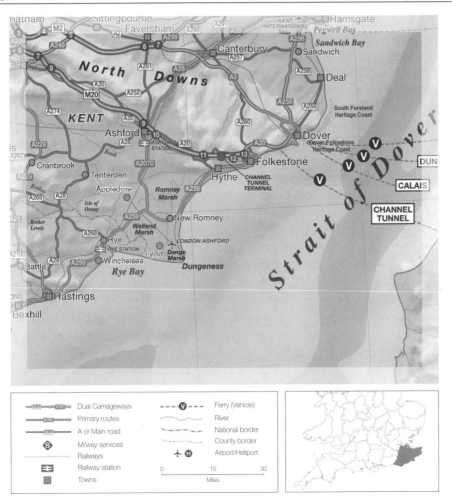

Dual Carriageways	Ferry (Vehicle)	
Primary routes	River	
A or Main road	National border	
M/way services	County border	
Railways	Airport/Heliport	
Railway station		
Towns	0 15 30 Miles	

Rye, situated on Rye Bay on the East Sussex–Kent border marks the western edge of Romney Marshes. Various parts of the Marshes have different names, such as the Walland Marsh and Denge Marsh, which are the two closest to Rye. The ancient town of Winchelsea is two miles west of Rye. Rye Harbour Nature Reserve, and most of Rye Bay from Cliff End to Dungeness, form a single 9,137-hectare Site of Special Scientific Interest (SSSI). This whole stretch of coastline has been spared development thanks to its combination of shingle ridges, mud flats, salt marshes, sandstone cliffs and sand dunes, mostly unique habitats that have long been under official conservation protection. The OS Explorer map 125 *Romney Marsh, Rye and Winchelsea, Tenterden, New Romney* (http://leisure.ordnancesurvey.co.uk/)covers the area in detail. Rye itself is a fortified hilltop town whose outline is a landmark that can be seen from the western

161

marshes. The River Rother meanders its final one and a half miles past Rye into the sea but, in the middle ages Rye stood on a promontory with river estuaries of the Rother and Tillingham on either side and an easy-to-defend entrance along a narrow isthmus. Over the centuries the river silted up and shingle banks formed at the estuary entrance. Rye Harbour, which was once part of the alliance of Cinque Ports, and strategically vital to the defence of the realm, gradually declined in importance but its maritime tradition lives on it its small fishing fleet. In summer, tourists flock in to wander Rye's cobbled streets and half-timbered buildings, and to admire the views over the Romney Marshes. Rye is great for walking, cycling, birdwatching, sailing and golf, and the old town is packed with wonderful historic inns and eateries. If you retired there, your daily needs would all be within walking distance and there are many interesting and enjoyable outdoor things to do in the surrounding area.

Writers and musicians have always been attracted to Rye. In 1899 when the writer Henry James bought Rye's grandest piece of real estate, Lamb House (now a National Trust property) he paid £2,000 for it, and was roundly ticked off by his brother for paying too much. His descendants might be wishing it were still a family asset. The problem with this gem of old England is the very high cost of property, so not many people, writers or otherwise, can afford the prices. For instance, for a three-bedroom terrace house in the old town, starting prices are £350,000. A potential tragedy on the horizon (literally) is the application to extend the runway at Lydd Airport to take large aircraft such as Boeing 737s and expand passenger services by millions. There is a local action group, Keep the Marsh Special Alliance, committed to opposing this, because of the adverse environmental impact it will have, particularly on wildlife and the area's tranquility (www.lyddairport-noexpansion.co.uk). At present, Lydd is used for flying lessons, flights over the bay, and commercial flights in small aircraft over the English Channel. Bus services and train services in the area are integrated, making use of public transport a feasible alternative to cars for getting around the area.

My experience...

Alec Richardson, a former mining engineer, now aged 70, moved to Rye from Leicester with his wife, 10 years ago.

The main reason for moving here was that we like this area. It wasn't our specific intention to move on retiring, although we had hoped we might move out of the city. We have lived in five English counties and abroad. We like the sea and walking and obviously there's a lot of scope for that down here. We also have relatives in

Kent, which isn't far away, and of course you always migrate south when you retire, because the weather, generally speaking, is better. Rye is quite secluded; there's not much noise or stress and very little air pollution and the roads are not crowded. The pace of life is slow and people down here live 10 years longer than the average. There are quite a number of interests we can pursue. Rye harbour, for instance, is a nature reserve and we are keen bird watchers. Living in the village has quite a lot of advantages because the social life is good. There are lots of things to do, like flower shows, luncheon clubs, farmers' markets, quizzes and then in summer it's a beautiful place and most people spend the summer in their garden. We also go to France quite often and we are only a few miles from Dover and Folkestone. That was another reason for moving down here.

When you retire, your cash is limited, so it is important to do your research. My wife's opinion of the cost of living down here, compared with the city, is that it is more expensive because there is less competition. Shopping in Rye is good because it has a supermarket and there are a couple of superstores on the outskirts. It is obvious that retired people need help getting to hospital appointments and the parish council pays for that. For instance, a few years ago I had a cataract operation and there's someone who takes people to the local hospital for appointments. I drive my own car, but it was obvious in that situation that I needed to be driven. As far as that system is concerned it works well.

We live in a bungalow, four or five miles from the sea, but it's in the woods because East Sussex is a very wooded county and there are lots of little villages tucked away in the woods. We are on the Tenterden to Hastings route and there is a bus about every two hours, which isn't much, but if you are retired, you can arrange your day according to the bus schedule. It would be better if Rye had better public transport, but I don't think lack of it is going to stop people coming here. I recommend that anyone thinking of Rye should see it in both summer, which is nice, and in winter, when there is frost and it drags a bit with the long nights. When 50%–60% of your day is spent going out or walking, it is important that you like the place in summer and winter, even though in winter it is not as nice. It doesn't stop us going out though; we're out in all weathers.

Rye fact file

Access: Hastings, 11 miles east on A259; Ashford; 10 miles

Average property price: £263,930

Airports: Gatwick, 80 miles; London City Airport (www.londoncityairport.com), 60.5 miles; London Manston Airport (www.kentinternational-manston.com), 38.5 miles; Lydd London Ashford Airport (www.lydd-airport.co.uk), 4 miles. Lyddair offers return flight Lydd to Le Touquet £86.62.

Bus services: Stagecoach (www.stagecoachbus.com), 711 route runs along the coast between Dover and Hastings. Connects with train timetable at Rye for fast trains to Brighton and Ashford International.

Climate: The climate of the Marshes is different from the rest of Kent and Sussex. Relatively cool and windy, especially at Dungeness.

Councils: Rye Town Council (www.ryetowncouncil.gov.uk); Rother District Council (www.rother.gov.uk)

Council tax: Band D £1,369.07; band E 1673.31

Crime: Quite high rates of burglary and theft from motor vehicles

Economic activity: The area between Rye and Folkestone is considered part of an area of relative economic deprivation

Ferries: Dover, 32 miles; Folkestone, 25 miles

Hospitals: Nearest general hospital with an A&E is the Conquest District General Hospital in Hastings (15 miles) (www.esht.nhs.uk); BUPA Hastings hospital is located on the same site and does private hip replacements. Rye has a partly charitable funded Memorial Care Centre (www.ryehospital.org.uk), which provides day care and inpatient care along with other non-acute facilities.

Percentage of people over 65: 32% (Rother area)

Population: About 16,000

Property prices: Detached £373,742; semi-detached £198, 684; terrace £182,888; flat £139,139

Railway station: Rye. Trains to London via Ashford International and services to Hastings, Eastbourne. Channel Tunnel 21 miles.

Specialised retirement property: Strand Court for the over-60s (one partner can be 50+) (www.homewise.co.uk). One-bedroom flats from £108,000.

South-west England

CORNWALL

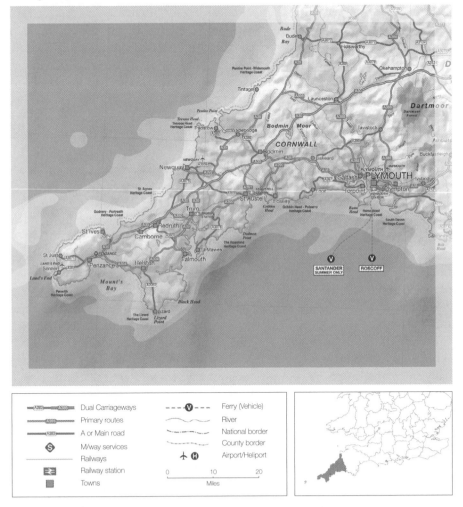

Dual Carriageways		Ferry (Vehicle)		
Primary routes		River		
A or Main road		National border		
M/way services		County border		
Railways		Airport/Heliport		
Railway station				
Towns				

0   10   20
Miles

Cornwall forms a peninsula at the south-western extremity of Britain and is home to a resident population of just over half a million people. Turn the map until the tip of Cornwall points downwards and you could easily mistake its outline for that of Italy. That's in shape, not in scale, since Cornwall covers a much smaller area at 1,357 square miles (Kent is 1,419 square miles). Cornwall's long narrow shape gives it a coastline of almost 300 miles. Many areas in Cornwall are designated Areas of Outstanding Natural Beauty (AONB)

SOUTH-WEST ENGLAND

165

amounting to a about a quarter of its total land and seascape. In boffin-speak, it is categorised as part of the 'Atlantic Arc' of Celtic lands: Brittany, Wales, the Isle of Man, Ireland and Scotland, but this demeans its uniqueness. It is preferable to think of it as the Cornish do, as a land apart, cut off from mainstream Britain, wrapped in its own remoteness; King Arthur's Kingdom, with folklore and fact so intertwined that historians struggle to separate them. Facts about Cornwall include the arrival of the Celts about 1000BC. It is widely credited that, centuries before Christ, the Phoenicians from the Middle East traded for tin in Cornwall and left their blue-eyed black-haired legacy in the genetic make-up of the people of the region. Even the legend of Lyonesse, about a lost land that sank beneath the waves between Land's End and the Scilly Isles, could be based on a real event such as a drastic change in sea levels. The Roman influence over Britain from 55BC barely ventured into Cornwall; the nearest Roman centre was at Exeter. Some say that ever since, Cornwall remained distant from the rule of London; until modern times and the founding of celebrity chef Rick Stein's seafood restaurant at Padstow. This is credited with starting the inflow into Cornwall of a larger section of the London and celebrity crowd. Cornwall is also receiving Objective I Funding from the EU, which rates it economically on a par with Sardinia. The heir to the throne is the hereditary Duke of Cornwall and the Prince Charles is the current holder of the Dukedom. The title and rights of the Duke are the subject of controversy in Cornwall.

The climate of Cornwall is tempered by the Gulf Stream, which keeps temperatures mild throughout the year. Tropical plants grow on the Scilly Isles situated 30 miles off the Cornish Coast, while in Cornwall itself, plant growth stops only for a few days a year. There is a north–south temperature divide within the county; the southern coastline is much warmer than the northern one. As anyone who lives there will tell you: it rains a lot in Cornwall. Days of mud and mire tend to come in yearly cycles from October to January; central Cornwall usually bears the brunt, but the west is generally wetter than the east.

The landscape of Cornwall is characterised by granite moors and a rugged coastline that has a history of causing ships to founder. There are also bogs and moorlands but precious little woodland. Cornwall is one of the least wooded (less than 5%) places in Britain. As a potential resident of Cornwall, you may have justified concerns about radon, a naturally occurring radioactive gas, which is emitted in particularly high concentrations (above 200 bequerels) in parts of Devon and Cornwall. North and south-east Cornwall are the worst affected, and householders in and around Gunnislake, Liskeard, Looe, Callington and Camelford are most at risk. Houses built where there is a high level of radon should have a special pump fitted indoors to dispel the gas out of doors. There are grants available for this.

Cornwall has long been a top tourist destination and a popular place for holiday homes but in the last decade or so, Cornwall has become one of the most popular places to retire to. However, according to a recent local government report

Roseland Parc:
Where every day feels like being on holiday

EVERY day feels like being on holiday at Roseland Parc retirement village on the stunning Roseland Peninsula in Cornwall. Just ask Roy and Julie Buckley.

The 72-year-olds from Surrey moved from another retirement development in favour of Roseland Parc, tucked away in the pretty village of Tregony near Truro.

"We saw Roseland Parc advertised in Saga magazine and thought we'd come and have a look round during a visit to see our son and daughter who live in nearby Camelford," said Julie.

"We never dreamt that by the time we left we'd have bought a new home," she smiled. "But we did and we love it."

"We've only been here a short while, but have already made lots of new friends," said Roy.

"I wander through the palm garden every day to go for a swim and we often go to the restaurant on Sunday for a delicious lunch. The food really is first class and nothing is ever too much trouble for the staff."

Roseland Parc offers 59 apartments and cottages built around the palm garden and croquet lawn. Central facilities include a swimming pool, hot tub, fitness area, hair salon, treatment room, restaurant and bar, shop and library.

Over half the properties are sold. Prices for independent living properties start at £245,000. Fully serviced, hotel-style living apartments are also available with prices from £170,000.

Retirement Villages Ltd has been developing and managing age exclusive communities for over 25 years and currently has villages in Cornwall, Devon, Somerset, Hertfordshire, Surrey, Warwickshire, Oxfordshire and Lincolnshire. More are planned.For more information about Roseland Parc call **01872 530888** or visit the company website: **www.retirementvillages.co.uk**

in Cornwall, 'No evidence substantiates the misconception that a large proportion of migration moves are by people approaching, or at, retirement age'.

What is not a misconception is that property prices have doubled in 10 years and developers are eyeing up new spots for apartments. There are considerable differences in prices, from trendy Newquay where two-bedroom apartments go for £500,000 pounds, to St Austell where you can buy a two-bedroom house for £206,000. The problem, if any, of retiring to rural Cornwall is its geographical remoteness and lack of large centres and amenities. Truro, the capital of Cornwall, has a population of just 21,000. Other towns of similar size are St Austell, Camborne, Redruth and Newquay. Towns such as trendy St Ives have a population of 10,000 or less and many rural villages have barely a couple hundred of inhabitants. The total population of Cornwall is just over half a million and over 46% of the population lives outside the towns. No wonder that tourists are called emmets (ants) because they swarm all over Cornwall in summer, vastly outnumbering the permanent residents. Rural life is great for the fit and active, but older people and those whose health deteriorates, or whose partner dies, might find it a struggle, or worse, experience loneliness. Also, if you are a non-driver, rural public transport, like the indigenous population, is pretty sparse. In 2005 Historic Cornwall carried out a detailed, informative and readable assessment of the 18 urban towns of Cornwall which can be accessed on their website www.historic-cornwall.org.uk. The following places in Cornwall are in the south-east of the county with access to both Cornwall and Devon.

Roseland Peninsula

Roseland is the name of the peninsula that is separated from the rest of southern Cornwall by the River Fal. It is located on the coastline known in tourist-speak as the 'Cornish Riviera' (www.cornish-riviera.co.uk), which includes St Austell Bay and Fowey. The widest part of the River Fal, where it blends into the sea, is called Carrick Roads, part of the busy Falmouth harbour, one of the largest natural harbours in the world. A delta of spiky branches of the Fal lead off the Carrick Roads, and it is one of these branches of water that flows along the northern edge of Roseland. The largest town in Roseland is St Mawes (population 2,000) while Truro is nearby, as is Falmouth, which can be reached by river ferry in 25 minutes. The Falmouth–St Mawes ferry is currently free for residents and students of Falmouth University College for Art, Design and Media. St Mawes has a well-preserved Tudor castle and hip hotels, especially the Tresanton, which has had a designer conversion. Crowds from London and the south-east and yacht crews can double the town's population in summer and it is an important centre for marine activities. Roseland has scenery different from the rest of Cornwall, consisting of coastal farmland and winding narrow lanes, with high hedges and passing places. The villages of Roseland are Portloe, Veryan Treworlas, Portscatho, Gerrans, St Just in Roseland, Philleigh, Treworga and Ruan Lanihorne. In many ways, Roseland is an ideal retirement place; a peaceful, mini-paradise of small fishing villages, sandy beaches, protected landscape, coastal walks with small friendly communities and a reasonable shopping centre at nearby Truro. Many properties are holiday cottages that are rented out.

My experience...

Peter Gane bought a holiday home in Roseland 10 years ago, with a mind to retire there eventually. He retired at 55 and is now 59 years old. He moved there permanently 15 months ago with his wife.

We stumbled on the Roseland 20 years ago. It isn't a place you'd ever pass through travelling on your way through Cornwall, it's the type of place you think 'let's go and have a look'. It's a very beautiful, peaceful part of the world. Because we'd been coming here for quite a long time, we knew the area pretty well. The Roseland's quite small, only about 10 miles long, so it's not difficult to find your way around once you get here. We came on holiday here every year for 10 years. We thought we would like to retire here, if we didn't go abroad. So we decided to buy a bungalow in Treworga, a hamlet of 20 properties, and use it for weekends, get ourselves established as semi-residents, before we finally moved here for retirement. I guess there is a large immigrant population here, but the Cornish people are very friendly to long-term residents and Roseland is a very communal sort of place. There is none of that resentment you might get in some places.

There are downsides, which we considered carefully. The nearest supermarket shopping is in Truro about 12 miles away. There are a couple of grocers, butchers and bakers on the Roseland, enough for basic daily needs. Our nearest shop is about two and a half miles. It isn't ideal for anybody who doesn't have their own transport. There are buses, but they are infrequent; there's a bus to Truro about every hour and a half. Also, family may seem a long way away. In Wiltshire, we were a few minutes' drive from our family. Now we have to prepare for visits in either direction.

It's just so different from anywhere 'up country'. It's the pace of life we like. We have dogs and it's a great place for walking. There are lots of little clubs pursuing different interests: music, several local history societies, cinema club and two very active amateur drama clubs. If you are interested in water activities it's absolutely fantastic; you've got the whole of the South Estuary and all the little creeks and boating activities that go with these. I am interested in family history and lead a family history group for the University of the Third Age (www.u3aroseland.org.uk). You have the time to focus on things you like; if you want to be involved with things you can; if you just want to be sitting outside enjoying the mild climate, you can.

SOUTH-WEST ENGLAND

Roseland fact file

Access: A390 St Austell to Truro road/A3078; London, 255 miles

Average property price: £190,000 (Cornwall)

Airports: Newquay (www.newquay-airport.co.uk); connecting flights to Bristol from £27 and Leeds/Bradford (www.airsouthest.com). New economic strategy for Cornwall includes expansion of Newquay airport to include flights to Europe. At present, the nearest international airport is Exeter (101 miles).

Bus services: Run by First Group (www.firstgroup.com) and Truronian (www.truronian.co.uk). Countywide Concessionary Fares Card is a free scheme for the over-60s for local bus services and through services to Plymouth and Devon. Details at www.cornwallpublictransport.info/gen_senior.asp.

Climate: Mild, tropical influence

Councils: Carrick District Council (www.carrick.gov.uk) based in Truro. Cornwall County Council (www.cornwall.gov.uk).

Council tax: Typically band D 1,210.21; band E 1,479.15 (St Gerrans)

Crime: According to Carrick District Council, crime was low anyway, but it has fallen again

Economic activity: Mainly connected with tourism. Other is low compared to the rest of the country.

Ferries: Year-round half-hourly ferry from St Mawes to Falmouth (King Harry's Cornwall Ferries) (www.kingharryscornwall.co.uk/ferries). Chain ferry between Philleigh and Feock. For all the other ferry and boat passenger services see www.falriverlinks.co.uk.

Hospitals: New primary care trust in 2006: Cornwall and Isles of Scilly Primary Care Trust (www.cornwall.nhs.uk). District general hospital in Truro (Treliske Hospital); also Derriford in Plymouth. Reorganisation of services and local hospitals and treatment centres in progress.

Percentage of people over 65: Out of six Cornish districts Carrick has the highest percentage of people over 65 (27%)

Population: 86,800 (whole Carrick area)

Property prices: Three-bedroom semi-detached period house £265,000

Railway station: Truro (approx 20 miles from St Mawes)

Specialised retirement property: Brand new retirement village Roseland Parc (www.roselandparc.co.uk) at Tregony 'gateway' to the Roseland Peninsula. 80 apartments. Full range of amenities including swimming pool and spa and personal trainers and classes. Prices from £170,000 (serviced) and from £245,000 (independent living).

St Austell

St Austell (pronounced 'St Ostel', except perhaps by Prince Charles) is on the south coast of east Cornwall, diagonally across from Newquay on the north coast. It has a population of just 22,600, and yet it is Cornwall's largest town. Nearby villages include Par, Biscovey, St Blazey, St Stephens and Tywardheath. Originally a medieval hamlet with a church, St Austell's fortune blossomed following the discovery, in the 18th century, of large deposits of porcelain-grade china clay, which transformed English pottery, especially when Wedgwood bought mining rights there. The town expanded throughout the 19th and early 20th centuries. Today, St Austell's china clay industry, although much diminished and foreign-owned, continues to supply kaolin for cosmetics, pharmaceuticals, paints and agricultural products, among other items. The white heaps that provide a somewhat lunar backdrop to St Austell are a reminder that clay mining is a wasteful process, producing five times as much waste as it does usable product. But St Austell and its environs are not languishing in the past. Quite the opposite, since the town and its nearby amenities are currently the focus of major development. The town centre is being modernised and rebuilt; Prince Charles' Duchy of Cornwall is building a faux-Victorian village on a disused railway yard in the town; and the St Austell Business Park on the edge of town will provide space for about 200 businesses. Nearby, the fabulous Eden Project (www.edenproject.com) opened in 2001 and has received worldwide adulation and visitors, while the controversial Carlyon Beach development (www.carlyonbaywatch.co.uk) of a massive beach resort, which includes more than 500 holiday flats, is in progress. There are misgivings over Carlyon, not only among environmentalists, but also among those whose awe of the ocean is greater than that of the developers; the complex is at beach level, just yards from the sea. The local astronomy club is worried about light pollution drowning out the stars, naturists have lost a popular beach, and naturalists mourn the destruction of habitat.

What is certain is that with so much happening in and around St Austell, it looks like it is shaking off its slightly dispirited air, even if many of St Austell's inhabitants think the revamp of the town centre is unaesthetic. It is a place in the throes of expansion, and while property prices are not cheap, they are on the lower end of prices in Cornwall. If you have the energy to take on a house in need of restoration, there are still bargains available, but there is competition from investors who want to convert them into holiday homes. St Austell caters well for the over-50s with a wide range of academic and leisure courses at the Cornwall College of St Austell (www.cornwall.ac.uk) and an active U3A. For the active there are wonderful cliff walks, an 18-hole cliff top golf course and all the other outdoor sights and sounds of the 'Cornish Riviera'. That said, Cornwall is two different places in winter and summer. Visit St Austell in winter as well as summer before deciding.

SOUTH-WEST ENGLAND

My experience...

Mr Cladingbowl, now 83, retired 18 years ago from South Africa, to the village of St Stephens near St Austell:

We were on holiday and visiting my daughter who was living in Exeter and we saw this house up for sale and bought it. We've been here ever since. I was quite happy as I had always planned to retire to the West Country, but St Austell was quite by chance and a very happy decision. We knew very little about Cornwall at the time, apart from a visit when we were first married. It is a lovely area to retire to, a nice place to live and the countryside beautiful and the air is fresh and clear because it blows in off the Atlantic, and of course it's very mild. We are right in the middle of Cornwall, close to the coast and the main road through Cornwall and a mainline railway station. We're actually four miles from St Austell, but close enough to be convenient. After we moved here we found there were lots of things for retired people to get involved with, particularly the U3A, which is very strong here and has helped us make lots of friends along with the local church. Our village has a couple of mini-markets, post office and hairdresser and a very good medical surgery and an excellent hospital eight miles away in Truro. I have personal experience of the local medical facilities because of lung problems and I can't speak too highly of them.

St Austell town centre is a bit of a wreck as they are rebuilding it. They are taking an awfully long time and haven't managed it very well in my opinion. The town is very good, on the assumption it will be finished one day. The only drawbacks I can see are that the place is overrun with visitors in the summer. It's obviously a popular place, but it's lovely when we have it to ourselves. There is a little resentment from locals towards people who move here. I think second homeowners are a different story because they push up house prices and are absent most of the year without contributing to the economy as we do. I've lived all over the world and I think the key is to make a point of becoming part of the local community. Oh, and you'll suddenly be very popular with friends and family coming to visit you. Unfortunately, this year we are moving away for health reasons to be nearer one of our children. It is with great reluctance that we are leaving; it is a lovely county.

St Austell fact file

Access: Via M5 and A390; Truro, 15 miles

Average property price: £217,968

Airport: Newquay (see Roseland for details)

Bus services: Run by First Group (www.firstgroup.com). Buses to the Eden Project, Truro, Bodmin, and other destinations in Cornwall and Devon, but you really need a car to live in this area.

Climate: So mild that it is possible to see flowers in bloom all year round

Council: Restormel Borough Council (www.restormel.gov.uk)

Council tax: Band D £1,194.82; band E £1,460.34

Crime: Antisocial issues among 10-19-year-olds and vehicle crime and violent crime.

Economic activity: Developments (see above) should increase local prosperity, which is second lowest in the UK at present

Ferries: Local ferry service May to September between Fowey and Mevagissey (www.mevagissey-ferries.co.uk). From Plymouth, Brittany Ferries to France and Santander (Spain).

Hospital: Royal Cornwall Hospital (also known as Treliske Hospital) on the outskirts of Truro (www.cornwall.nhs.uk). Large general hospital.

Percentage of people over 65: Above average due to incomer retirement

Population: 34,000 (whole St Austell bay area)

Property prices: Flat £177,224; detached £257,954; semi-detached £185,263; terrace £178,600

Railway station: St Austell

Specialised retirement property: Several new housing developments not necessarily aimed at – but suitable for – retirement including New Homes Development (0845 402 4454), Edgcumbe Road, one and a half miles from city centre and The Wentworth, three and four-bedroom homes built by Wainhomes (0845 408 3283) on site of old clay works. Chisholm Court (01726 76243) is a warden-controlled complex.

SOUTH-WEST ENGLAND

Torpoint

In 1848, the Topographic Dictionary of England said of Torpoint, 'Though small it is highly respectable; and in the vicinity are many genteel seats'.

Topography, aided by national landscape conservation and private land ownership, have all contributed to ensure Torpoint has remained small. It is situated on a peninsula on the western side of the Tamar Estuary, opposite the naval dockyards at Devonport, part of an industrial area of the large city of Plymouth over the other side of the River Tamar. There is a 24-hour passenger and car ferry service between Torpoint and Plymouth. North of Torpoint is Saltash, the first town in Cornwall, at the end of the toll bridge from Plymouth. Some people might find the aspect of Torpoint too industrial, but the river frontage is very attractive. Even if the view towards the dockyard is grim on a grey day, the view looking back at Torpoint from Plymouth is quite the reverse. Shopping trips to Plymouth are probably a necessity as Torpoint does not have a wide selection of shops. It does have its own leisure centre – reopened with much fanfare in 2004 – the Garden Sports and Leisure Club (01752 816800), complete with swimming pool, restaurant and spa treatments. There are a high proportion of older and retired people in Torpoint and they must see advantages in retiring to Torpoint that easily outweigh the lack of a perfect view or a branch of Marks & Spencer. It is a cosy, friendly town with spectacular wider surroundings such as the larger peninsula of Rame (www.rame-cornwall.co.uk), on which Torpoint is located. Like the Roseland, Rame is an Area of Outstanding Natural Beauty, not on the way to anywhere, and the majority of tourists ignore it as they rush over the Tamar into deeper Cornwall. In consequence, Rame is a peaceful gem consisting of landscape with wide bays and small villages with evocative names including Cremyll, Crafthole, Freathy, Kingsand and Cawsand. The South West Coastal Path starts at Cremyll and meanders through the 800 acres of the very beautiful Mount Edgcumbe Park. There is a cliff-top golf course overlooking Whitsand Bay that runs down the western side of Rame peninsula. Other advantages are not hard to find: there is a single route into Torpoint and so no through traffic. It is on the border of Cornwall and Devon and is thus a gateway to both counties. Torpoint is also very conveniently situated to explore the Tamar Valley and Dartmoor National Park in Devon and Bodmin Moor in Cornwall. Historic Cornwall's 2005 report on Torpoint is well worth reading for anyone thinking of retiring there (www.historic-cornwall.org.uk).

Property is expensive in Torpoint in relation to local incomes, but compared with the most popular places on the coast, such as Newquay, Rock and St Ives, it is considerably cheaper.

My experience...

Ted Murphy, aged 60, has recently moved from Torpoint for personal reasons and explains what Torpoint conjures up for him.

I lived in Torpoint for many years, even now it's a great place to grow up in and a nice place to bring up kids. The downside is that property is expensive and the cost of living, coupled with low wages can be hard going for some people. If you can afford it it's great. When people look at the holiday brochures they see all these lush gardens; what they don't realise is that this is because it is always raining, believe me it is. On the other hand, it is relatively warm and seeing palm trees and sub-tropical plants in people's gardens is normal.

The Torpoint ferry has been running since 1791 when it was established by an Act of Parliament. It was the most important part of the development of Torpoint as a viable town. For the residents of Torpoint, it can be a bit of a pain having the ferry because it can put as much as two hours on travel time during summer when it's busy. But it does keep the place quiet at night; not much traffic.

Torpoint fact file

Access: Via A374 which ends in Torpoint. Plymouth, 3 miles.

Average property price: £180,423

Airports: Plymouth City Airport (www.plymouthairport.com), 5.5 miles. Domestic flights including to Gatwick, Leeds Bradford and Jersey all from £38 with Air Southwest (www.airsouthwest.com). Exeter Airport (www.Exeter-airport.co.uk), 68 miles, for international flights to holiday destinations.

Bus services: Devon and Cornwall buses run by First (www.firstgroup.com)

Climate: Typical milder climate of Cornwall

Councils: Caradon District Council (www.caradon.gov.uk); Cornwall County Council (www.cornwall.gov.uk)

Council tax: Band D £1,268.23; band E £1,550.06

Crime: 744 Crimes per 2,000 head of the population in 2006, so on the high side

Economic activity: Quite high compared with Cornwall as a whole. Innovative schemes include the Trevol Business Park on a former Ministry of Defence site and the Torpoint Enterprise Court for small businesses.

Ferries: Torpoint car/pedestrian ferry operates between Torpoint and Devonport (www.torpointferry.org.uk). Brittany Ferries operate from Plymouth to Roscoff (France) and Santander (Spain).

Hospitals: Part of Cornwall and Isles of Scilly Primary Care Trust (www.cornwall.nhs.uk). Local hospital, St Barnabas at Saltash, has minor injuries unit. Nearest large hospital is Derriford Hospital, Plymouth.

Percentage of people over 60: 20%

Population: Approximately 11,000

Property prices: Detached £175,000; semi-detached £150,000; terrace £118,483; flat £79,000

Railway station: Plymouth

THE WEST COUNTRY

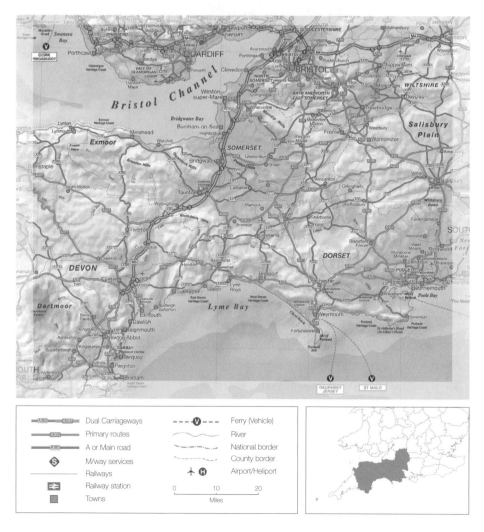

Dual Carriageways
Primary routes
A or Main road
M/way services
Railways
Railway station
Towns

Ferry (Vehicle)
River
National border
County border
Airport/Heliport

0   10   20
Miles

SOUTH-WEST ENGLAND

The West Country (Wiltshire, Somerset, Devon and Dorset) is a state of mind as well as an area of England. Somewhere around Salisbury, the air changes and you begin to breathe in another atmosphere. The A303 is still the main trunk road to the West Country, and the A30 runs parallel to it. These roads partly follow the historic routes from London to the West Country, from the days of coaching, post chaises and unsurfaced roads. The A303 has been widened, diverted and resurfaced countless times to take on the endlessly increasing motor traffic that is now made to loop around the town centres or bypass them completely, away from the welcoming courtyards of the coaching inns that once furnished weary travellers with rest and sustenance. The A30, meanwhile, has been demoted to a slow road for local traffic, or anyone who wants to join a cavalcade behind an unpassable caravan. The M5, which ends at Exeter in Devon, is the main artery of access for the holiday traffic that pours down from the north in the summer months. The West Country is a popular holiday destination and retirement area perhaps since FL Löhr and D Eardley-Wilmot penned their once popular and inspirational song for the First World War, *Little Grey Home in the West:*

> I forget I was weary before
> Far ahead, where the blue shadows fall
> I shall come to contentment and rest
> And the toils of the day will be all charmed away
> In my little grey home of the west.

If you are looking forward to an active retirement in your own 'grey home in the West', you will have chosen an especially good part of the country for those who love the outdoors. Devon and Dorset have picture postcard coastal villages, beautiful beaches, the desolate beauty of Dartmoor and Exmoor and busy seaside towns: Exmouth, Poole, Torquay, Sidmouth, Swanage and Weymouth to name but a few. Much of Dorset is designated an Area of Outstanding Natural Beauty. There should probably also be a designation for appealing place names, which Dorset excels in, including Piddlehinton, Chaldon Herring, Briants Puddle, Toller Percorum, Plush, Tincleton and Puncknowle; all watered no doubt by the famously named River Piddle. Bucolic and pastoral are adjectives that spring to mind when you see the soft landscapes of Devon and Somerset unfurl their hills dotted with sheep and cattle, and your thoughts can roam lazily as far as the wide horizons you view. Somerset is known for apple growing and dairy produce, particularly cider and cheese making. Cheddar and more recently Somerset Brie are some of the better-known cheeses from the area. There is fine hill walking in the Mendips and Quantock Hills, on paths along steep cliffs and through wooded river valleys.

The cities of the West Country are exceptional: Georgian Bath with its famously Roman origins is one of the most beautiful English cities and is a gateway to the west, as is Salisbury with its iconic cathedral spire. Plymouth on the south coast is strongly associated with the giants of British maritime history, including Sir Francis Drake, the Plymouth Brethren (who set sail for America from there) and the people's admiral, Lord Nelson, probably Britain's most popular hero. Not as remote as Cornwall, and without that county's wild and rugged beauty, the West Country is considered by some people to be the best place in England to retire to for its healthy air, mild climate, good access routes and the excellent healthcare support for the rising population of older people who live there. Its popularity is, however, reflected in the property prices and the rising cost of living. Property with a sea view is very expensive, and Poole and Weymouth are some of the most expensive spots in the West Country and Britain.

Bath Spa

Retiring to Bath is not a new idea. According to www.Roman-Britain.org:

> *The Roman city of Bath was (and still is) known throughout the civilised world for its complex bath-house built around natural hot springs. The baths were dedicated to the goddess Sulis Minerva, and was one of the most sought-after retirement places in Roman Britain, being surrounded by a plethora of country villas and several temples.*

The development of Bath into the Georgian city of neo-classical design, is an appropriate reflection of its Roman 'undercity'. Take Walcot Street, which archaeology has revealed was a street of Roman shops leading into the city; today it is still a street of quirky and individual shops. Seeing the elegance and classical geometry of the honey-coloured buildings of Bath for the first, or even umpteenth time it is easy to imagine it peopled with characters from Jane Austen's romantic, satirical novels, two of which were partly set in Bath, or Becky Sharp, the resourceful and scheming heroine of Thackeray's novel *Vanity Fair,* who retired to genteel Bath, post Battle of Waterloo to take tea and sympathy in the Pump Room. Bath is not only glorious to look at and nice to live in, but also saturated in history and layered with historic imagery. The entire city is a Unesco World Heritage site, which means that very little can be done to spoil it, although it is not without a few blemishes from the age of concrete.

The construction of Georgian Bath, including the Royal Circus and other iconic Bath buildings, took place over more than a century, from the early 18th century up to 1825. Victorian Bath continued to grow outwards to the outlying suburbs, all of them built in the honey-coloured stone that gives Bath its unique homogeneity. At the end of the 18th century, long after the Georgian dandy, gambler and social butterfly Beau Nash had been largely instrumental in making Bath fashionable and a rival to the London social scene, Bath went into decline. The aristocracy left and the middle classes began to come to Bath for retirement. The Victorians 'rediscovered' the original Roman baths in 1880 and made them a tourist attraction. Bath still wears an air of comfort and gentility, where anything slightly vulgar might cause the vapours, but it also has a thriving modern arts scene including the Bath Fringe Festival (www.bathfringe. co.uk) and the International Music Festival (www.bathmusicfest.org.uk). The cultural scene is a strong component of the Bath lifestyle and is one of the big attractions of Bath for those with the leisure time to enjoy it. Jane Austen's legacy of lovelorn heroes and heroines lives on in Bath's romantic attraction for today's youth: Bath has become a hotspot for 'Bridget Jones' weekends and has a thriving trade as a wedding venue. The final accolade (for some) is that the immensely winsome Hollywood star Johnny Depp, fell in love with Bath while filming nearby and is rumoured to have bought a manor house just outside Bath and enrolled his children at Bath schools, as an antidote, he says, to exposing them to the violent ills of America.

Despite the bustling arts scene and wonderful shopping, Bath has a downside, which includes serious traffic congestion (especially on the London Road), and lack of parking in the city area. In the outlying areas of Bath these problems are less significant. Property prices are high, but not completely outrageous. For instance, on the edge of town you can find a three-bedroom Georgian terrace house for under £400,000, and it may still be possible to find a property in need of renovation somewhere in the square mile of the city centre. The ambience is much the same if you live in the centre or up on one of the seven hills that Bath is spread out upon. Be warned that the Romans were on to something; properties in Bath sell faster than hot Bath buns. There is a useful website www.housesforsaleinbath.co.uk which has a wide range of properties on it to give you some idea of prices in the different areas of the city. If you are thinking that a dip in the Roman Baths might be one of your regular retirement treats, that is sadly no longer possible. However, a brand new spa building, the Thermae Bath Spa, has just been opened with sessions from £19 (15% discount for Bath residents). Bath has a large retired and older population and Bath University has a large university campus a mile from the city centre, which balances out the young–old ratio. The university also runs a centre for lifelong learning near the city centre (www.bath.ac.uk/lifelong-learning/parttimecourses) (01225 328703). Bath also has hundreds of clubs and societies covering a wide range of interests.

Georgian houses in Bath

My experience...

Prethee Hillary was forced to retire early (she is now 55) due to ill health and found Bath a good alternative to London.

I was living in London and had been looking for a flat or small house there. Then I realised that for the same amount of money, I could get something in Bath that was better value, since the further out of London you go, the more horrible it gets. I thought that I may as well move right out. I also thought that it can take two hours to cross London on a bad day, and that's what it takes from Bath to London anyway.

Bath is a town with its own identity and sense of importance. I knew Bath was a nice town; I didn't have to spend a lot of time making up my mind about the place. It's really interesting and has festivals on all the time and there's a lot to do. There's a theatre, Theatre Royal, which has a lot of pre-West End plays, which is good, an Odeon and art house cinema, lots of parks and some good museums including the Roman Baths and the Costume Museum. Bath is especially good if you play bridge as there is a lot of bridge played here. It's also nice because when you're in town you can look up from any point and see hills so you feel a sense of being in the countryside, even though you are in a city.

I moved into a house in the centre of town and for me it's perfect. At the end of my street there are four restaurants; Bath has lots of restaurants for all budgets and tastes. Waitrose is a seven-minute walk. Living in the centre of Bath, you never have to use a car; my car sometimes sits outside for a week or two at a time because everything I need is a few minutes' walk away. I suppose at the weekends it can get a bit rowdy and noisy. I'm not sure that there is enough for young people to do really, so they can get a bit wild. But I like living here and the experience has been very positive because I live in such a friendly area. We get lots of tourists in the summer, which I don't mind, but if you don't like being among multilingual hordes, Bath might not be for you.

Bath Spa fact file

Access: Junction 18 off M4 (10 miles). M4/M5 interchange north of Bristol gives fast access to the West Country. London, 115 miles.

Average property price: £253,364

Airport: Bristol International approximately 35 miles. Bus goes from airport to Bristol station (30 minutes). Train Bristol to Bath (15 minutes).

Bus services: Local services run by First Somerset & Avon (www.firstgroup.com/ukbus/southwest/somerset/home) and Faresaver Buses of Chippenham. Also Somerbus (01761 415456).

Climate: Inland so avoids the winds and fog of seaside places. Slightly colder than the coast in winter and still air makes it uncomfortably hot and sticky in summer.

Council: Bath and North East Somerset County Council (www.bathnes.gov.uk)

Council tax: Band D £1,254.35; band E £1,533.09

Crime: Late-night drinking and crime and disorder, especially at weekends, has been a problem in the city centre in recent years

Economic activity: The Bath economy thrives on tourism, 67% of tourism is from the UK

Ferries: Southampton (62 miles)

Hospital: Royal United Hospital Bath (www.ruh-bath.swest.nhs.uk)

Percentage of people over 65: Approximately 19%

Population: 84,000

Property prices: Detached £365,492; terraced £234,336; flat £204,294

Railway station: Bath Spa

Residents' on-street parking permit: £80 per year

Specialised retirement property: Many flat developments and conversions suitable for the retired (at a price)

Dorchester

Dorchester is a large market town and also the county town of West Dorset. It is situated on the River Frome, 20 miles from Poole and eight miles north of Weymouth. The other main towns of the area are Bridport, Lyme Regis, Beaminster and Sherborne. West Dorset is affluent and consistently Conservative with a big 'C'. This is ironic considering that in the 19th century, rural Dorset was a byword for extreme hardship and poverty, after the villagers of Tolpuddle formed a (legal) trade union to protest against their pitiful agricultural wages. In 1833, the 'Tolpuddle Martyrs' were tried and punished on a trumped-up charge brought by a local landowner, who saw shades of the French Revolution in their action. The Trades Union Congress (TUC) commemorates the Tolpuddle Martyrs with an annual village festival. Dorset has seen some of the steepest property price increases (244%) since 1996, which puts it just below Oxfordshire and West Sussex in the Halifax property price table for England. However, Dorchester, being a little inland, is a slightly cheaper option to the very expensive coast of Dorset.

Like Bath, Dorchester was founded by the Romans who called it Durnovaria, and it has famous literary associations. Thomas Hardy's rustic idylls with a gloomy essence, such as *Tess of the D'Urbervilles*, (published in 1891), were set in and around Dorchester and Dorset – referred to in the novels as Casterbridge and Wessex. Nowadays 'Wessex' is a marketing concept for businesses in the area such as Wessex Water. In the century before Hardy, Daniel Defoe, made a tour of England and opined that, 'A man that coveted a retreat in this world might as agreeably spend his time, as well in Dorchester as in any town I know in England'.

It is hard to know what Hardy or Defoe would have made of Poundbury, the Duchy of Cornwall's creeping urban extension of Dorchester expected to be completed in 2025. Poundbury will add 5,000 to the population of Dorchester and include factories, offices and general facilities such as a school and leisure centre. There is nothing ersatz about Dorchester's lively community Arts Centre and there is a local golf club founded in 1895, based at the curiously named Came Down Golf Course.

My experience...

Dorchester has good facilities that are widely appreciated by the elderly, as ex-soldier **Tom Fitches,** who moved to Dorchester three years ago aged 82, explains:

We moved to Dorchester because my son and two great-granddaughters live here and they wanted me and my wife to be nearer so they could visit us more easily. We've got a nice little ground floor flat with a kitchen/dining room and a big bedroom. It's in a complex for retired people run by Magna Housing. The surroundings are nice and we've met lots of people and have no end of friends; all retired here from all over the place. We already knew the area well and I used to drive here quite a bit when we had the car. I don't drive anymore, but bus services are very good and we have a bus stop just up the street. I can just go up the road and get a bus to anywhere from there; bus services are very good and even better with a bus pass.

Dorchester is a lovely little town. At one time there was a thriving cattle market but this was closed down years ago. There is a main hall where we have weekly bingo and high teas. Twice a week we go to the Dorchester day centre. Dorset people are friendly; we don't get much trouble here or anything like that. There are some nice public houses and shows and things in the evenings. The best part is that it is near places like Weymouth and Bournemouth. For anyone who wants to retire, I don't think you could do much better. I have breathing problems so the only problem for me is the hills. I can't walk very far. But we are near the hospital and there is help on hand where we live.

Maiden castle, Dorchester

SOUTH-WEST ENGLAND

Dorchester fact file

Access: On the junction of the A35 (south coast trunk route), and the A37 to Yeovil and north. One of four English counties that does not have a motorway. Weymouth, 9 miles; Yeovil, 20 miles.

Average property price: £231,272

Airports: Bournemouth International (www.bournemouthairport.com), 30 miles

Bus services: First Bus (www.firstgroup.com); Wilts and Dorset (www.wdbus.co.uk) operates in an area from Bath to Dorchester and Andover to Bournemouth

Climate: One of the highest sunshine records

Councils: West Dorset District Council (www.westdorset-dc.gov.uk); Dorset County Council (www.dorsetforyou.com)

Council tax: Band D £1,348.11; band E £1,516.62

Crime: Regarded as a low crime area

Economic activity: Unemployment is low and there is a lot of light industry and high-tech businesses operating from business parks

Ferries: From Weymouth and Poole, Condor Ferries (www.condorferries.com) to the Channel Islands and St Malo (France). From Poole, Brittany Ferries (www.Brittany-ferries.co.uk) to Cherbourg (France).

Hospital: West Dorset General Hospital Trust, which manages Dorset County Hospital (www.dch.org.uk) in Dorchester, and Weymouth Community Hospital, is rated excellent for managing waiting lists

Local newspaper: *Dorset Echo* (www.dorsetecho.co.uk)

Percentage of people over 60: Approximately 25%; 19.9% are aged 45–59

Population: 16,580

Property prices: Detached £411,325; semi-detached £227,978; terraced £198,637; flat £150,273

Railway stations: Dorchester South (on the South West Trains line to Bournemouth and Southampton). Dorchester West for Bath and Bristol.

Residents' on-street parking permit: £60 per year

Specialised retirement property: Magna Housing Group (01305 216000; www.magna.org.uk). Sheltered housing complex Dorchester (also in Sherborne, Bridport, Lyme Regis and Beaminster).

Exmouth

Exmouth is the largest town in East Devon and is made up of two parishes, Littleham and Withycombe. The central area of town is technically known as Littleham Urban. This corner of Devon has a famous two-mile beach, and fabulous views from the Beacon cliff area, which are the focus of its appeal as a seaside holiday spot. The town occupies the point where the River Exe joins the sea on the wide curve of Lyme Bay. Directly opposite Exmouth, on the other side of the estuary is the Dawlish sand spit. Exmouth is only 10 miles south-east of Exeter, with links by rail and road. Some of the most picturesque and popular seaside towns of the south-west are nearby. To the south-west are Dawlish, Teignmouth, Torbay, Brixham and Dartmouth, while to the east is Budleigh Salterton, Sidmouth, Seaton and Lyme Regis.

Local historians believe that the lack of any early human history in the Exmouth area can be attributed to its exposed position. It is subject to the prevailing south-west winds; a providence utilised by a 13th-century miller, who built a windmill on the point that juts into the estuary. In the 12th century a manor house stood where Phear Park is today. Over the centuries, Exmouth's function as a port was very restricted and only when it became fashionable for the wealthy and unhealthy to take seaside holidays in the 18th century, did the town begin to materialise on the map. It claims to be the oldest seaside resort in Devon. The walks and parks along the Beacon Breccias and Beacon Terrace were created around the 1790s. Lady Hamilton (long-suffering wife of Admiral Lord Nelson) is buried in the cemetery on the Beacon. In 1861 the first train arrived and the increased tourism that followed provoked much of the construction that makes up the ambience of Exmouth today. The main dock area on the point was built in 1825. During the summer season, fishing and pleasure trips leave from there, and the ferry from Starcross on the other side of the estuary docks at Exmouth. The area around the dock basin that was once home to trades connected with boats and shipping has been replaced by a brand new marina development. It's a far cry from the scene that must have made up the start of Sir Walter Raleigh's New World expeditions, which once left here with Good Queen Bess' blessing. The Dorset and East Devon World Heritage site, a kind of Jurassic Park with ancient rocks and fossils (but no rampaging dinosaurs) begins here at the Exmouth cliffs and runs along the Dorset coast.

SOUTH-WEST ENGLAND

My experience...

Brian Price, now aged 73, retired from Buxton after having notched up 40 years working on the railways and moved to Exmouth with his wife.

We moved to Exmouth to be near our sons, who are both in the Marines, did their basic training here at Lympstone, married local girls and bought property here. For 16 years before I retired we used to visit two or three times a year. After a few visits, I realised that I really loved the place, being near the sea and the winters are a lot milder here than in the north. We met one or two local people and Exmouth was the only place we wanted to retire to. If we couldn't have found somewhere here, we probably wouldn't have moved. Before I retired I had to work usually two out of three weekends. My wife came down here and she sussed out the area, bus and train services and property to find out where was the best place to live. We bought a bungalow because my wife had hip replacements 18 years ago and we didn't want the bother of stairs. It is at the top of a small close and we have a very big garden, because the land was earmarked for another bungalow that never got built. There is a bus stop nearby where a service runs to Exeter every 12 minutes, and we have about a dozen local shops near us. As a former railwayman, I get free rail travel, which also covers my wife. Exeter Airport is only 25 minutes away.

Gardening is my main hobby and I spend a lot of time working in our huge garden and greenhouse, and I grow plants for neighbours. My wife is a churchgoer and when she was up in Buxton was in the Mothers' Union. When she found out the Exmouth branch had closed down she restarted it and has been running it ever since. She's also in the WI, a gardening group that she started and the Exmouth flower club as she is an expert flower arranger. Over six months she located all these different activities and she's on most committees She is unable to drive now, because of poor eyesight and I am very pleased she has found something she enjoys so much. At the moment, I still drive, but there are quite a lot of hills and it could be a problem getting about if you were infirm and didn't have a car. We have a local hospital in Exmouth but the main hospital is in Exeter. They were brilliant when my daughter-in-law had a brain tumour and my wife had a problem with her hip replacements. Hospitals are very good here in my experience.

Exmouth has many residents who moved down here, say, over the last 25 years; three new lots of people arrived in our neighbourhood last year; they all say the same thing about how clean and quiet it is.

Exmouth fact file

Access: Junction 30 off the M5 to Exeter, then A376. Exeter, 10 miles.

Average property price: £206,319

Airports: Exeter International (www.exeter-airport.co.uk), 12.5 miles

Bus services: Stagecoach Devon (stagecoachbus.com)

Climate: Mild microclimate

Councils: Exmouth Town Council (www.exmouth.gov.uk); East Devon District Council (www.eastdevon.gov.uk)

Council tax: Band D £1,296.08; band E £1,584.10

Crime: Highest level of crime in East Devon, but low compared with rest of the UK

Economic activity: Rolle College in Exmouth, part of the University of Plymouth, is being relocated to Plymouth in 2008, with expected repercussions for the local economy resulting from the loss of 3,000 students and staff. The nine-acre campus is a target for developers.

Ferries: Local Starcross/Exmouth ferry over the estuary. Plymouth (40 miles) ferries to France and Spain.

Hospitals: Exmouth Hospital has a minor injuries unit. Large general hospital Royal Devon and Exeter Hospital in Exeter (www.eastdevon-pct.nhs.uk).

Percentage of people over 65: 28.1%

Population: Approximately 35,700

Property prices: Most property in the £100,000 to £200,000 bracket

Railway station: Exmouth linked to Exeter St David's (25 minutes)

Specialised retirement property: Pegasus Homes (www.pegasus-homes.co.uk) are in the process of getting planning permission for 40 flats in Salterton Road, Exmouth and expect them to be ready for occupation in late 2008. A similar development and timescale is planned for Exeter. At the time of press there flats were for sale at their development in Topsham.

Isle of Portland

The famous lighthouse that sits on a rocky outcrop off Portland Bill, is at the tip of the beak-shaped, windswept, limestone mass of the Isle of Portland that projects southwards, four and half miles out into the English Channel. As the poet Drayton put it, 'Where Portland from her top doth over-peere the maine, Her rugged front empal'd on every part with rocks'.

Barely an island, it is connected to the rest of the Dorset coast by a slender neck of land attached to a road bridge (the original was built in 1839; the newest opened in 1985), and by the 18-mile long shingle stretch of Chesil Beach. To the west of Chesil Beach is Lyme Bay. Portland is a geologically and historically fascinating spot: dinosaur footprints have been found imprinted in its rocks and there are signs of human habitation going back 7,000 years, probably thanks to obvious natural defence properties. Despite its small size the Isle has several villages: Fortuneswell, Chiswell, Southwell, Grove, Wakeham, Weston and Easton. At one time its inhabitants preferred to maintain their isolation and were known as 'the slingers' because they used stones to keep strangers away. Stone is synonymous with Portland and has been quarried there since the 12th century. After the Great Fire of London in 1666, tons of the stuff was ferried to the capital to be used in reconstruction, most notably St Paul's Cathedral. It was also used for many additional churches and buildings in London and latterly for war memorials and headstones across Europe. The island's breakwater is a feat of Victorian engineering begun in 1849, and took 23 years using convict labour. It is the largest artificial harbour in the world, covering 2,000 acres, originally built for naval use but now a popular place for water sports and due to host water sports events for the 2012 Olympics. There are still prisoners residing on the Isle, occupants of HMP Verne, a former Victorian citadel, which houses category C prisoners (those who are not likely to try and escape, but are not in open prisons). Portland is an out-of-the-ordinary retirement place, with exceptionally well-constructed cottages built by the skilled masons of the area. There is a very elderly couple of Portlanders who have never been off the island in their entire lives. At the end of 2006 a Grade II listed cottage with no bathroom or mod cons was for sale for £157,000 in Wakeham.

The rugged beauty of its cliffs and seascapes with castles, quarries and on-the-water activities attract walkers, ornithologists, canoeists, windsurfers, and geologists. The Isle's special qualities have also lured a permanent thriving artistic and musical community to live and work there. Cultural life need not mean a trip to nearby Weymouth, as Portland has its own well-equipped amateur theatre. Retiring to Portland might not suit all types of people, but with its excellent transport connections and reasonably priced property it is definitely worth considering as a less expensive option to Poole or Swanage. There is no campsite or holiday caravan park on the Isle so you could consider running a B&B, as five-bedroom terraced Victorian houses, which could be suitable for this purpose, are relatively inexpensive on Portland.

New building is very restricted on Portland. There is a development of luxury investment/holiday apartments, Ocean Views, at Castleton with prices from £199,000 for a one-bedroom flat. Weston Park Homes site is five miles from Weymouth on the western side of the island and is affordable as John Clayton found (see below). However, since Portland is largely 'undiscovered' it is likely to become the next big popular retirement place. Now is the time to move in, if it appeals to you. For detailed and fairly scurrilous insider information on Portland go to http://travel.ciao.co.uk/island_of_Portland_Review_5569437.

My experience...

John Clayton, now aged 73 and originally from Birmingham and Lincolnshire, moved to Portland with his wife in 2002 when they found a park home for sale at Weston Park Homes, a small, new site for retired people. Before retiring he worked variously in railways, construction and in a factory.

My wife used to go over to the Channel Islands from Weymouth twice a year in the 1960s with our lad, and we always thought we'd like to retire in the south-west. Our son is in the Navy and he married a Portland girl while stationed down here, and when we retired they suggested we moved nearer them. Like most people living in cities inland we wanted to move to the coast. It was mainly the family link that made us move here, but if I'd known what it was like down on the island, even if he hadn't married a local, I would have seriously considered it because it is such a lovely island to live on. We already knew Weymouth quite well because of our trips there over the years, but we had very little to do with Portland itself. Now we live here, we've found that you can go for walks all over the place; you never seem to get tired of them. My wife and I have gone out at 1 pm and haven't got back till half past six, having walked all across the other side of the island and walked back overlooking Lyme Bay; it's an absolutely fabulous view.

Property on Portland isn't on the market for long, but it's basically people looking for holiday and second homes. Moving north to south is a wrong move financially, and it just so happened we were here in Christmas 2001 and heard about a little development on the Island. We went to see it and did a deal that weekend. We actually like living in a park home; there are 15 of them tucked away from the main road. Everybody on this one is retired and children are not allowed to live there permanently, only for holidays. It just so happened to be in the right place at the right time and well within our price range. Although we did little research before moving here, we had a rough idea from our regular visits about the cost of living. Most of our shopping is done in Weymouth because we have no big supermarkets on the Island; but for good shopping you really have to go to Poole, Bournemouth or Southampton. We have small shops on the island, Co-ops, Londis and village shops, but they work out quite expensive. We have a new post office here. Travel is good; there's a bus every eight minutes.

The funny part is that although we are sociable, we don't actually mix that much. Both my wife's and my interests tend to be away from the home. There's plenty going on community-wise. I am involved with the Portland Community Swing

(Continued on following page)

SOUTH-WEST ENGLAND

189

(Continued)

Band and play with a big band in Dorchester once a week. I belong to the University of the Third Age and my wife has her keep-fit, and she also goes to Weymouth and helps out at a school there. We were told when we moved down here that we wouldn't like the people of Portland because 'they're a funny lot', but we've had no problems whatsoever. I believe there's still a feud with certain families between what they call 'Underhill' and 'top hill'. At one time a Weymouth person would never marry a Portland person and vice versa; there are still some families that harbour such feelings, but nothing like it once was. There is a downside though, it is very, very windy and very wet at times, and we did have our caravan stolen. We've been caravanners for over 25 years; we'd only been here six weeks. I can't think how they got it off the island, but I'd say 99.9% of our contact with islanders has been positive.

Isle of Portland fact file

Access: Via the A354 from Weymouth or the B3157 via Wye Regis. Weymouth, 6.5 miles.

Average property price: £205,422 (for Portland and Weymouth combined)

Airports: Bournemouth International, 44 miles

Bus services: Buses every 10 minutes between Weymouth and Easton on Portland

Climate: Windswept, but claims to have as much sunshine as the Scilly Isles

Council: Weymouth and Portland Borough Council (www.weymouth.gov.uk)

Council tax: Very high. Band D £1,432.04; band E £1,750.

Crime: Caravan stealing? (see account above). Some fairly insalubrious areas, for more see Travel Ciao review (web page given above).

Economic activity: Low unemployment but also low incomes

Ferries: Condor Ferries (www.condorferries.co.uk) from Weymouth to the Channel Islands and St Malo, France

Hospitals: Portland Hospital in Castletown is a community hospital with A&E facilities. County Hospital is in Dorchester (www.dorset-pct.nhs.uk).

Percentage of people over 65: 22% (Weymouth and Portland)

Population: Approximately 13,000 on Portland

Property prices: Two-bed terrace house from £164,950; semi-detached three-bedroom house from £269,950; detached £315,000

Railway station: Weymouth

Specialised retirement property: Weston Park Homes, Weston Road, Portland

Minehead

Minehead's name has nothing to do with mines, but derives from Old English 'myned' meaning hill. It has two miles of sandy beaches looking out over the Bristol Channel from the North Somerset coast and is on the north-eastern edge of Exmoor National Park (www.exmoor-nationalpark.gov.uk). The neighbouring area includes Watchet and Lynmouth and Porlock on the coast as well as the Brendon Hills and Quantock Forest. The town spread from a small feudal settlement and for much of its history up to recent times, the harbour area was owned by the local Luttrell family. Predating any historic records there were plentiful Bronze Age settlements in the area, although most remains have long since been overlaid with the sprawling suburbs of modern Minehead. The fortunes of Minehead rose and fell with its activities as a port for the wool, livestock and fishing trades, as well as the inevitable smuggling activities. The harbour proved very expensive to maintain and was poorly managed and liable to silting. By the end of the 18th century, Minehead's various vicissitudes, including a fire in 1791 that destroyed 80 houses, had reduced its economic activity to rock bottom. Even by the early 1800s, when seaside places had begun to be fashionable, Minehead was not attracting the *haute monde* (the A-list celebrities of the times) as Bognor and Brighton were. However, it did become popular with Romantics of the Wordsworthian kind, and the more impecunious members of gentle society found its lodgings affordable. Thus from the mid-19th century it had already become a place to retire to, just prior to the commencement of grand municipal works of the kind Victorians are famed for, such as sewers and public buildings, which began in the 1860s. The steam railway arrived relatively late in 1874, and was probably the greatest single factor in the revival of Minehead's economic fortunes as it brought Victorian and Edwardian holidaymakers, until the arrival of Butlin's flagship holiday development in 1962. There are many Victorian and Edwardian buildings and many larger ones have been converted to apartments, some of them very pricey. The vestiges of steam rail remain today in the form of the private, volunteer-run West Somerset Railway, (www.wsr.org.uk), which runs from Minehead inland as far as Bishop's Lydeard three miles from Taunton.

Minehead would be an ideal place for an active and fit retirement, because it is surrounded by fantastic walking, cycling and horse riding country. You can begin an Exmoor walk from the town and be in spectacular surroundings on the North Hill in minutes, and the South West Coastal Path begins in Minehead. However, while it is bustling from April to October, the winter months can be rather quiet. The predominantly rural area lacks facilities, but there is a year-round theatre, used by both professional and amateur companies, a golf course and a health and fitness centre. North Somerset towns, such as Bridgwater, Shepton Mallet, and even once prosperous Taunton, are known for a high level of delinquent and criminal behaviour. Property is not cheap in Minehead, but considerably cheaper than in the most popular south coast resorts. In 2007 a range of two-bedroom apartments were on sale in the town with prices from £139,000–£295,000, and there are also some new retirement developments with prices from £118,000. The west Somerset area has one of the highest proportions of retired people, care homes and facilities in the south-west, and employment in the care areas is growing.

My experience...

Mrs Lang is a widow in her 70s, who moved to Minehead 12 and a half years ago from Berkshire.

After my husband died, I decided to move somewhere more suitable than Berkshire, which is a busy area and not really a retirement place. My mother lived in Minehead. I liked the town and wanted to move there in 1991. My husband had had a stroke and I thought it would be brilliant for him but he didn't want to move. I moved there a few years later. It's got a nice feel to it with wonderful countryside and the sea nearby, and it's the gateway to Exmoor. Even when I moved here, I didn't realise at that stage how much Minehead has to offer. It had everything I wanted and I expected that it would cost me less to live here than in Berkshire.

I'm nearly a mile out [of the town]; within easy walking and cycling distance. I normally cycle because parking is always a problem in small towns. Minehead has lots of individual local shops, although we have some small supermarkets too. There are many cafés, and in the countryside nearby there are lovely places for cream teas. There are limited rural bus services so to make the most of the countryside you really need a car and it's good to be reasonably agile. You can also join a club for the elderly that goes on occasional outings. There's an excellent local theatre run by volunteers, a film society and of course Butlin's. There's a local cottage hospital with a minor injuries unit but otherwise the nearest main hospital is in Taunton. There's a bus to and from Taunton every hour. I've heard it gets very crowded in summer, which is a problem if you are reliant on the bus service. I joined the University of Third Age as a founder member after someone suggested the idea of starting a branch here in 1998, and it snowballed from then to become a very successful group. Now I'm membership secretary, a member of six groups and I run one of them. There are lots of other clubs and societies for different interests.

The best things here are the beautiful countryside and the pace of life. You go into town and you smile at people and they smile back, and after the third time you meet them you start chatting away like you've known them for ages. The only disadvantage is that Minehead is a bit of a way off the main routes, so getting away and back can be difficult. On the other hand, if the roads were better we'd have a huge influx of people, so I guess it's both a downside and an upside.

Minehead fact file

Access: A39 from Bridgwater and A358 from Taunton. Bridgwater, 25 miles; Tiverton, 30 miles.

Average property price: £237,907

Airports: Bristol (www.bristolairport.co.uk)

Bus services: Good bus service from Taunton Railway station to Minehead

Climate: Sheltered by North Hill and temperate year round

Councils: Minehead Town Council (www.minehead.co.uk); West Somerset District Council (www.westsomersetonline.gov.uk)

Council tax: Band D £1,300.47

Crime: Minehead is one of several Somerset towns, including Bridgwater and Taunton, which have high levels of crime and disorder

Economic activity: £1 million is being invested in Minehead by the Regional Development Authority to boost the economy, including development of a brownfield site on the edge of the town.

Ferries: From Ilfracombe and Barnstaple to Lundy Island (www.lundyisland.co.uk). Discounts for senior citizens.

Hospitals: Minehead hospital has a minor injuries unit. Nearest general hospital is Musgrove Park in Taunton (www.somerset-health.org.uk).

Percentage of people over 60: 33%

Population: Total for Minehead, Dulverton and Watchet is 35,500

Property prices: Detached £277,333; semi-detached £225,000; terraced £143,000; flat £150,472

Railway station: Nearest mainline station is Taunton. The privately run West Somerset Railway goes only as far as Bishop's Lydeard. There are buses to Taunton from Bishop's Lydeard from April to October.

Specialised retirement property: Fulford Court, Millbridge Gardens retirement flats from £118,000; Carlton Court (0845 0130655)

SOUTH-WEST ENGLAND

Poole

Poole is in Dorset west of Bournemouth, in the affluent retirement conurbation formed by Poole, Bournemouth and Christchurch, south-west of Ringwood and south of the Wiltshire Downs. What makes Poole unique is its vast and beautiful natural harbour (second only to Sydney in size), which is large enough to accommodate commercial shipping, a fishing fleet, yachts and water sports areas and a variety of wildlife habitats. It also helps that Poole has seven miles of award-winning clean, sandy beaches lining Poole Bay, from Studland Bay in the west on the Isle of Purbeck to Sandbanks in the east. As if this were not a surfeit of amenities, it also has an exceptionally high level of care services for the elderly; a case of demand plus affluence producing supply. It is probably no surprise that Poole is one of the top retirement spots in Britain.

The port of Poole has an illustrious history, particularly from the end of the 17th century up to the end of the Napoleonic Wars. During this time transatlantic trade, including fishing around Newfoundland, saw the burghers of Poole flourish as they supplied the Catholic countries of Europe with salted fish. Gracious Georgian buildings grew up around the town from the profits of highly successful merchant activities, and the harbour was filled with a few hundred ships. The peace dividend after Waterloo favoured only French and American traders who assumed the trade in fish with Europe, and bit by bit forced the Poole élite into bankruptcy. The arrival of the railway in 1847 was a further blow as it removed the need for coastal shipping. Decline was also hastened because the harbour was unsuitable for newer deep-draught vessels, which used Southampton, Liverpool and Plymouth instead. Probably the next distinction bestowed on Poole was in 1939 when BOAC (forerunner of British Airways) flying boat services were moved from Southampton to Hamworthy in Poole, at the outbreak of hostilities of the Second World War. They remained there until after the War. Poole was badly bombed, but the docks were not obliterated as in Southampton. By the end of the War, much of the housing was in a parlous state and Poole began a period of reconstruction. Thanks to a modicum of farsightedness, not all the historic buildings at the heart of the old town were ripped down, even though many of them were in a state of dereliction and near collapse. A preservation area was declared and restoration of a section of this area means that Poole has been able to keep its distinctive character, despite having borne its fair share of post-war philistine architecture. Latter day expansion has meant that Poole has blended at the edges with Bournemouth, although its strong sense of separate identity means that it was made unitary authority in 1997 under the local government reorganisation.

Poole has not failed to move with the times. It has a new shopping centre, a huge modern Barclays Bank building (Barclay Towers), and is a busy ferry port, arts venue, and a top place for water sports. If your retirement includes a lot of sailing then you will be spoilt, as Poole is the UK's biggest sailing centre. Not only are motor yachts built here, there are three sailing clubs: the Lilliput, Parkstone and Poole yacht clubs. The proximity of Bournemouth and the Dorset countryside are added bonuses. Residents covet the views from the top of Evening Hill and Constitution Hill and crossing the harbour mouth on a chain ferry and walking along Studland Beach, delicately avoiding the part allocated to birthday suit enthusiasts. Perfection comes at a price, though: the Sandbanks peninsula that forms the eastern side of the harbour mouth is dotted with exclusive real estate. It has the fourth highest land value in the world (by area), so unless you are a footballer or have won the lottery you probably won't be able to retire to this particular small select area of Poole. A useful contact for new developments (not necessarily retirement specific) in Poole is Key Drummond (01202 700771; www.keydrummond.com/new_deve.html).

My experience...

Ray Merrell moved to Poole in 1999 from Worcester Park in Surrey. He is a professional trainer and is semi-retired.

I used to work in the Poole area many years ago, and knew the area very well as I had a number of friends here, and we used to holiday here a lot. I've always wanted to live by the sea. This was my life's dream. I'd done a lot of diving and things like that and used to work in Bournemouth in the high diving show. We did look at property costs and at that time, they were similar to where we were living in Surrey and we could just about afford it. I've always wanted to live in a bungalow and that's what we got. We live in Lilliput; that's one up from Sandbanks. It's a very friendly area. We have unusual surroundings as we have the sea on both sides and we can be at the sea in five minutes. As a family, we have always been aquatically minded, particularly sailing, so we've got the best of all worlds. It's like a permanent holiday here. We can also cycle everywhere from here and there are lots of places to visit. Poole centre is about 20 minutes' walk from where I live and the hospital, 15 minutes. From the rail station there are direct services to Waterloo and good bus connections to Bournemouth (10 minutes) and Swanage (one hour) and elsewhere. The shopping in Poole is very spread out and we tend to go to Bournemouth, where the big chain stores are. Poole has a nice character. We did consider Bournemouth for retirement, but Poole has the Quay area with lots of different events every week during summer. Each town has different values but for marine surroundings, Poole is the place: for the Quay, all the boats, the Old Town, the New Town ... There are lots of clubs: bridge, chess, social clubs, a lot of golfing and yacht clubs. I like the cleanliness, the fact that people have more time. It is hilly here and so may not suit those with mobility issues.

SOUTH-WEST ENGLAND

Poole fact file

Access: A338 from Ringwood, A35 from the west. Bournemouth, 5.5 miles.

Average property price: £266,368

Airports: Bournemouth (www.airportdirecttravel.co.uk/bournemouth/), 11 miles

Bus services: Wilts & Dorset Bus Company (www.wdbus.co.uk) operates throughout the area. Yellow Buses (www.yellowbuses.co.uk) operate Poole to Christchurch services. Free bus travel for senior citizens throughout Dorset including Bournemouth, Poole and Christchurch.

Climate: Milder microclimate similar to Bournemouth

Council: Poole Borough Council (www.poole.gov.uk)

Council tax: Band D £1,278.99; band E £1,563.21

Crime: Poole has problems with drugs misuse, burglary and antisocial behaviour, particularly in deprived areas of the town

Economic activity: Employment is very low (3.4%), but wages are also low, consistent with wages in the south-west

Ferries: Brittany Ferries to Cherbourg in France; Condor Ferries to Jersey, Guernsey and St Malo

Hospital: Poole Hospital NHS Trust (www.poole.nhs.uk) district general hospital. Has had one of the shortest waiting times in England (84 days wait for hip operation).

Percentage of people over 65: 21%

Population: Approximately 138,000 (36,000 aged over 60)

Property prices: Detached £365,115; semi-detached £205,220; terrace £187,125; flat £222,476

Railway station: Poole (direct to London Waterloo in 1 hour 50 mins)

Residents' on-street parking permit: £30 per year

Specialised retirement property: Lots, including Churchill Retirement Homes' Churchill Lodge, Andover Lodge (29 flats with resident manager, 01202 732616) and McCarthy & Stone's Branksome Park (01202 761094)

Salisbury

Wiltshire has only one city and Salisbury is it. Old Sarum, the historic site two miles north of Salisbury is its prototype, which included a cathedral, ruined by storms then abandoned in the 13th century, and rebuilt at the new site of Salisbury using some of the masonry from Old Sarum. Legend surrounds the reasons for the refounding of Salisbury, but there is probably a clue in the fact that the second site is at the confluence of the Avon and Nadder rivers; an abundance of water replacing a previous lack of it? These rivers combine to form the Hampshire Avon, which flows into sea on the south coast at Christchurch. The spire of the Cathedral is the tallest in Britain. Painted by both Monet and Constable, it soars up to 404ft, and you see it well before you see the city itself. The mysterious upright and lintel stones of nearby Stonehenge sprout from Salisbury Plain, brought there, who knows how, by those of an ancient religion, long before Christianity caused Salisbury Cathedral to be built.

Salisbury is a small city by modern standards, but in late medieval times up to 1500 it was one of the largest cities in England, with a population of about 8,000. For three centuries or more, the wool trade was the mainstay and cause of its prosperity. After a period of decline, which lasted until the Restoration, the city experienced a social revolution that brought scientific pioneers and other notables of the time (Boyle and Pepys among them), in whose wake polite and affluent society followed. The Cathedral Close, which had for centuries been home to the well-off, grew larger in the age of gracious architecture from the late 17th to mid-18th centuries, and the many new buildings came to be inhabited by the gentry. With *noblesse oblige*, a spate of charitable foundations for the poor and needy were founded, including a hospital and many almshouses. The city developed as a tourist spot and then, as now, coach passengers passing through were encouraged to buy local high quality crafts such as lace and cutlery. Restoration funds were also lavished on the cathedral, which was visited by an approving George III in 1792. The railway arrived in 1847 making a return journey to London possible in a day, sounding the death knell of the coaching trade. During the latter part of the 19th century Salisbury experienced the biggest spate of growth in its history, bursting its medieval confines and reaching approximately half of the population and size of today.

Nowadays prosperity is based on newer industries, such as technology, management consultancy and English for foreigners, as well as the old ones such as tourism, insurance, estate agency and finance. Bright city lights are accessible in most directions. Bath, Bristol, Bournemouth and Southampton are all less than an hour's drive. The Royal Artillery has its gunnery training school at Larkhill on the edge of Salisbury plain, an army training area since 1899, and so frequently tank swarms, soldiers and low flying helicopters can be seen and heard there. Salisbury city is a regular rest and recreation place for army types

SOUTH-WEST ENGLAND

and their families. The city has a racecourse and an annual International Arts Festival held from late May to early June. It is not a hip place, but what it lacks in cutting edges it makes up for in friendly locals, beauty and timelessness.

My experience...

Hans-Dieter Scholz, 66 and a former management consultant, moved with his wife to Salisbury from inner London 16 years ago.

We moved to Salisbury because I was looking for a place with a bit of cultural life that was within easy reach of the coast and major airports. What really spurred me on to move was that although we lived in a very nice part of London, even on Sundays, you couldn't leave the house after 10am because of traffic gridlock. I was working at the time and we visited the city purely as a theoretical exercise. I fell for the place immediately. It took us nearly a year to organise moving and to sell our house in London. We bought an early Victorian house in a marvelous location bordering the Cathedral Close. It's close to Salisbury's huge cathedral and I can walk to the shops in town within six or seven minutes. From experience I know that the NHS hospital in Salisbury is a good one and only five minutes' drive. Less than 30 minutes' drive away there is beautiful countryside and it takes only 16 minutes to get to the New Forest.

Since moving to Salisbury, I've found it very satisfying culturally, considering it's a smallish place. The community aspect couldn't have been better. It seems to me that the whole place is welcoming to newcomers. Salisbury has a large ex-military community, so a lot of military families pass through here because of Salisbury Plain training area being so close. They spend off-duty time here and there's a surprising number that settle for civilian life here. The downside is that in the 1950s and 1960s the beautiful medieval city was ravaged by planning and development. The place is still beautiful, but if you look at what could have been done and what could still be there, it makes you angry. Transport links are good. I've noticed that the trains have considerably improved in my time here. The journey time has been cut by 15 minutes these last 10 years and there is now a modern and very acceptable train service.

Salisbury fact file

Access: Several roads converge at Salisbury : A30, A36 , A338, A360 and A345. It is one mile from the A303. London, 80 miles.

Average property price: £259,312

Airports: Bournemouth, approximately 24 miles; Heathrow, 75 miles

Bus services: Wilts & Dorset Bus Company (wdbus.co.uk)

Council: Salisbury District Council (www.salisbury.gov.uk)

Council tax: Band D £1,332.83; band E £1,629.02

Crime: Lower than average

Economic activity: Low unemployment. South Wiltshire is one of the least deprived areas in the UK.

Hospital: Salisbury District Hospital (www.salisbury.nhs.uk) has a 24-hour A&E

Percentage of people over 65: 20%

Population: 43,000

Property prices: Detached £356,296; semi-detached £216,823; terrace £196,049; flat £159,421

Railway station: Salisbury is on the main Exeter–London (Waterloo) line

Residents' on-street parking permit: £30 per year

Specialised retirement property: Bemerton Farm, Salisbury (Beechcroft; www.beechcroft.co.uk); Homesarum House (www.homewise.co.uk)

Seaton

Seaton lies on a flat site, south of the Blackdown Hills in the Lower Axe Valley of East Devon, between Axmouth harbour and the white chalk cliffs of Beer. It shares the valley with the towns of Branscombe, Colyton and Colyford. To the west are the coastal towns of Sidmouth, Budleigh Salterton and Exmouth, while to the east is Lyme Regis. Seaton has been a tourist town for more than a century and has some attractive Victorian and Edwardian hotels and villas and the wonderful Axe Estuary, now silted up but a magnet for wading birds. It has a seafront entirely lacking in aesthetic appeal, but to dismiss Seaton on this count as a retirement spot would be shortsighted. The partly pedestrianised town is full of old-fashioned, individual shops of the kind that have long since disappeared from most country towns. The mile-long shingle beach with its concrete esplanade is sheltered in summer and battered by forceful seas in winter, to the extent that sand is revealed beneath and the shingle itself is continually reshaped by the sea. The harbour at the end of the estuary, located at the eastern end of the beach, has been used since before Roman times and the Romans used it to invade the area. Significant Roman remains have been found locally, including mosaics at Honeyditches farm on the edge of the modern town. The town was once known for fishing and shipbuilding, but these trades have largely disappeared.

Seaton has never really had a heyday and has remained a quiet spot. In recent years, it has taken off in modest way as a place for retirees. This is not surprising, since places such as Lyme Regis and Sidmouth have become very busy and have very expensive property. Seaton is, at present, more affordable. It is quite possible to find a two or three-bedroom semi-detached property for around £230,000, or even a detached bungalow. Steeply built Lyme has the added problem of suffering severe subsidence, which recent radical engineering work is aimed at trying to counteract. Seaton is situated in the same Area of Outstanding Natural Beauty as Lyme and it is also part of the Jurassic Coast, which has been declared a World Heritage site. Some large retirement developments have been built near Seaton seafront, which is entirely flat and highly suitable for the older and less mobile of retirees. The town has several old fashioned eateries that cater for the tastes of older people. Seaton is a friendly spot. Even in summer when holiday families are present in large numbers, it is possible to escape to comparative solitude in the cliff gardens, or by walking a leg of the South West Coastal Path which runs through Seaton to Beer. There is an active sailing club and golf course and the usual watersports activities.

My experience...

Jean Slack, who is 87, has lived in Seaton for two and a half years with her second husband, after moving there from Chard. Before that she had lived in Portsmouth and Edinburgh with her first husband who was in the Services.

I initially retired to Chard, about 15 miles inland, with my first husband, but I later remarried and moved to Seaton in 2004. Wanting to move closer to the sea was part of it, but my husband had lost his sight and Chard became unsuitable for us. We'd visited Seaton and a friend of ours bought a retirement flat there and we were most impressed by it. Seaton has a very long frontage and it's flat. When my husband and I go walking, I have to guide him, so we have to be somewhere level and this is ideal for us. We bought a two-bedroom flat in a retirement development and found it well planned. We have our own laundry but not meals and there is a manager living on site Monday to Friday, plus an on-call facility if we need anything. When you reach our circumstances, it's nice to know you can call for help if you need to.

Seaton is quiet, nothing like as busy as Lyme Regis or Sidmouth, but we find we have everything we need here. We can walk 100 yards to the Co-op, the dentist and doctor and especially the seafront. Seaton is also very good on buses. We don't use them yet because of my husband's difficulties, but other people here have gradually got rid of their cars. There's a lot going on. We have a cinema club and places where people go to play bridge, but personally I love the sea. I can sit there in the afternoon and just look at it.

It's a very friendly area, which I have found to be true of the south-west generally. Where I live you have to walk through the communal lounge to get out of the building and you meet people on the way, which is nice. I do miss the garden that I used to have; we have just a little balcony here with some plants on it. Seaton gets busy in summer, but many people are day visitors so it is quiet in the early morning and evening. If I were younger, I am not sure I would want to live here as there are a lot of older people, but it's a good place to retire to and we are very happy here.

Seaton fact file

Access: Via A3052 or B3172. Lyme Regis, 7.5 miles.

Average property price: £249,753

Airports: Exeter, approximately 20 miles

Bus services: First Devon & Cornwall, South and West Devon (www.firstgroup.com/ukbus/southwest/). The journey to Exeter takes approximately an hour.

Climate: Typically mild south-western climate

Council: Seaton Town Council (www.seaton.gov.uk)

Council tax: Band D £1,023.93; band E £1,251.47

Crime: Low crime area

Economic activity: Lower economic activity than the rest of the region. Largest industries are retail and wholesale and tourism-linked activities.

Ferries: Weymouth (to France and Channel Islands)

Hospitals: Seaton Community Hospital (www.eastdevon-pct.nhs.uk). Large general hospital in Exeter, Royal Devon and Exeter (www.rdehospital.nhs.uk).

Percentage of people over 65: Seaton has an older than average population: ages 45–64 (26.8%); 65–74 (16.4%) and nearly 22% are older than 75

Population: Approximately 7,000

Property prices: Detached £305,416; semi-detached £233,800; terrace £222,225; flat £178,452

Railway station: Axminster, 10 miles

Specialised retirement property: Jubilee Lodge (Churchill Retirement Homes)

Sidmouth

Sidmouth, in south-east Devon, sits at a narrow valley opening to the sea with other towns in its vicinity: Beer, Seaton, Honiton, Ottery St Mary, Budleigh Salterton and Exmouth. It is known for its mild climate, which, in part, derives from its sheltered position and thanks to immense red sandstone cliffs that book-end it on either side. In the 17th century it was described as an 'especialest fisher town' and was sustained by the fruits of the sea and of the land, which furnished a market for both of these. Various schemes to make it a bigger working port ended in failure. From the 1780s it began to enjoy the attentions of polite society and joined the small group of fashionable Regency seaside towns, which included Torquay and Brighton, in the new craze for sea bathing. In 1820 the Revd E Butcher enthused:

> *Bathing, that salutary and pleasant custom, that chief avowed reason for which such numbers every year quit the towns, and crowd to the coast of our island, and so important an article to the invalid, is, at Sidmouth, both commodious and reasonable.*

The Napoleonic era brought a wave of prosperity to Sidmouth. The upper classes, who were deprived of European travel by Napoleon's enmity and wide-ranging ambition to dominate all of Europe, began to build themselves seaside homes. These were in the style of *cottages-ornées*; essentially rustic fantasy houses where they could play at being country folk in the manner of Marie Antoinette, but without losing their heads for it. Several of these are still in use today as hotels including the Knowle and Royal Glen. During the Regency period, terraces and lodging houses were built and the town doubled in size. Sidmouth retained its reputation as a spot for the discerning minority throughout the 19th century. However, it never achieved the massed family appeal of other Victorian resorts such as Torquay, in part because the railway arrived late (1874) and stopped short of Sidmouth; a deliberate move to keep the trippers and gawkers away. The age of the popular motor car took all that élitism away and helped to make Sidmouth a thriving holiday and retirement place, especially during the latter part of the 20th century.

Although its population has grown by only a few hundred in the last decade, reinforcing the idea that it has a preponderance of older folk and does not attract younger blood to replace them, this is not entirely accurate. The main sources of local employment are tourism and care services, both of which require a younger element of the population. While it may not have a skateboard park, for such a small town Sidmouth has a lot of other amenities, including a cinema and theatre and some interesting individual shops, although serious shopping is best done in Exeter (16 miles). There is a busy social life to plug into, generated by the many clubs, such as sailing, golf, tennis, cricket, croquet and gardening, and quiet discourse can be pursued in the many tearooms. A fuller listing of social entrées can be found at www.sidmouthdiary.co.uk. The town's medical facilities are provided by a small local hospital, The Victoria. Sidmouth's international renown revolves around the annual events of the International Festival and the Folk Week, which attract an influx of spectators and participants from around the world. The main drawback is the price of property, which is about 35% more expensive than a few miles inland.

My experience...

Mr Davis from Cornwall, retired to Sidmouth in 2004.

I retired from Cornwall County Council, where I had lived in the same cottage for 50 years since going to school there, but it had a big garden and was gradually falling down and a bit isolated, so not ideal for retirement. I wanted to move, but to stay in the West Country, somewhere further to the east. Transport is tricky in Cornwall and airports are miles away. I took a week to go around staying in bed and breakfasts in different counties: Somerset, Dorset, Devon ... As I was coming back along the south coast of Devon I stopped at Seaton (I quite liked Seaton) and then Sidmouth, which I thought was the best place on earth. The ambience, the vibe, the feel of the place was so wonderful. It's a small town that sits in a valley running to the sea. It hasn't got high-rise buildings or multiple shops; it's got small, old-fashioned shops, a lovely promenade to walk along, there's no rubbish and litter lying around and the whole place felt right. The bus service is wonderful; every half-hour there are local buses to Exeter, Honiton, Seaton and longer distance ones to Bournemouth and Plymouth. Despite living in the West Country all my life, I don't recollect ever having been here before I decided to come here. If I'd stayed in Cornwall I would have become very isolated as I got older. Sidmouth has an enormous number of facilities for the retired. There are lots of clubs for a whole range of interests; I've never known a place with so many clubs. I have a list of about 150 organisations here and they drop a booklet called Sidmouth Diary through your letterbox.

There's nothing I don't like about Sidmouth, but the property is expensive because it's by the sea. I'm in a flat quite near the centre. It was the best I could get for my money, but I'm quite happy with it; it's low maintenance and cheap to run. I'm just under a mile from the sea. I would say about 60% of the population is retired. It's a retirement town really, which is ideal. Younger people do tend to move away but there are some young people here. Most of my friends have come to Sidmouth to retire; about 40% to 50% of them from somewhere else. It does get busy in the summer, around the time of the Sidmouth Folk Festival in August, which is a fantastic thing. The town goes mad for a week; it's real entertainment. Oh, and it doesn't snow in Sidmouth.

Sidmouth fact file

Access: A3052 and A375 from Honiton. Exeter 15 miles.

Average property price: £311,158

Airports: Exeter (www.exeter-airport.co.uk), 27 miles; Bristol, 105 miles

Bus services: Frequent, including regular Sidmouth to Exeter service. Complete bus/train timetable from Devonbus (01392 382800; email devonbus@devon.gov.uk).

Climate: Mild enough to grow sub-tropical plants

Council: Sidmouth Town Council (www.sidmouth.gov.uk); Devon County Council (www.devon.gov.uk)

Council tax: Band D £1,366.13; band E £1,669.71

Crime: Petty crime and vandalism is a problem, as is alcohol abuse among the young

Economic activity: Mainly tourism and care homes

Ferries: Poole (50 miles). Run to Channel Islands and France.

Hospitals: Victoria Cottage Hospital has a casualty department. Nearest large hospital is in Exeter (Royal Devon & Exeter NHS Trust; www.rdehospital.nhs.uk).

Percentage of people over 65: 65–74 (16.1%); 75+ (21%)

Population: Approximately 14,000

Property prices: Detached £449,329; semi-detached £289,762; terraced £241,345; flat £250,000

Railway station: Honiton (8 miles)

Residents' on-street parking permit: £90 per year

Specialised retirement property: A lot

Swanage

Swanage is one of three towns (the others being Wareham and Wool) on the Isle of Purbeck, a quiet rural area some 60 miles square in Dorset. Purbeck is surrounded on three sides by the sea, and is therefore an island by name, and a peninsula by fact. The peninsula is dotted with a baker's dozen of interesting and picturesque villages including Corfe (famous for its castle), Studland (famous for its bay), Langton and Worth Matravers, Kingston, Kimmeridge and Steeple, and landscape features including the Purbeck Hills, Wytch and Newton Heaths. The coast of Purbeck on which Swanage is situated is part of the Jurassic Coast World Heritage Site. Its principal attractions have some of the biggest 'wow' factors England has to offer, including Durdle Door and Lulworth Cove, which lie between Swanage and Weymouth. Purbeck has been battled over since Viking times, but after the English Civil War of the 17th century it pursued first its agricultural and then its entrepreneurial destiny in relative peace. In the Victorian era two gentlemen called George Burt and John Mowlem began supplying Purbeck Stone, a kind of polishable limestone, sometimes erroneously called marble, for buildings in the streets of London and elsewhere. The resulting firm of Mowlem is still in existence.

Long before Purbeck Stone became the rage, ball clay mining had been a local industry for nearly 2,000 years and the development of the Swanage Railway (www.swanagerailway.co.uk), built in 1885, is strongly connected to this industry. The railway has been lovingly restored during this Millennium, with the ultimate aim of restoring the rail link between Swanage and Wareham and a connection to mainline services. The clay was, and still is, used for fine pottery and everyday items. Former examples include clay pipes, and present ones include washbasins and fillers. The nodding donkeys at Wytch Farm are not the gentle dejected Eeyore kind, but part of the mechanics of the largest onshore oilfield in Western Europe. Drilling by BP started in the 1970s, and massive tree planting and landscaping has helped to reduce the visual impact of the wellhead and linked drilling paraphernalia. All this forms the fascinating hinterland of Swanage, which despite all the surrounding mercenary activity is a holiday town par excellence, with safe, sandy beaches, the newly restored railway, walking, sailing and other water sports against the backdrop of one of the most celebrated areas of coastline in England.

Swanage is a beautiful town to live in, unspoilt, unique with quaint alleys and historic buildings and with a character of its own out of season. Some retirees might find that the lack of a sports or fitness centre, adult education facilities, a large supermarket and of upmarket shops and restaurants a step too far into the wild. Those who value what Swanage has to offer in terms of quality of outdoor life and community will find its appeal is year round. There is a local hospital and anyone retiring there would find the community spirit and friendliness of the inhabitants make it easy to integrate. Club life for all ages and interests is very active; go to www.virtual-swanage.co.uk for a foretaste of clubs and their agendas. Swanage does have litter and traffic, particularly parking problems and public transport needs to be greatly improved. A car would be probably be essential, even though nearly a quarter of the people living on Purbeck manage without one. Needless to say, as part of the Poole, Bournemouth, Christchurch area, property prices have rocketed in recent years and the council tax is very high. Many properties have been converted into flats, as these are relatively more affordable. Most of the flats are two-bedroomed and prices start at £169,000 although most are over £200,000.

My experience...

Eileen Hobdell, aged 81, moved on her own from Broxbourne in Hertfordshire, having worked previously for Marks & Spencer.

I chose to retire to Swanage because my son had moved down here, and the fact that I would be near him was important. I didn't know much about the area before I moved here, although I had visited it some years ago and I remembered that I liked it. My son told me about the day centre before I moved, but otherwise I didn't know much about what was on offer for my age group. I moved into a nice little flat, about one and a half miles from the centre of Swanage. The post office where I get my pension is just around the corner and my son and his wife bring me most other things I need. I used to drive into town, but I had an accident and gave up the car. I occasionally take the bus into Swanage but they are not very frequent. My son and I usually go into town where there are lots of cafés and restaurants. We also go into the countryside, which I enjoy. I used to go to the day centre, but they changed the registration categories and I stopped going, although I really miss it. There are some other clubs, and with a little help from my son, I'm looking for one that will suit me.

The best thing about Swanage is how compact it is. Bournemouth is huge and very spread out; but Swanage is not like that at all; it's a nice, quiet little place. The area is very friendly and people always stop and greet you, so you don't feel an outsider. I would say it's a very rural area and quite different for me, coming from London.

Swanage fact file

Access: The A351 runs down the spine of Purbeck. Poole, 20 miles.

Average property price: £322,000

Airport: Bournemouth, 14.6 miles

Bus services: Wilts & Dorset (www.wdbus.co.uk). Hourly service between Swanage and Bournemouth.

Climate: Mild microclimate

Council: Swanage Town Council (01929 423636; www.swanage.gov.uk). Purbeck District Council (www.purbeck.gov.uk).

Council tax: Very high, band D £1,474.93; band E £1,802.69

Crime: Swanage has a very low crime rate

Economic activity: Higher than Dorset average

Ferries: Local ferry to/from Sandbanks (Poole) every 20 minutes, all year round (www.sandbanksferry.co.uk). From Poole harbour ferries to the Channel Islands and St Malo.

Hospital: Swanage Community Hospital. Nearest large hospital is Poole General Hospital (www.southandeastdorsetpct.nhs.uk).

Percentage of people over 60: 29% aged 60–84; 34% if you add the over-84s

Population: 11,000

Property prices: Detached £500,000; semi-detached £339,000; terrace £311,830; flat £223,929

Railway station: Nearest is Wareham on the London Waterloo line (2 hours to London)

Specialist retirement property: A lot of care homes

SOUTH-WEST ENGLAND

Torquay

Torquay is situated on the Devon coastline, on the northern promontory of Torbay, while Brixham occupies the southern promontory; nestling in between the two is Paignton. Today these three towns nearly form a conurbation around Torbay, which goes under the marketing tag of 'The English Riviera', a reference to its famously mild climate. The medieval Torquay or Tor Quay was literally that: a small quayside built by Torre Abbey, tucked just inside the promontory. Torquay owes its development as a seaside resort in part to the navy and in part to Regency aristocrats' predilection for healthy sea air, to counterbalance their London lifestyles. Torbay bites so deeply into the coast it forms an ideal sheltered anchorage, large enough to hold a fleet of British warships. In Napoleonic times such a gathering of ships was held ready so that, at the drop of a sail, it could head for a face-off with Napoleon's navy. Summer villas were already being built in Torquay from the 1780s, and the wives and relatives of the ships' officers repaired to these. Many of these were visiting Torquay to be in the vicinity of their menfolk. This swelling of polite company increased demand for suitably glamorous lodgings. It helped spread commendation of Torquay as a pleasant place to pass the time, and a possible alternative to Continental travel during the Napoleonic wars, or as a visitor in 1794 put it, 'Here enjoy carriage rides, bathing, retirement and a most romantic situation'.

Throughout the 19th century Torquay enjoyed continuous popularity as a place for the healthy and wealthy and those unwell with consumption to enjoy themselves, or to recover their strength. From the early part of Queen Victoria's reign up to the 1870s, the bulk of grand terraces and buildings were constructed. This period of architecture most typifies Torquay and reflects the type of upper class clientele for which they catered. By about 1880 though, most of the grander tourists were taking their holidays abroad and Torquay was forced to cater for a less distinguished type of visitor. By the end of the 19th century it had more or less absorbed all the surrounding villages and parishes into one municipal borough of Torquay. It still retains some of the splendour of its 19th-century heyday and is held up as a model of Victorian town planning.

My experience...

Anne McKinnon, aged 62, retired to Torquay in 2000. Formerly she worked in adult education and lived in Fleet in Hampshire.

It's always been a dream of mine to live by the sea. My parents had retired to the general area about 20 years ago and I used to visit them often. I really liked the area, and I always felt better here. It's a degree or so warmer and the temperature suited me, it sowed a seed in my mind. I had no ties except my elderly parents, so I thought, 'why not move here?' It happened quite quickly once I had made up my mind. Also property is cheaper here than in Hampshire. I was on a visit and while looking at the local paper I found something I wanted, so I sold my flat and bought a house out the outskirts of town, 10 minutes' drive from the sea. I wanted a new house because I thought there is less to go wrong. So I bought a plot on a new development near a retail park with a big Sainsbury's and Marks & Spencer, and then had to wait for it to be built. There is a bus from here linking in to the main town bus services, but I usually drive as I have a mobility problem. I've actually found out more about the town after moving here. The more you live here, the more you discover. The main part of Torquay that you see as a visitor is only the half of it. There's the big harbour and marina and main beach, but there are about eight small beaches and lots of places to explore and find out about.

Coming from Hampshire and one of the most expensive postcodes in Britain, I thought I can only be better off and being on your own there's only one lot of expenses to consider. I didn't know anyone else here apart from my parents and I saw a friendship group advertised in the paper. It's for singles, not like a dating agency; it's for friendship. You can't join if you're a married couple because you don't have quite the same need of making friends. I joined that one thing I saw in the paper when I got here, and also the University of the Third Age and really I know everyone now. The U3A is a good starting point for anyone of retirement age. There is so much to join in and do. It's very different from the town I moved from, where people just haven't got the time. It's a friendly area. If you stop someone to ask a question they'll chat to you for 20 minutes. As it's a tourist town there are always things going on. You can look in the local paper any day of the week and there'll be live music, theatre and cinema. The theatre here is very good; I arrange group bookings for the U3A as it's one of my main interests.

Most of the people I know here have come from another part of Britain. It might not suit everyone because we are so far down in the south-west that it's a long way before you get into what I call civilisation. From Fleet, London was fairly accessible, but from here you have to add on hours. I've never had a moment's regret about moving here.

Torquay fact file

Access: M5. A380 Exeter to Torquay trunk road or A379 coast road. Exeter, 22 miles.

Average property price: £175,717

Airport: Exeter, approximately 19 miles

Bus services: Mostly run by Stagecoach (www.stagecoachbus.com)

Climate: Warm local climate. Snow falls are rare.

Council: Devon County Council (www.devon.gov.uk)

Council tax: Band D £1270.78; band E £1553.18

Crime: Problems of alcohol abuse on harbourside (where the pubs and bars are) are being tackled

Economic activity: Torquay is in the throes of regeneration

Ferries: Plymouth (Brittany Ferries to Roscoff and Santander)

Hospital: Torbay District General Hospital (one of the five national flagship hospitals) is run by South Devon Healthcare Trust (www.sdhct.nhs.uk)

Percentage of people over 65: 23%

Population: 65,000

Property prices: Detached £385,684; semi-detached £218,828; terrace £189,190; flat £179,536

Railway station: Torquay

Residents' on-street parking permit: £20–£30 per year depending on car size

Specialised retirement property: Lots, many sold through Torquay Real Estate Co Ltd (0845 1175914)

Weymouth

Weymouth lies south of Dorchester on the coast of Dorset, with Chesil Beach to the west and Weymouth Bay to the east. South of Weymouth and connected to it by bridge is the Isle of Portland. Weymouth embraces the once separate parishes of Melcombe Regis, Weymouth and Radipole. The harbour town of Weymouth and Melcombe Regis were united into a single borough by Royal Charter in 1571. The harbour is infamous as the port (or probably one of several ports), through which the highly contagious bubonic plaque (the Black Death) reached the shores of Britain, before wiping out an estimated 45% of the population of England, Wales and Scotland in medieval times. The town of Weymouth grew up around its harbour, which although not as important, or on the scale of Plymouth and Bristol, nevertheless saw a share of New

World departures, particularly to New England where another Weymouth was founded in the 17th century.

Today the harbour is one of the most picturesque in Britain and is used by ferries, fishing and recreational boats. In the 18th century an act of 1751 greatly increased alcohol duty and deprived the locals of their usual bibulous recreation. The effect was to pit wily local smuggling gangs against His Majesty's rapacious Customs, especially around Osmington and Ringstead Bay just east of Weymouth. Evidently not holding a grudge, George III favoured Weymouth with a royal visit in 1789 after his first bout of madness (the result of an illness now thought to be porphyria), and entered the water in a bathing contraption (a shed on wheels pulled by a horse). He enjoyed his stay so much that he bought a house on the seafront and made regular visits there until 1805. In his wake, the rich and fashionable followed and with them the town's prosperity grew. Fully recognisant of the beneficial effect on the town's fortunes, grateful townspeople erected a statue of him on the seafront in 1810 in the year of his reign's silver jubilee. The railway arrived in 1857, and in 1889 an extra line was built down the carriage route, connecting the station with the passenger ferry terminal at the harbour. The newest bridge linking the two ports of Weymouth and Melcombe Regis dates from 1930 and is a drawbridge, raised at two-hourly intervals to allow the passage of shipping. Ferries go from Weymouth to the Channel Islands of Guernsey, Jersey and St Malo in France. Over the last 10 or so years part of the harbour area has been given a facelift; a new marina and harbourside apartments are among the modern improvements. The seafront is Georgian, and the bathing beach below is a sweeping arc of golden sand. Sand sculptures and traditional pursuits such as donkey rides and Punch and Judy shows vie with more modern events such as beach volleyball, a kite festival, fireworks and motocross events.

SOUTH-WEST ENGLAND

My experience...

Pauline Carter, aged 64, retired from being a museum assistant and moved with her husband David to Weymouth, from Horsham.

We had bought a holiday flat in Weymouth. We kept that for five years and we bought it to see whether we would like retiring to Weymouth because we were happy in Horsham and could have retired there. We both have a love of the sea, and we wanted to own a boat and it was an affordable place to get moorings. We knew we could afford it and we knew from listening to other people in Horsham that some people just up sticks and retire to somewhere they don't

(Continued on following page)

(Continued)

know, just because they like the look of it. We wanted to make sure that we would like being in Weymouth 365 days a year. Once we had made the decision to move, it was about two years in the planning. My husband is a diver and he worked for some years on a marine archaeological project in Weymouth Bay, and I had cousins in Weymouth and had visited as a child so we knew Weymouth quite well. We already belonged to the Weymouth museum friends and volunteers are always needed at the Royal Society for the Protection of Birds (RSPB) to monitor the bird reserve on Chesil Bank.

The cost of living here is actually cheaper than Horsham. On the other hand, Weymouth doesn't have a huge range of shops. I go to Dorchester to shop and there is a good arts centre there. We have a corner shop and a post office close by. Our flat is on the harbour and we can see right out over Weymouth Bay. From our home we are within walking distance for everything. We wanted to get away from traffic and motorways. We love walking and we had done all the walks in Horsham so we had to go further and further in our car to find somewhere new. Weymouth is so different. We can walk from the town on a nice walk inland or along the coast. Because we are in the Jurassic World Heritage Area the coastal bus service is good. You can take a bus and stop for coffee in Lyme Regis, and then hop on the next bus to Seaton. We have a local hospital and we actually think the medical services here are better than in Horsham. I went to Shepton Mallet treatment centre for my hip operation. It was quite a way to go but the treatment was excellent. If you don't have your own transport, travelling distances like that could be a problem. The U3A here do excellent courses at Weymouth College and in summer we like to get out on boats; if you're a yachtsman, you couldn't come to a better place. I've heard other people say there's nothing to do here, but I think that's because you have to put yourself forward and seek out groups. If you are retired, you have got to get out and about and David and I are quite friendly people. We know that every day when we walk into Weymouth we'll meet someone we know; we'd been in Horsham for 23 years and it didn't happen.

Weymouth fact file

Access: A35 to Dorchester and then A354 from Dorchester. Dorchester, 8 miles.

Average property price: £205,422

Airport: Nearest is Bournemouth, 43 miles

Bus services: First (www.firstgroup.com) run services along the Jurassic Coast between Exeter and Bournemouth; 01305 783645 for timetable information.

Climate: Generally mild, even in January. A few miles inland from Weymouth, Dorchester has a colder climate.

Council: Weymouth and Portland Borough Council (www.weymouth.gov.uk)

Council tax: Band D £1,499.82

Crime: Lower than the English average

Economic activity: 2012 Olympic Games water sports activities and other regeneration, including a relief road afoot

Ferries: Condor Ferries from Weymouth to the Channel Islands and on to France

Hospitals: Weymouth Community Hospital (www.dch.org.uk). Nearest general hospital with A&E is Dorset County Hospital, Dorchester.

Percentage of people over 65: 25.9% (whole of Dorset)

Population: Approximately 63,648

Property prices: Detached £308,080; semi-detached £222,102; terraced £181, 690; flat £152, 387

Railway station: Weymouth (direct links to London and Bristol)

Residents' on-street parking permit: £45 per year

Specialised retirement property: Lots including McCarthy & Stone's forthcoming retirement flats at Hardy's Court, Weymouth from £193,950 (01305 779359)

SOUTH-WEST ENGLAND

West central England

THE COTSWOLDS

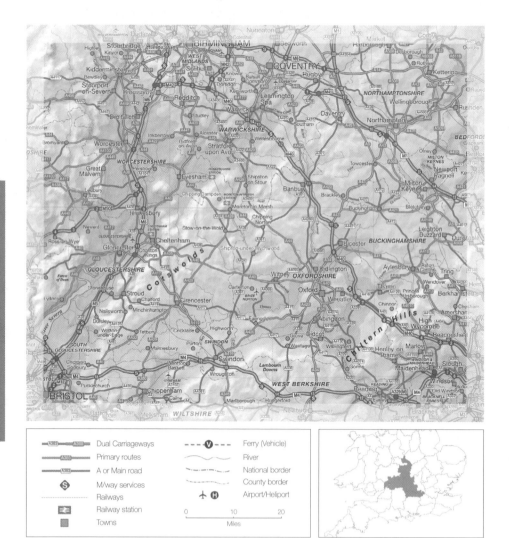

Dual Carriageways		Ferry (Vehicle)	
Primary routes		River	
A or Main road		National border	
M/way services		County border	
Railways		Airport/Heliport	
Railway station			
Towns		0 10 20	
		Miles	

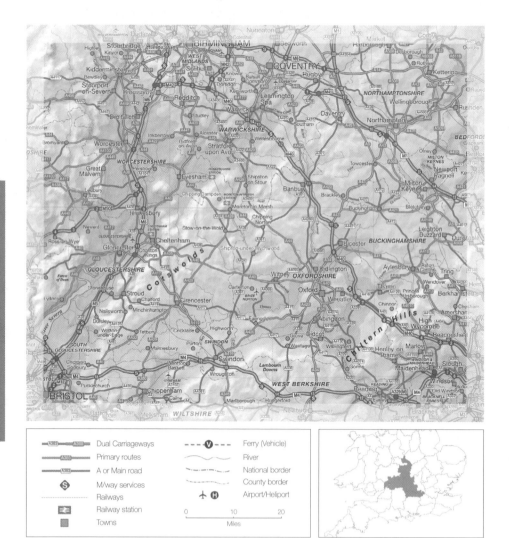

The Cotswolds area is based around the Cotswold Hills, which are just east of Cheltenham in Gloucestershire. The main towns of the Cotswolds include Stroud, Wotton-under-Edge, Tetbury, Cirencester, Fairford, Lechlade, Burford, Bourton-on the Water, Shipton-under-Wychwood, Stow-on-the-Wold, Moreton-in-Marsh and the Chippings (Chipping Campden, Chipping Sodbury and Chipping Norton). Bath is just off the south-west corner of the Cotswolds. The M5 forms a rough boundary to the western side of this whole area. In tourist literature, the Cotswolds includes Stratford-upon-Avon, Banbury, Oxford and Witney, all of which are within easy travelling distance. The famous Roman road, the Fosse Way, stretches from Exmouth and Exeter and goes straight as an arrow across the Cotswolds north-eastwards towards Lincoln. It forms the basis of the modern A429 through Stow-on-the-Wold, and in the guise of the B4455 continues on its trajectory just east of Stratford-upon-Avon. How many motorists consider what a feat of ancient backbreaking engineering this was and how its remains are now literally a few feet below their tyres? The Cotwolds are criss-crossed with routes on higher ground worn into the landscape by human passage since Neolithic times. Some were once used by drovers herding huge herds of cattle from as far away as Wales to market in London. When land had to be enclosed in the 18th century, dry stone walls were built without mortar and are a particular feature of the Cotswold landscape, although not unique in England.

The Cotswolds are an amazingly picturesque place to retire. The towns and villages have substantial buildings in honey-coloured Cotswold limestone, and their size and abundance are a legacy of the wealth generated by the sheep that produced sought after wool in the Middle Ages. The whole of the Cotswold area is designated an Area of Outstanding Natural Beauty and it is certainly one of the most beautiful, but expensive, areas in which to retire. This is the price you pay for excellent lifestyle components. For those with a serious inclination towards the arts, Cheltenham, Bath, Stratford-upon-Avon and Oxford with their theatres, literature and music festivals would provide enough choice for even the most dedicated culture vulture.

Cheltenham Spa

Cheltenham Spa grew into prominence in the first part of the 18th century after the discovery of natural springs there. Tradition has it that in 1716, local pigeons were seen pecking at the mineral deposits from the waters and were observed to exude a resultant air of well being. These perky pigeons are commemorated on the town's coat of arms. The springs, with their medicinal properties, were flocked to by the rich and celebrities of the time, hoping to alleviate their various maladies of excess. A royal seal of approval established the town's pre-eminence as a spa; George III, kingly entourage in tow, took the waters there in 1788. This gave the town a popularity boost, which was followed by a construction

WEST CENTRAL ENGLAND

boom in the late 18th and early 19th century. It included new wells, a new pump room, elegant Regency terraces and visitor accommodation, which form the gracious heart of the city today. Modern-day tourists most probably expect to see endless elegance when they visit the city. However, Cheltenham is no Bath, and modern development has been widespread, making Cheltenham as much business centre as heritage city. It has excellent shops of the 'bling' boutique kind, which have, some say, put it firmly on the map for chavs. It is hard to say what new 'style' legacy this might bequeath to Cheltenham. The 'horsey' set is much in evidence about town, which is to be expected since Cheltenham is within a stone's throw of eventing and horseracing. Badminton, Gatcombe and Hartpury horse trials are local and may appeal greatly to those who like plodding around cross-country courses and waiting for riders to tumble into water jumps. Cheltenham racecourse, home to one of racing's most prestigious events, the Cheltenham Gold Cup, is a big draw for lovers of turf events (and 'bling' exhibitionists). There are also various horse-centred events held at the National Exhibition Centre (NEC) in Birmingham, which is within easy distance. There are also various college campuses in the town and some famous public schools.

Culture addicts will find solace in the annual Times Cheltenham Literature Festival held in October, which claims to be the biggest event of its kind in the country. There is a jazz festival in May and various other arts festivals as well, so there is no lack of food for thought and for the soul.

My experience...

Inga Moss Jones, now 67, and her husband moved from Buckinghamshire to Cheltenham. She had been retired for 10 years before moving but her husband, now aged 74, was still working part-time and they delayed moving until he too retired.

We had already decided that we'd like to retire to the Cotswolds, where we had been quite a few times. We'd never lived in a village and as we are getting on, especially my husband, we thought we would try to find a town house not far from the town centre. We didn't want to live in a retirement development, and we were looking specifically for a house in a quiet spot with no through traffic, as my husband hates noise. We considered Bath as well, but property there is about 20% more expensive than Cheltenham, and it was impossible to find anywhere quiet with a garden within walking distance of the centre. We spent a weekend in Cheltenham and we both liked it; the Promenade and lovely boutiques; the shopping is really excellent. I used to go shopping in London but you don't have the individual boutiques that

Cheltenham has there. We spent about six months researching, getting the local newspaper sent to us in Buckinghamshire. We found out that there are quite a few festivals and we liked that very much. The Literature Festival in the autumn for 10 days, Science Festival in spring, the Cricket Festival, Chess, Music, Folk Festival.

We noticed that property prices in Cheltenham were similar to Buckinghamshire. The house we bought is ideal because we overlook the park at the back and the little garden reaches the River Chelt at the front, so nothing will ever be built there. We're in a small development of 24 houses and there is a short street that goes right under the London road, which is the main route into London and the bus route too. The bus stop is two minutes' walk away. One thing I did find quite unpleasant; it's dirty. So many people eat on the streets and they just throw down their fast food containers. After a Friday or Saturday night the streets are covered with litter.

Since moving to Cheltenham, we've been more active and joined different groups. I've started to learn Italian and I belong to various groups for art appreciation, philosophy and biography. We joined the Ramblers. Cheltenham is very good for rambling, wherever you go north-east, south or west, the countryside is so beautiful. Some of it you can actually walk to from our house or you can take the car to one of the Cotswold villages where there are very beautiful walks. I would say that people as a whole are friendlier, they have more time. I've found that the closer you get to London, the more stressed people are and they haven't got the time to talk. People call this the 'best county', and so it is.

WEST CENTRAL ENGLAND

Cheltenham Spa fact file

Access: M5 (junction 10); A46; A40. London, 120 miles.

Average property price: £224,972

Airports: Birmingham International (www.bhx.co.uk), 40 miles; Bristol, 45 miles

Bus services: Swanbrook (www.swanbrook.co.uk) provide local bus services around Cheltenham and further afield eg Cheltenham/Gloucester–Oxford. Also Stagecoach (www.stagecoach.co.uk).

Climate: Cheltenham is in a sheltered position between the Cotswold Hills and the Severn Vale giving it a mild, pleasant climate

Council: Cheltenham Borough Council (www.Cheltenham.gov.uk)

Council tax: Band D £1,302.44; band E £1,591.87

Crime: Lower than the national average

Economic activity: High in Cheltenham, but not for Gloucestershire as a whole

Ferries: Nearest Portsmouth, Southampton

Hospital: Cheltenham General Hospital (01242 222222; www.gloshospitals.org.uk)

Percentage of people over 65: 17%

Population: 95,000

Property prices: Detached £373,645; terraced £200,204; flat £168,064

Railway station: Cheltenham Spa (London Paddington 2 hours 10 mins)

Residents' on-street parking permit: £54 per year

Specialised retirement property: Park Garden consisting of 31 flats (020 8901 0300); Pegasus Court consisting of 46 flats (0870 600 5560 Peverel agent). The retirement builder Pegasus has its headquarters in Cheltenham (www.pegasus-homes.co.uk).

Chipping Campden

Chipping is a recurrent village name in the Cotwolds, and occurs elsewhere in England. It comes from the Middle English 'chepynge', meaning long market. Chipping Campden is on the edge of the Cotswolds in north Gloucestershire at the centre of a triangle formed by Stratford-upon-Avon (12 miles), Evesham and Stow-on-the-Wold, and near the village of Broad Campden. It has a famously beautiful and historic high street with buildings from the Middle Ages to the 17th century, and a much-photographed arched and timber-roofed market hall that was built in 1627 for the wool traders. Already, by the 14th century Chipping Campden was a prosperous town where fleeces from the surrounding Cotswold countryside were traded and transported to London, before being shipped off to the Continent. Several of the oldest of the medieval buildings in town were built by wool merchants. In 1902, at the height of the Arts and Crafts Movement, over 100 craftsmen from the East End of London arrived in Chipping Campden, formed the renowned Guild of Handicrafts, and established their workshops in an abandoned silk mill. Although the Guild subsequently closed, many of the craftspeople stayed on and the tradition of high quality objects and artistry remains very much a part of Cotswold life today. Cultural events in Chipping Campden are not all of the rural kind, although morris dancers (www.chippingcampdenmorrismen.org.uk) and maypole festivals are much in evidence. The town also has an annual music festival (www.campdenmusicfestival. co.uk), which is held mainly in St James' church, a 'wool' church built on a grand scale denoting the former wealth of the town, and flaunting a 120-foot steeple. For walkers, Chipping Campden is quite a hub, including the start of the Cotswold Way, which is just over 100 miles long and finishes in Bath. Many other Cotswold walks are in the vicinity and the area is also renowned cycling territory.

Although Chipping Campden is a good place to retire, you will need to have ample financial resources as property prices in the town and the surrounding area reflect its desirability; council tax is also very high. Chipping Campden is something of a centre for the area of small Cotswold villages that surround it. It has good facilities for a small town, including a sports centre, library, banks and interesting shops.

My experience...

Diana Evans, aged 68, has lived in Chipping Campden since 1994. She moved from Gerrards Cross in Buckinghamshire and was formerly a school administrator.

We ended up in Chipping Campden because we had family connections here. My in-laws retired here before us; part of my mother-in-law's family have actually been here since 1902 when they came with the Arts and Crafts movement, and we knew the area very well. We hadn't given much thought to actually moving here until, as we neared retirement, it became the obvious place to be. Gerrards Cross is very much commuter-land and although we still keep in touch with our friends there, for us it was time to move on. By then we'd decided to move to Chipping Campden; it's a beautiful place; the buildings, the surrounding countryside and the people are very friendly to incomers. We live in the High Street, three minutes from the shops. There are a couple of convenience stores, two bakers, a butcher, post office, greengrocer; everything you need to survive without driving out. There are Tesco stores in Stratford and Evesham, about eight miles away, but you don't need to leave Campden for anything. There are eating places, cafés, pubs and a town hall that is used for all kinds of events and gatherings. There's also an old police station that's used for counselling sessions and has the tourist information. The local history society also has an archive there. There's masses to do here, you can't fit it all in! I play with two bridge clubs, I'm active in the history society archive centre and part of another history group. I'm also helping my husband with an international museum that's being opened and is dedicated to the Arts and Crafts Movement.

Living in Chipping Campden we find we do have to use our cars a lot. There are buses on the hour, or every two hours on certain days to Stratford-upon-Avon. Although there are ways of getting to villages like Moreton-in-Marsh as well as Stratford, public transport isn't that regular and you can't really do without a car. Having said that, the worst thing about Chipping Campden is the nightmare car parking. Moreton-in-Marsh has the nearest train station; you can get a bus there and there are lots of local taxi companies.

Chipping Campden fact file

Access: B4035, B4081. Chipping Campden is not on any main road but is just off the A429 and the A44. Cheltenham, 23 miles.

Average property price: £330,091

Airports: Birmingham, approximately 40 miles

Bus services: Local bus services include to Stratford-upon-Avon (Johnsons), and Evesham (Cresswell, Henshaws)

Climate: Westerly influence means fairly mild all year round. High rainfall in autumn.

Councils: Gloucestershire County Council (www.gloucestershire.gov.uk); Chipping Campden Town Council (www.chippingcampden.co.uk)

Council tax: Band D £1,357.92; band E £1,659.69

Crime: Other Cotswold towns have more problems

Economic activity: High level of economic activity and small business creation. High level of day visits from tourists.

Hospital: Evesham Community Hospital, is 8 miles. The nearest general hospital is in Cheltenham (www.gloshospitals.org.uk).

Percentage of people over 65: Cotswold area 33%

Population: 2,200

Property prices: Two-bedroom £237,017; three-bedroom £323,205. Limited prospect for new building in the town itself except for conversions. Barratt Homes has a new housing development at Mickleton, a couple of miles north of Chipping Campden with prices from £262,000 (0845 375 1225 enquiries).

Railway station: Nearest are Honeybourne to the north-west and Moreton-in-Marsh to the south-east, each about 4 miles away

WEST CENTRAL ENGLAND

THE EAST MIDLANDS

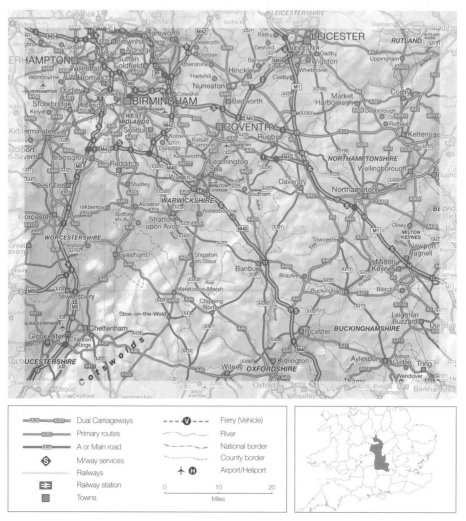

	Dual Carriageways	--- V ---	Ferry (Vehicle)
	Primary routes		River
	A or Main road		National border
S	M/way services		County border
	Railways	✈ H	Airport/Heliport
	Railway station	0 10 20	
	Towns	Miles	

The East Midlands area has long been associated with being a heartland of mining and manufacturing, and the home of many famous products of British industry from aircraft to lace. The historic counties of the region are Derbyshire, Leicestershire, Lincolnshire, Northamptonshire, Nottinghamshire and tiny Rutland, and within these are the once begrimed cities of Derby, Nottingham, Coventry, Birmingham and Leicester. North-east Warwickshire nudges into the East Midlands area and, in complete contrast to the industrial metropolises of that region, it contains the elegant spa town of Leamington, characterised by white stucco neo-classical architecture. A surprising find perhaps, considering the proximity of Coventry and Birmingham. The East Midlands have excellent transport links (except Lincolnshire) to the rest of Britain by road, via the

M42 and M40 motorways and railways. For trips further afield, it is near both Birmingham and Coventry airports. The grand scale of the old manufacturing conurbations means it is easy to overlook that the East Midlands are 90% rural, with Lincolnshire forming a large chunk of its non-industrial territory. There is also no shortage of heritage sites. Around Coventry for instance are Stoneleigh Abbey, Packwood House, and the National Agricultural Centre at Stoneleigh, with its regular local and national shows. The arts are also thriving: Birmingham has long since upturned its industrial image to excel as a major centre for the arts and for prestigious exhibitions and events held at the National Exhibition Centre (NEC). You would expect no less from Britain's second largest city.

Leamington Spa

Royal Leamington Spa is an attractive medium-sized town in Warwickshire, south-east of Birmingham, and 10 miles south of Coventry. Other towns in the area include Warwick (including Warwick Castle and Warwick University campus), Rugby and Stratford-upon-Avon. Until about 1800, Leamington, or Leamington Priors as it was then, was a hamlet of 300 souls on the south bank of the River Leam. It had saline springs, which had been known about from medieval times, when springs were places of pilgrimage. Visitors of the commercial sort began coming from 1784, when taking the medicinal waters became fashionable, but it was soon obvious that an expansion of facilities was needed if the increasing fame of the springs was to be fully exploited. New springs were discovered in about 1810 on the north bank of the river and the Royal Pump rooms were constructed over them and opened in 1814. The new town began to expand from there. It was carefully planned with the quality of life of its citizens and visitors at the forefront, and this is its legacy to our more stressful times. By 1848, the popularity of the spa was declining and another phase of construction was undertaken to provide additional facilities, including Turkish baths and a swimming pool to attract visitors. The Pittville Pump Rooms nowadays house the art gallery and museum, as well as the town library and tourist information centre. The former assembly rooms have been refurbished and are used as an attractive venue for music and other events. You can still drink the waters, pumped from about 80ft down, but water-based treatments have not been offered since the 1990s. Leamington is a beautiful town with fine individual shops, lots of bars and restaurants and green spaces; the renowned Jephson gardens are such a peaceful place to wander that you might not need to have your own garden. There are also pleasant walks from Leamington Spa to Offchurch and Cubbington. These cross Newbold Common, which has an 18-hole golf course and a miniature golf course, as well as a leisure centre and swimming pool.

Leamington is not a retirement town in the sense of being favoured by the retired. In fact it appeals to all ages. The advantages of Leamington as a retirement place include pretty surroundings, excellent local facilities, the great transport

WEST CENTRAL ENGLAND

connections, as well as the fact that property is still affordable compared with places such as Poole or the Cotswolds. You can still rent allotments at the top of Campion Hill with a special rate for pensioners and for paying dues early, which makes them available for as little as £13.50 per year.

My experience...

Dan moved to Leamington about seven years ago from north Birmingham with his wife. He was formerly involved with heavy vehicle engineering.

My daughter was already living in Leamington, so we got good reports from her about it. We visited quite a lot. I was actually quite settled to retire where we were living, so it was more my wife's decision to move to Leamington. The area of Birmingham where we had been living for nine years was very nice, but had deteriorated to the state where we were burgled twice and my wife was mugged while shopping.

At the time we moved to Leamington it was in the middle of a £3m renovation to improve certain parts and we are reaping the benefits of that, with things such as a miniature golf course and a fitness centre. It's a wonderful place if you like walking; there are canals, a river and a wonderful park, and activities such as rowing. There's a variety of clubs of all sorts and wonderful theatres nearby in Stratford and Birmingham. Access by car is good; the A46 goes straight to Stratford and Coventry. My wife was a florist all her working life and she loves the beautiful gardens and horticultural clubs. We joined two: one in Leamington and one in Offchurch. I'm a bowler; crown green bowls and all that. We had a lovely open space where we lived before, a catchment area for reservoirs. Unfortunately it had become unsafe to wander there because of youths with motorcycles and other hazards, so we love that you can wander here safely.

We bought a two-bedroom bungalow in a residential area. We do have a bus service into Leamington centre, but you can walk there in a couple of minutes. There's a regular bus service to Coventry. The nearest hospitals are in Warwick and Coventry. I didn't find it a particularly friendly place when I moved here. In Birmingham, people are very friendly; in and out of each other's houses; here in Leamington, people are more reserved. It could be our Birmingham accent, or just that people here have high hedges and secluded gardens and like to keep themselves to themselves. We did join different organisations like the University of the Third Age where you get to know people and then you get connections to other organisations, and begin to socialise with people living a few minutes away.

Royal Leamington Spa fact file

Access: M40 (London 90 minutes), A46, A452, A425, A4189, B4453. Birmingham, 35 miles.

Average property price: £226,659

Airports: Coventry, 9 miles; Birmingham, 18 miles; East Midlands, 48 miles

Bus services: Regular local services to Stratford and Coventry

Climate: Typically mild. A tornado was spotted near Leamington in August 2006.

Councils: Warwickshire County Council (www.warwickshire.gov.uk); Royal Leamington Spa Town Council (www.leamingtonspatowncouncil.gov.uk)

Council tax: Band D £1,339.51; band E £1,637.17

Crime: Doesn't share the high crime levels of the East Midlands generally, but crime in Warwickshire is going up

Economic activity: High business activity, probably in one of the most vibrant business areas in the country

Hospital: Brand new large, University College Hospital Coventry (www.uhcw.nhs.uk)

Percentage of people over 65: 16%; Average age of area is 40

Population: Approximately 42,000

Property prices: Detached £370,295; semi-detached £209,749; terrace £202,404; flat £166,612

Railway station: Leamington Spa (Leamington to London Marylebone 1 hour 30 mins)

Residents' on-street parking permit: £10 per year

Specialised retirement property: Lots of retirement developments. Also new homes (not necessarily for retirement) by Barratt, Antler and Crest Nicholson from £220,000.

WEST CENTRAL ENGLAND

THE MALVERN HILLS

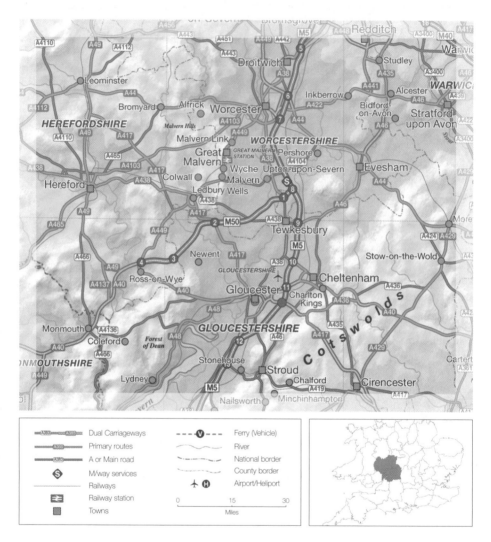

Dual Carriageways	Ferry (Vehicle)	
Primary routes	River	
A or Main road	National border	
M/way services	County border	
Railways	Airport/Heliport	
Railway station	0 15 30	
Towns	Miles	

The Malvern Hills is a range of hills whose character is conserved as an Area of Outstanding Natural Beauty, partly in Herefordshire, partly in Worcestershire and a tiny part in Gloucestershire. The village of Knightwick marks the northern tip, while Brown's End in Gloucestershire marks the southern limit. Towns and villages within this area include Alfrick, Suckley Green, Longley Green, Storridge, Cradley, West Malvern, Great Malvern, Upper and Lower Wyche, Malvern Wells, Little Malvern, Wellend, Ledbury, Hollybush, Eastnor and Camer's Green. It is an area as much of springs as hills, whose Celtic name was 'Moel-Bryn', meaning bare hill, which later became 'Maelfern'. It is an area that has inspired poets from the 14th-century epic *Piers Plowman* by William Langland, to WH Auden who, in the 1930s, taught in a local school and wrote his poem *The Malverns* while there:

> Here on the cropped grass of the narrow ridge I stand,
> A fathom of earth, alive in air,
> Aloof as an admiral on the old rocks
> England below me.

The rock of the Malvern Hills is indeed old; pre-Cambrian and some of the most ancient in the country. Its formation is estimated to have taken place 600 to 1,000 million years ago, so this not a place for Creationists to retire. The highest point is the Worcestershire Beacon at 1,295ft. There are many holy wells and springs in the Malvern Hills and there is a very active society, the Malvern Spa Association, which is concerned with their preservation, refurbishment and continuing use. However, some of the water may have a high content of bacteria, so be circumspect in your consumption from any historic spout you may come across; great for mopping your brow on a long walk, though.

Great Malvern

Great Malvern, often just called just Malvern, became a popular spa town in the 18th century, although the supposed curative powers of the waters had been known of since at least the 17th century. When Dr John Wall analysed the mineral content of the water in the 18th century, he found it low in mineral content, which did not, however, prevent a whole industry growing up around it that is still going strong today. Bottled Malvern water is splashed into glasses the length and breadth of the land and beyond. Malvern began to be seen as a desirable place to live and visit from the early 1800s, when the first baths, hotels and houses were built. However, it was as a Victorian spa town that it really took off and expanded in a major way. In 1842 Victorian enterprise arrived in the form of doctor practitioners of the 'Water Cure', who set up practice to promote their new treatments. The railway arrived in 1861, increasing accessibility and visitor volume. There may be something special in the water after all. Malvern was the home of the composer Sir Edward Elgar, who composed many of his best-known works including *Pomp and Circumstance* Marches 1 and 2 while living there between 1904 and 1912. No doubt he drew his inspiration from the Malvern Hills where he frequently went walking, climbing and cycling. In the 1920s the Malvern Festival was founded and the literary giant of his day, George Bernard Shaw, premiered several of his plays there, some of which he wrote specially for the festival. The arts are still a big part of Malvern life and leisure, with the focus on the Malvern theatres comprising the original Victorian Theatre, The Forum modern theatre with seating for 1,000, and a cinema. On the industry side, Malvern is the home of the Morgan car and of the government radar research establishment. The latter is much diversified and commercialised under the brand name Qinetic.

Malvern is in a deeply rural area that has good communications and transport connections, which has prompted Londoners to buy up property in the area. The rolling folds of Malvern's hills provide not only an inspirational backdrop, but are the source of many wonderful walks and explorations. People don't really want to tell you what a great place Malvern is for retirement, as that would let the cat out of the bag about how great it really is.

My experience...

Mary Gardener and her husband moved to Malvern from the Stoke-on-Trent area in 1997. She retired from teaching, but continued to work in other fields.

I'd been thinking we should move from where we were. Transport wasn't very good and we wanted to be somewhere nearer the shops, and Malvern is a beautiful place with lovely buildings everywhere and an interesting history. There's also the fabulous countryside, which is very important to us. My two daughters moved to this area, one after the other, so I visited the area quite a bit and got to know it. They seemed very settled and unlikely to move away. I really liked the place, so I asked a friend in Malvern to keep a look out for houses and she spotted the house where I now live, just as it was coming on the market.

I am now within walking distance of the shops and train station. There is a lot to do in Malvern; loads of eating places and it has a cinema, theatre and concert hall; not all on the same site but close together, which is very handy. Shopping is actually a bit limited, but there are lots of other places to shop and an excellent train service to Birmingham. There is also a direct service to London Paddington. I can walk to the bus stop and get a bus to Worcester, as they are pretty frequent. The other useful connection is that you can get a National Express bus from Malvern Link to London Victoria.

For active people, Malvern is great. The other thing I looked for when I came was a church to belong to and the Church here was very welcoming and that helped. I joined the University of the Third Age here, and we have everything from walking, bridge and art, to a nuclear physics group. I help to run the art group. Malvern has a very good college for art and the prospect of art classes was another thing that drew me to Malvern. I am also just about to join the WI.

I love the general beauty of the place and its surroundings; its openness. It is a nice mixture of town and country. It's a bit like living in an overgrown village, so you quickly get to know people and meet them in all sorts of different contexts. In the local shops, if you visit a second time, they recognise you.

Great Malvern fact file

Access: M50, M5, A449. Worcester, 10 miles.

Average property price: £266,162

Airports: Birmingham, approximately 47 miles

Bus services: Malvern Hills Hopper circular route around Malvern Hills villages; First Midland Red (www.firstgroup.com) services to Birmingham, and Worcester

Climate: Some of the UK's warmest summer temperatures

Council: Malvern Hills District Council

Council tax: Band D £1,337; band E £1,634

Crime: Most people in Malvern feel safe in the day and if they are out at night. Vandalism can be a problem.

Economic activity: Very active, including Malvern Hills Science Park on the edge of town

Hospitals: Malvern Community Hospital (www.worcestershirehealth.nhs.uk). Acute hospitals part of the same NHS trust are: the Worcester Royal, the Alexandra at Redditch and the Kidderminster Hospital.

Percentage of people over 65: 24.31% (Malvern Hills)

Population: 31,640

Property prices: Detached £346,858; semi-detached £192,739; terrace £200,571; flat £147,029

Railway stations: Malvern has two: Great Malvern and Malvern Link on the Hereford–Worcester line. Some direct services to London Paddington.

Specialised retirement property: Several developments including Santler Court (McCarthy & Stone), Churchill Retirement Living's new development at Malvern Link and Crellin House (flats in Priory Road)

THE MARCHES

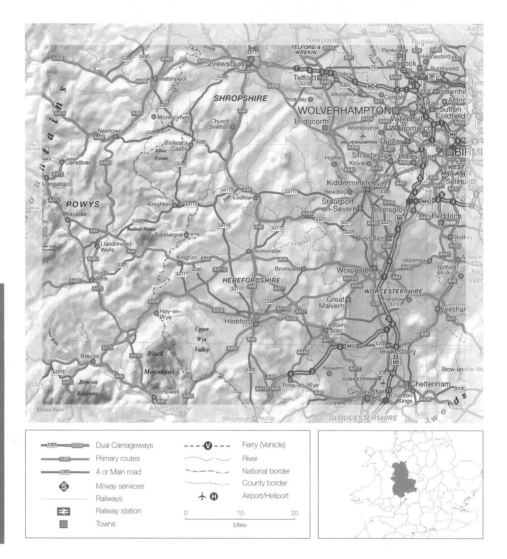

Symbol	Description		Symbol	Description
A385 A388	Dual Carriageways		---V---	Ferry (Vehicle)
A388	Primary routes			River
A329	A or Main road			National border
Ⓢ	M/way services			County border
	Railways		✈ Ⓗ	Airport/Heliport
⊠	Railway station			
■	Towns			

0   10   20

Miles

In European history, marches are buffer zones of defended territory between regional powers, an idea that probably grew out of Roman military strategy. In English history, the Welsh Marches are the borderlands, mainly on the English side, between these two countries and they include the counties of Shropshire and Herefordshire, sometimes called the Central Marches. Cheshire further north and Gloucester further south, also share borders with Wales. Some time in the first century AD, these regions formed the western limit of the Roman Empire, and excavations in Herefordshire have revealed the remains of Roman fortifications. In later medieval times, England expanded further into Welsh territories and those awarded lands in the region were known as Marcher Lords, and had the title of 'Lord of the Marches' added to their nomenclature. The Welsh were fiery opponents and the Marches of England and Wales produced a string of fortifications constructed along the edge of the region. These remain much in evidence and include the magnificent castles of Ludlow and Chepstow, which in tribute to their builders, remain virtually intact. Towns of the Central Marches include Leominster, Hereford and Shrewsbury.

Hereford

Hereford justly claims to be one of the country's most historic and ancient cities, founded in the seventh century, or possibly earlier. It sits almost exactly midway between Leominster to the north and Monmouth to the south, and is surrounded by landscape betokening rural activities from cattle-rearing (including the eponymous Hereford supreme beef breed, now found in 50 countries worldwide), fruit growing and cider-making. However, these days nearly half the Herefordshire farmland supports arable farming, rather than cattle. There is also extensive forest cultivation. Hereford is a gateway to mid- and South Wales and lies to the east of the English border town of Hay-on-Wye, which is on the edge of the Black Mountains. To the west are Malvern and the Malvern Hills, which form the eastern boundary of Herefordshire. Also within easy driving distance are Ross-on-Wye and the Forest of Dean. Hereford also has excellent transport connections by road and rail to South Wales and north-west England.

Hereford Cathedral dates from the 11th century and is dedicated to St Ethelbert. During the 12th century it was a place of pilgrimage, second only to Canterbury. Hereford is also a guardian of valuable artifacts including the Mappa Mundi, a world map used to instruct the illiterate, presumably in a very misleading way, as it is a wild mixture of fact and imagination. Rare manuscripts and early printed books make up the rest of the collection. Hereford High Town is where the medieval market, modelled on a Norman French one, once stood. Through various vicissitudes, including fire and war, Hereford lost some of its older buildings and had its city walls demolished. However, there are still a sufficient number of medieval and Jacobean buildings, and a medieval bridge, to give a feel of those older times. During the late 18th century much of Hereford's trade with the outside world was carried out via the River Wye and the arrival and departure of river traffic, mainly barges, would have been a daily sight. The railway arrived in 1853.

The fact that the region around Hereford has great rural charm and is unspoiled, is one of the main benefits of living in or near Hereford, along with good transport connections. The Wye valley is quite rightly considered some of the most beautiful landscape in England. The Wye itself meanders for 154 miles through several counties and has its outlet in the Severn at Chepstow. House buyers and those who wish to retire have recently been buying up farmhouses and cottages in rural Hereford, pushing prices above the national average. It is likely that you would find property cheaper in the city itself, where there is a good assortment of retirement flats and other flats that would be suitable for retirees.

My experience...

Marjorie Stockley who is now 78, has lived in Hereford since 2004; before that she was in Leintwardine near Ludlow.

My husband and I used to come to Hereford from Leintwardine for shopping and we had fallen in love with it. It wasn't my intention to move to Hereford, but as I'm on my own now, I thought the time would come when I would not be able to drive and I wanted to be near amenities. I had a choice between moving to Litchfield or Hereford, and Hereford won hands down for two reasons; it's a cathedral city and I think that always gives a special feeling, an ethos of its own; and it's on the flat, which I thought was important if I began to find walking difficult. I moved to a retirement development in the centre of town, 500 yards from the cathedral and four minutes' walk from Marks & Spencer. It's not a place where you have Tuesday night bingo, but it does have the security with the orange cords, and a manager who visits three times a week.

Living in the centre of town, I've met people because I joined lots of things. There's plenty to join in Hereford: the U3A, of which I'm now chairwoman; the WI and lots of societies. There really is masses going on and everyone is very friendly. There are also the usual things: library, museum and rather good shops. There's also an arts centre that shows films and they do breakfast showings with coffee and pastries. The Three Choirs Festival is held in Hereford every third year. Then there's The High Town, which is absolutely something else; if you're depressed and you go in there; you immediately perk up. There's just this feeling that it's the heart of the city and a marvellous space. The other thing is we are very close to Malvern, which has a theatre and gets pre-West End shows.

The traffic can be heavy in the mornings and evenings, because there is only one bridge across the river, but it's really only a problem for people getting to work. Summer brings an influx of visitors around the Cathedral area, but you don't get overwhelmed by tourists as you do in some places, and in any case this is a county town so you've always got people coming in from outside. They could be tourists or locals; you can't always tell which.

Hereford fact file

Access: A49, A438, A465, A4103. Ross-on-Wye, 16 miles; Brecon, 43 miles; Worcester, 27 miles; Abergavenny, 26 miles.

Average property price: £215,208

Airports: Birmingham is the nearest, 50 miles; also Cardiff and Bristol. Heathrow can be reached in 3 hours.

Bus services: To obtain public transport information for Hereford, email public.transport@Herefordshire.gov.uk; local bus service enquiries (01432 260211)

Climate: Warmer than average microclimate suitable for fruit growing

Councils: Hereford City Council (www.herefordcitycouncil.gov.uk); Unitary Authority of Herefordshire (www.herefordshire.gov.uk)

Council tax: Band D £1,334; band E £1,631.42

Crime: Regarded as a safe area with low crime

Economic activity: Fragile economy as mainly rural

Hospital: Hereford County Hospital in Hereford (www.herefordshire.nhs.uk)

Percentage of people over 65: 26% (Herefordshire overall)

Population: Approximately 56,000

Property prices: Detached £294,931; semi-detached £294,931; semi-detached £188,730; terraced £153,279; flat £127,235

Railway station: Hereford. London–Paddington 2 hours 50 mins); Cardiff (1 hour); Manchester (2 hours 15 mins); Worcester (40 mins)

Residents' on-street parking permit: £25 per year

Specialised retirement property: Includes Jamieson Court, Melrose Place and the Rose Garden Independent Living Scheme for the over-55s due to open in 2008 with over 90 flats (for local people)

WEST CENTRAL ENGLAND

Shrewsbury

Shrewsbury, which was once known as Salopsbury, is in Shropshire encircled within easy distance by the towns of Whitchurch, Oswestry, Welshpool, Ludlow, Market Drayton, Telford and Bridgnorth. Birmingham is slightly further (an hour's drive) away to the east. The historic town of Shrewsbury was probably founded in the fifth century and is of Celtic origin, although later Saxons and then the Norman lord, Roger de Montgomery became its holder. When Roger received Shropshire in its entirety, as a gift from William the Conqueror, he made Shrewsbury his stronghold by building a castle and an abbey there in the 11th century. For two centuries after, Shrewsbury was the focus of Welsh aspirations, as they repeatedly tried to take the town. A very bloody battle took place in 1403, which claimed the lives of 6,000 soldiers; an extraordinarily high body count for the times, which steeped Shrewsbury's history forever in blood. During the Tudor and Elizabethan times the town became a very prosperous centre for the wool and flax trades. These eras gave rise to the many black-and-white mansions that line the streets, and with which Shrewsbury is greatly associated. The town probably contains more listed buildings (over 600) than any other town in England. A river runs through it in the form of the gently looping Severn, which historically provided the town's natural defence barrier. Shrewsbury's most famous son is Charles Darwin, whose theory of evolution rocked the Victorian religious establishment and still provokes pathological denial in Creationists today. He was a pupil at the famous Shrewsbury public school and a 'Salopian', (a person who hails from Shrewsbury) born and bred.

Shrewsbury is in beautiful countryside with the Shropshire Hills to the south-west, the Welsh coast within easy distance and close to the West Midlands and Birmingham. It is in the middle of the north–south rail network. Shrewsbury has an annual arts festival: Shrewsbury Summer Season (www.shrewsburysummer.co.uk) and an annual folk festival. There is also a privately run institution, The Concert Bus (01743 790400), which arranges trips to the Symphony Hall in Birmingham and major arts events and provides a door-to-door service.

My experience...

Betty Green, now 86 years old, moved alone to Shrewsbury from Pembrokeshire, nearly 20 years ago.

I felt it was time to move from Pembrokeshire as I had a house that was too big for me and I wanted somewhere smaller. I also wanted to live in a medium-sized town, rather than a big city. I looked at places from Kent to Oxford, but they were too expensive for me. Shrewsbury is a lovely medieval town, which I had already been to a few times before I moved here. I came to stay with a friend in Shrewsbury and started visiting estate agents. Within a week, I found a Victorian-style two-bedroom house and found myself moving in a few weeks later.

I'm about a mile from the town centre and there is a good, regular bus service. When I first moved here, I found myself with time on my hands, as you do when you move somewhere new. I started joining everything I could. I've dropped a lot of them now, but in the course of doing that I met someone who wanted to start a U3A group in Shrewsbury. They'd had a few attempts without much success, but we managed to get that off the ground and now I'm involved with its gardening groups, an art history group and I'm still on the committee. There are now 260 members. There's a lot going on here and things for you to join: restaurants, cafés, good hotels, multiplex cinema and a lovely small cinema in a medieval building. There are also lots of churches and a wonderful abbey.

I don't want to be a whinger and resistant to change, but there is a lot of traffic congestion, new road planning and some modern buildings which look out of place. On the good side, there is still a lot of medieval Shrewsbury and some very good modern buildings, which haven't impinged on the views at all. It was a very good choice to move here and I've never regretted it. Since moving here I have found nothing but kindness and help. I remember one morning my curtains were still closed a bit late and somebody actually tapped on the door to see if I was all right. It is still like that; we all look out for each other.

Shrewsbury fact file

Access: A profusion of roads fan out around Shrewsbury and these include the A49, A53, A458 and A5l. Birmingham, 47 miles.

Average property price: £188,392

Airports: Birmingham, 57 miles; Liverpool, 6 miles; Manchester, 63 miles

Bus services: Arriva, Midland Red

Climate: Mild enough to nurture the grapes at Wroxeter Roman vineyard, 4 miles east of Shrewsbury

Councils: Shrewsbury & Atcham Borough Council; Shropshire County Council

Council tax: Band D £975.66; band E £1,192

Crime: Vandalism and criminal damage problem

Economic activity: Mainly focused on the service sector and tourism and as a regional shopping centre

Ferries: Holyhead (120 miles). Ferries to Dublin (www.stenaline.ferries.org).

Hospital: Royal Shrewsbury Hospital (Royal Shrewsbury Hospitals NHS Trust, www.sath.nhs.uk)

Percentage of people over 65: 14%, over-70s; 30%

Population: Approximately 100,000

Property prices: Detached £267,717; semi-detached £178,426; terraced £151,244; flat £132,462

Railway station: Shrewsbury

Specialised retirement property: Many flat developments (not specifically aimed at retirees) from about £195,000 for two bedrooms

WEST CENTRAL ENGLAND

Wales

THE UPPER WYE VALLEY

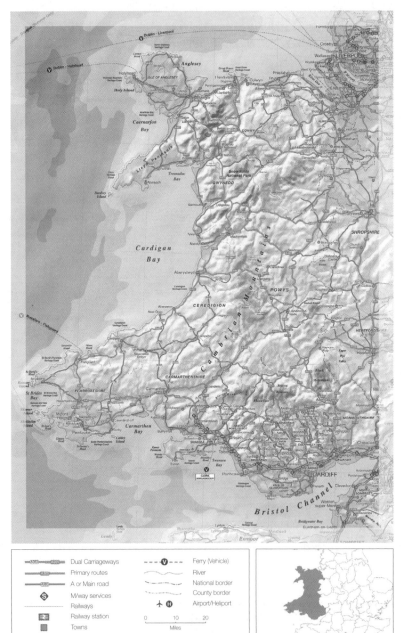

Dual Carriageways		--- 🅥 ---	Ferry (Vehicle)
Primary routes			River
A or Main road			National border
🆂	M/way services		County border
Railways		✈ 🄷	Airport/Heliport
Railway station			
Towns		0 10 20	
		Miles	

WALES

The area around Builth Wells, Llandrindod Wells and Rhyader in Powys lies in the Upper Wye Valley. It is so called to distinguish it from the lushly wooded depths of the Wye Valley of the English Marches, which is further south and takes in the downstream section from just south of Hereford, to its outlet at Chepstow. At Hereford, this great river bends westwards into the heartland of Wales and passes just east of the Elan lakes. The Wye's source is further north still in Ceredigion on the spongy slopes of Plynlimon Mountain, where legend has it somewhere deep below the embedded sheep droppings the Wye river god stirs. The area of the Upper Wye Valley is surrounded by the mountain, river and lake scenery of wild Wales, forever under the eyebeam of buzzard, red kite and other birds of prey. Hill walkers and coarse and fly fishermen (and women) are attracted here by the lure of the wilderness of places such as the southern part of the Cambrian mountains, or the rich fishing grounds of the Wye, its tributaries such as the Irfon and the Ithon, and the impressive reservoirs created by Victorian dams in the Elan Valley. Fishing fans can get more information from the Rhayader and Elan Valley Angler Association (www.rhayaderangling.co.uk) and walkers from www.wyevalleywalk.org or the Mid Wales Ramblers (www.fourwells.powysramblers.org.uk). There is a 24-mile new extension of the Wye Valley walk in the upper Wye Valley from Rhayader via Llangurig to the slopes of Plynlimon, where it joins the Severn Way.

Builth Wells

A Norman castle, of which nothing but the site remains, was built in the 13th century on a strategic point of the River Wye. It is considered to be the origin of the town of Builth Wells, although not the name Builth, which was the name of a 'cantref', or area of administration, which was in existence before the town was built. Builth is an English translation of Welsh words that probably meant 'the ox of the wooded slope'. A town grew up in the shelter of the castle and was granted a charter in 1277. Even by the 1800s it was a place of no more than 700 souls. In 1779 a splendid bridge was built across the Wye and a new road was put through the town in the 1820s, linking north and south Wales. However, the town experienced its biggest growth during the Victorian and Edwardian eras, which are the periods most represented by the town's architecture today. Prosperity was linked directly to commercial exploitation of the restorative springs, some of which had been known about since at least 1740. In 1830 discovery of both saline and sulphur springs prompted the arrival of an increasing number of visitors to try them, and in order to accommodate the demand for baths, lodgings and shops the town duly expanded. Its heyday came after 1860, when the railways delivered visitors *en masse* and the word Wells was added to its name.

For a small town, Builth Wells has good amenities, including a cinema, theatre, sports centre and a golf course on the outskirts. As it is a popular visitor destination in summer it also has a good selection of restaurants, pubs and cafés.

Builth Wells is also the warm heart of the sparsely punctuated wilderness of Mid-Wales, including the Brecon Beacons, the Black Mountains, Radnor Forest and the Elan Valley. At the same time it is easily accessible from other Welsh towns.

As a retirement place Builth Wells is not typical as it is a small town where the average age is 40, rather than 60+. However, it is a very friendly place and there is also a park home site, suitable for retirees aged 50+, in the grounds of Caerwnon House, overlooking Builth Wells and three miles from it. The area is outstanding for walking, fishing, wildlife watching and other outdoor pursuits. The Royal Welsh Show (www.rwas.co.uk) has a permanent showground nearby. All in all, a bit of a hidden secret for retirement, but remoteness from bright lights may not appeal to some.

My experience...

John Gaze, age 71, an antiques dealer from London, moved to Builth Wells in 1988 with his wife.

We wanted to move out of London and looked in quite a few places including East Anglia, where we put in an offer for somewhere and were gazumped. We also looked at Norfolk, Leicestershire and north Lincolnshire. Having not found what we wanted we took a week's holiday in Wales. We travelled along the south-west coast and then inland, ending up in Builth Wells, which we knew almost nothing about. We carried on travelling in Wales, but had to come back to Builth, as I had left my wallet in a pub there. The landlady had contacted the police and I was so impressed with her honesty that we decided we liked the place and left our details with a couple of estate agents in the town. We then made a day trip to Builth Wells to look at a property. We didn't like the one we looked at but saw something in an estate agent's window that looked interesting and was near the estate agent. To cut a long story short, we made an offer on the spot. It was a Victorian house equipped as a B&B, which we ran for a while. After four and a half years, we moved just outside Builth Wells to Aberedw, as heavy traffic had been diverted to the road we lived on and disturbed us through the night. This is not typical of Builth and many people find it a quiet place.

Builth is a friendly place and it has the Wyeside Arts, including a cinema which sometimes shows previews, and a small exhibition space. We are only 16 miles from Hay-on-Wye, where there is the famous literary festival. There is adequate basic shopping in Builth, but for a big shop we go to Hereford, 20 miles away, or to Abergavenny. There is a Community Hospital in Builth Wells that the powers that be are trying to close down, and there is a major local protest in progress. There is a slightly larger hospital in Llandrindod Wells, but for other acute things you have to go to different places. Brecon Hospital is the main cardio unit about 17 miles away.

Builth Wells is in the lovely setting of the Wye Valley, which is beautiful countryside. It brings a lot of walkers in summer. The only downsides of living here are that you cannot manage without a car. There is a bus service, but it is very limited and goes at ridiculous times. For instance a service for Hereford once a week that leaves at 10.30am, so half the day is gone by the time you get there. Fuel is also very expensive. Here we pay about £0.98 per litre; in Hereford it is £0.90, so that is a major expense.

Builth Wells fact file

Access: A470, A483, A481. Llandrindod Wells, 8 miles; Hay-on-Wye, about 14 miles; Brecon, 12 miles; Aberystwyth on the Welsh coast, 50 miles

Average property price: £173,405

Airports: Cardiff approximately 52 miles,

Bus services: Local companies Browns (01982 552597) and Cross Gates (01597 851226)

Climate: Lots of rain, cold winters

Councils: Builth Wells Town Council (www.builth.com); Powys County Council (www.powys.gov.uk)

Council tax: Band D £946 approximately; band E £1,157. Further info by emailing revenue@powys.gov.uk

Crime: Low crime. Residents feel safe. Strong community spirit.

Economic activity: Mainly revolves around agriculture and tourism

Hospitals: Builth Wells Cottage Hospital with 12 beds and minor injuries unit (www. builthsurgery.co.uk). Nearest hospitals for specialist treatment such as Hereford, Abergavenny and Carmarthen are all approximately 45 miles away. Builth Wells community support provides volunteer transport for those unable to make the journey they need to on their own.

Percentage of people over 65: 20% (whole of Powys)

Population: Approximately 2,350. Average age 40 years.

Property prices: Four–bedroom detached house £225,000–£235,000; three-bedroom bungalow £239,500–£270,000; one-bedroom apartment from £92,000. Park home in Ash Way from £62,000.

Railway station: Builth Road (2 miles north of Builth Wells on A470). Heart of Wales Line. About four trains a day to Swansea and Shrewsbury where you can join mainline services.

Specialised retirement property: There is a good supply of flats in converted buildings and newly built ones, although not specifically for retirement

WALES

ANGLESEY

The Isle of Anglesey, often just called Anglesey or 'Ynys Môn' if you are a Welsh-speaker (60% of islanders are) is 20 miles by 16 miles, and 27 miles around the edge. It lies off the north-west coast of Wales, from which it is separated by the Menai Straits, which are spanned by two bridges, the Menai (suspension) Bridge and the Britannia (railway) Bridge. The marvellously scenic Lleyn peninsula of Gwynedd juts out into the sea, south-west of Anglesey, in a curious echo of the shape of Cornwall far away in the south-west of England. The great expanses of Wales' premier national park of Snowdonia is within easy distance east of Anglesey on the mainland. Anglesey has an appropriately fabulous setting for a place believed to be a chief seat of the ancient Druid religion. While the Romans wiped out the Druids and called it Mona, the Anglo-Saxon name was Angle's Eye (Eye meaning island). It is rich in mineral deposits, including copper, which was mined there from the Bronze Age to the 18th century. There are signs of human habitation on the island, going back 8,000 years, including stone burial chambers, standing stones and hill forts. The Isle of Anglesey has its own island, Holy Island, off the eastern coast and reached via the A55. This island is sacred to both pagan and Christian religions, and it is also the embarkation point for ferries to Ireland from Holyhead.

Anglesey is dotted with towns and villages and has been comparatively populous for more than a century. In 1901 when the main source of work was agriculture and fishing, it supported a population of 50,738; 100 years later it has grown by a fairly modest 17,000 souls, to 66,828. The main towns are Amlwch, Beaumaris, Cemaes, Benllech, Holyhead, Llanerchymedd, Llangefni, Pentraeth and Rhosneigr, and it has not one, but three golf courses and a fantastic coastal path. The lack of intensive farming on Anglesey means that it is a haven for wildlife, particularly birds and butterflies, and sailors may find themselves watched by soulful sea lions, or chased and sported with by bottlenosed dolphins.

Moelfre

Moelfre is a former fishing village on the east coast of Anglesey. Although the name is an ancient one from the area and means 'bare hill', the village itself grew only in the early 19th century when it attracted seafaring folk to settle there, thus expanding the community from a few cottages. Moelfre has an especially illustrious lifeboat tradition going back to 1848. Apart from being an attractive village, what singles out Moelfre from a retirement point of view is that three-quarters of its residents are seniors, and it has become a byword for how a community best looks after the interests of older people. The Moelfre Community Project based in the village school, provides activities including a

WALES

lifelong learning programme for seniors, as well as a mobility programme for the less agile and a social programme and day care centre. For those who crave peace and quiet, it is possible, even in summer, to find nearby beaches with just a few people on them. The town also has a bakery, restaurant and several pubs and the village is connected by various excellent bus services to the rest of Anglesey and mainline railways.

My experience...

Brenda Frost, a retired accountant, moved to Moelfre from the West Midlands near Birmingham, in 2001 with her husband, a former engineer. She loves it there, but her husband who 'gets bored easily' – wants them to move to Spain.

We decided we were going to move and we were very systematic about the whole process. My husband spent a couple of years taking days off to have a good troll around the coastline of Britain. We eventually decided on the east coast, but our move fell through. We decided to have a look round Anglesey. We went on a bus trip and when we were leaving the area, I noticed how everyone there looked relaxed and happy and I said 'I think I could live here'. There was a slower pace of life. We came to look at a house and it is a lovely house that we now live in. We didn't know Moelfre particularly well, but we couldn't have chosen better; it's a beautiful place and there is a wonderful social life here. We can walk down to the bay and the sea in three minutes. We've got a pub, restaurant, bakery and a fabulous shop where there is also a small restaurant. We do our main shopping in Bangor. The buses here are very good; every half hour to Bangor, which is also a central point for buses all over North Wales.

There's lots to do here and I haven't time to join in everything that's on offer. I am involved with the WI and volunteer one afternoon a week with the lifeboat's gift shop. I'm also a member of the Benllech Flower Club and the Ladies' Club. They are a kind of breakaway group, ex-WI without the red tape. The best things about living here are that you feel very safe if you are an older person and that Anglesey is just such a beautiful island. We have an unusual climate and get various butterflies that are not found elsewhere in the British Isles. The main drawback is that wherever you go from Anglesey, it's a long way. If you wanted to go to Spain, for example, the nearest flights are from Cardiff or Liverpool.

WALES

Moelfre fact file

Access: B5025. Bangor, 13 miles.

Average property price: £181,082 (Anglesey)

Airport: Nearest international one is Cardiff. In May 2007 Highland Airways launched flights between Cardiff and Anglesey Airport (www.angleseyairport.com) – flight time is one hour.

Bus services: Numerous bus services, especially to the coastal places

Climate: Mild maritime climate

Council: Isle of Anglesey County Council (www.anglesey.gov.uk)

Council tax: Band D £948.62; band E £1,159.42

Crime: Safe place to live but problem with rural crime and theft of trailers, tools and other everyday equipment

Economic activity: Mainly tourism and services

Ferries: Holyhead to Dublin

Hospital: Cefni Community Hospital (01248 750117) in Llangefni. Nearest general hospital is Bangor on the mainland.

Percentage of people over 65: 75%

Population: Approximately 1,000

Property prices: Detached £229,228; semi-detached £149,687; terraced £106,764; flat £147,590

Railway station: Anglesey is well-served by railways, which reach the island via the George Stephenson (son of 'Rocket man' Stephenson) Victorian railway bridge. Nearest station Llanfairpwllgwyngyll, whose full name seems as long as the station platform, is on the route to Holyhead, or train to Bangor on the mainland by the Menai Bridge and then to Moelfre by bus. Holyhead to London (Euston) takes 4 hours 20 mins.

Specialised retirement property: Limited property available at any one time in Moelfre, but suitable 1970s bungalows are sometimes on the market. At the time of writing there were two: 5-bedroom detached £339,500 and a 4-bedroom detached part bungalow £349,950.

NORTH WALES COAST

The North Wales Coast is the narrow strip at the top of North Wales in the county of Conwy. Nearly half of Conwy is taken up by the magnificent Snowdonia National Park and the other half by the borderlands of Wales. Spare a thought for the sheep and those who consume them, as the government admitted in 2006, that 20 years after the Chernobyl nuclear disaster Welsh sheep are still grazing on land, including Snowdonia, which is contaminated from the fallout. For the elderly and retired, this is probably not a problem; it is more worrying for families with children. Anglesey is often included in the area of North Wales, even though it is very definitely separate both in geography and spirit. The North Wales coast is approximately 20 miles long and stretches from the Menai Bridge as far eastward as Prestatyn on the border with Flintshire and just across the water from the Wirral Peninsula. It is where 80% of the county's population of 110,000 lives. Prestatyn also marks the northern end of (King) Offa's Dyke, the once massive eighth-century earthwork that bulwarked the 170-mile English–Welsh boundary stretching from Chepstow to Prestatyn and passing through the Clwydian Range just south of Prestatyn. The Clwydians are great walking country known also for hill forts. Half a dozen of these eagles' nest lookouts dating from 600BC to the 1800s are perched on various Clwydian high points.

Most of the North Wales coast consists of long, sandy beaches interrupted by the great jutting headland of Great Orme Head at Llandudno. From west to east the resorts of the North Wales coast are Penmaenmawr, Llandudno, Colwyn Bay, Rhyl and Prestatyn.

Llandudno

Llandudno is an attractive Victorian seaside resort between the hills and the sea, just north-east of the estuary of the River Conwy. The town's most outstanding feature, apart from the beaches and the views, is the Great Orme headland, which rears up nearly 700ft. This is the location of most of the town's ancient history, having been mined for copper from the Bronze Age until the mid-19th century when the ore was finally exhausted. Fortunately for Llandudno (named after St Tudno who brought Christian religion to the area), the rise in popularity of seaside towns enabled it to expand and prosper from more airy pursuits throughout Victorian and up to Edwardian times. The resort was largely planned by a scion of the local Mostyn family to attract visitors from Society, including minor European royals, ex-royals and others mentionable in the Court Circular, such as Otto von Bismarck. The arrival of the railways to Llandudno in 1858 popularised the resort and increased its clientele, but the pier, completed in the same year to allow passengers from Ireland to disembark in Llandudno, was less fortunate. One of the worst storms in British maritime history hit Llandudno in 1859 and wrought havoc on the pier and other town structures. A new pier, all 2,300ft of it, was opened in 1875, and is the one standing today. Llandudno has a long flat promenade, which curves around the base of Great Orme. The town also has the Great Orme Tramway opened in 1902, which is still carrying passengers up to the summit today. The towns in the immediate surrounding area are Conwy (which has an outstanding castle), Deganwy, Colwyn Bay, Old Colwyn and Llandudno Junction. Llandudno Junction is three miles outside Llandudno and has a cinema and the railway station for Llandudno. Not for nothing is Llandudno referred to as 'Queen of North Wales Resorts'. It has reinvented itself as a conference and top arts venue with the Venue Cymru, which seats 1,500 and is a multipurpose theatre whose fare includes starry West End productions and the Welsh National Opera. It is also a haven for the retired, with around a third of the population of pensionable age.

My experience...

June, now aged 64, moved to Llandudno in 2001 from Chesterfield in Derbyshire. She and her husband are both retired teachers.

We always said that when we retired, we'd like to live by the sea. We also love walking so we wanted somewhere that was good for that. The east coast is too cold and the South Coast too expensive, but we loved North Wales and although we didn't know Llandudno itself, we were familiar with the area. We had some friends living there and they invited us to visit. After looking around we decided that Llandudno had everything we needed, plus it's on the edge of Snowdonia. At the time, property prices were slightly lower and when we bought, we were lucky enough to afford a nice house. We live about half a mile from the sea. We are higher up so we overlook the town and the views are spectacular. We're within walking distance of the town centre and there are lots of shops, including a new shopping development. We find public transport is brilliant.

We knew about the University of the Third Age before we moved, but we've joined lots more things since being here; we became involved in walking groups and learned to bowl. We're volunteer stewards at the theatre and I also volunteer at the local hospice. We had very good neighbours and when we came they introduced us to the Lions International, a volunteer organisation of which we are now members. We are very busy!

Llandudno has lots of cafés and things as it's a tourist centre, mainly for older people. We've got a fantastic promenade with beautiful Victorian buildings; there are no shops allowed on the front so it's retained its lovely Victorian charm and there's a fantastic pier in a beautiful bay. The best things for me are probably the climate and the fact that it's a pretty place in a beautiful setting. I can say now, that there's the friendliness of it as well. Although the town itself is very flat, the immediate hinterland is very hilly so those with zimmer frames can manage and

WALES

yet there is scope for the more agile to do some challenging walking. If you need to, you can get around on the excellent bus service. If you like the big city buzz, then Llandudno wouldn't suit you; it's much slower moving and there are no designer boutiques; you don't come here for the sophisticated life or the cocktail hour.

Llandudno fact file

Access: A470. Bangor, 23 miles.

Average property price: £181,000

Airports: Liverpool nearest. Manchester, 50 miles; Birmingham, 80 miles

Bus services: Local bus services for North Wales are excellent. Arriva Wales and other operators. For information on tourist use of public transport go to www.greatorme. org.uk/transport.html to see where you can go from Llandudno.

Climate: Drier and sunnier than many parts of Wales, thanks to the mountains to the south. Can be 'invigorating' when the wind blows for days on end.

Council: Conwy County Council (www.conwy.gov.uk)

Council tax: Band D £916.03; E £1,119.59

Crime: Low crime area

Economic activity: Llandudno has a busy retail, tourism and conference scene (www.wales.nhs.uk)

Ferries: Holyhead (40 miles) to Dublin; Liverpool to Douglas IOM, Belfast and Dublin

Hospital: Llandudno General, currently the subject of passionate local protest at plans to downgrade services and move them to main district hospital in Bangor. Some services, including coronary care, have already been moved.

Percentage of people over 65: 26%+

Population: Resident approximately 22,000 (triples in summer)

Property prices: Detached £241,000; semi-detached £180,000; terrace £167,760; flat £143,273

Railway station: Llandudno Junction (3 miles). Direct trains to/from Chester, Birmingham and Shrewsbury and onward connections to all parts of the UK.

Residents' on-street parking permit: £60

Specialised retirement property: Many retirement flat developments with prices from £45,000 and other flats not specifically aimed at the retired such as Becks conversion in Church Walks of flats, cottages and duplexes (£185,000 to £400,000 for two to three bedrooms).

Rhyl

Rhyl is a Victorian brick-making village, reborn as a seaside resort. Located in the north-eastern corner of the North Wales coast in Denbighshire, just west of Prestatyn, with which it shares miles of unbroken sandy beach. From Craig Fawr (the mountain you can see just inland) at the start of the Clywydian Range (known locally as the Prestatyn Hills), you can see Rhyl and Prestatyn laid out before you like a devil's temptation, along the flat strip of the coast. This is just one of the area's beautiful hikes and walks with fantastic views. Easy to reach from Rhyl are Chester and the metropolitan areas of the Wirral and Liverpool.

As a resort Rhyl began welcoming visitors from about the 1830s and attracted an upmarket clientele. In the 20th century it became a popular family resort, until the increase in foreign holidays and cheap travel abroad reduced its clientele. The fabric of Rhyl has deteriorated in the last decade, but it is an unpretentious place with some very decent folk who are mostly at verbal war with their council. It hasn't helped that the council allowed unscrupulous local landlords to rent out rundown accommodation to drug abusers and those just released from prison, creating a ghetto-like effect in some parts. The upside of this is that property in Rhyl is comparatively cheap, so it could be a place to plan to retire to, rather than to retire to this year or next. The reason for optimism is that money is being invested in the seafront and Rhyl could easily become as desirable as its surroundings within a few years. It has many good points such as its transport connections and amusements, two theatres including one for children, a cinema, a community college and decent shops. More seafront buildings are coming on the market having been converted to flats, and contractors are moving in to build new developments in other parts of town. Rhyl could well turn out to be a bit of a find for retirement, and you don't have to speak Welsh there as the town is not predominantly Welsh-speaking.

Many people buy caravans on local caravan sites. These are not meant for permanent living. The regulations say that you have to leave between 6 January and 1 March, as the caravan parks are obliged to close then. In fact, many people seem to live in the caravans for most of the year and then rent a flat locally for the closed period, or they may go abroad, or stay with friends.

My experience...

Terry Slater, 71, moved to Rhyl from Greater Manchester in 2002 as a widower.

After my wife died I found myself alone in a three-bedroom house with all my children married and leading their own lives. Previously, my wife and I had had a holiday caravan at Rhyl. After she died I bought a new caravan in Marine Holiday Park. I found that I was coming to Rhyl on a weekly basis, so moving here seemed the natural thing to do. Also my knees were getting arthritic and Rhyl is nice and flat, and it's less expensive living here than where I was before. I sold my house in Manchester and bought a bungalow on Kinmel Bay, which is a popular place to live, and separated from Rhyl by the River Clwyd; you cross the bridge to get there. I live three-quarters of a mile from the sea and near the harbour. I was lucky that I already had a lot of friends down here from when I was in caravans and I knew a lot of people in the pubs and clubs. A lot of people come to retire here from Liverpool, Merseyside and Stoke-on-Trent as the motorway makes it accessible.

Rhyl has a lot of character, but it's looking a bit jaded. But there has been a spurt of investment recently and a lot of semi-derelict buildings have been converted to high-class flats with underground car parking. There are plans to demolish the old fairground and replace it with better amenities and a supermarket superstore. Things are definitely looking up. Unfortunately a lot of the former B&Bs have been multiple-occupancy lets for some years. They are rented by people with problems such as alcoholism and drug dependency, so they can't work and are on benefits. So some areas are quite dangerous. It's such a shame as they are really nice old houses.

There's lots going on in Rhyl apart from the pubs and clubs, we have the Pavilion Theatre on the Promenade, which has an excellent variety of shows and drama. This is a beautiful area to live with loads of open country and lots of great day trips. You can be in Snowdonia in half an hour, and the weather's reasonable – better than the Pennines!

WALES

Rhyl fact file

Access: B5119, A525, A548; Rhyl is just off the A55 North Wales Coast road. Chester, 32 miles.

Average property price: £158,914

Airports: Liverpool, 65 miles; Manchester, 74 miles

Bus services: Main company is Arriva Wales (0870 608 2608; www.arriva.co.uk)

Climate: Locals say the Vale of Clwyd gets more sunshine than the rest of Britain

Council: Denbighshire County Council

Council tax: Band D £1,132.83; band E £1,384.57

Crime: Some poor housing, unemployment and drug-related and petty crime

Economic activity: One of the lowest wage areas of the UK but Rhyl is reinventing itself as a day trip and short break destination which will need supporting services and boost the local economy.

Ferries: Holyhead (fast ferry to Dublin); Liverpool, but nearest is Mostyn Quay (to/from Dublin) near Prestatyn

Hospitals: Conwy & Denbighshire NHS Trust (www.cd-tr.wales.nhs.uk) has two in Rhyl: Royal Alexander (elderly care; paediatrics); Glan Clwyd (A&E).

Percentage of people over 65: About 20%

Population: Approximately 26,500

Property prices: Detached £177,841; semi-detached £133, 013; terrace £119,905; flat £132,547

Railway station: Rhyl. Virgin Trains to London Euston. Arriva Wales to Chester, Crewe, Manchester, Birmingham and across North Wales. Also services to Cardiff and South Wales via Shrewsbury and Hereford.

Residents' on-street parking permit: £20 per year

Specialised retirement property: There are many newly built homes at Rhuddlan just outside Rhyl. Approximately 16% of current Rhuddlan residents moved there for retirement.

SHOW FLAT OPEN NOW

THE WELSH COLLECTION
Y Casgliad Cymraeg

Overlooking the River Pembroke and opposite the majestic medieval Pembroke Castle, is the exclusive new Thornsett Group development at North Quay.

With only 20 luxurious one and two bedroom contemporary apartments, all with private parking and access to a variety of communal terraces and private balconies, North Quay is already proving to be very popular.

Contact **Thornsett Group** on:

01834 869 142

or visit
www.**welshcollection**.co.uk

THORNSETT GROUP
REALISING THE POTENTIAL

www.thornsettgroup.com

Best of Britain series

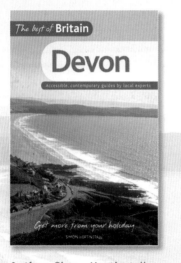

The Best of Britain guides are a series of exceptional books that do Britain justice and showcase its most unspoilt areas in their full glory. Today's Britain competes as a holiday destination on every level, with exciting boutique hotels, superb Michelin starred restaurants, and a range of fresh, locally produced food and drink for self-caterers. From Devon and Cornwall to the New Forest and Isle of Wight to East Anglia and the Lake District, these guides will help to create a tailor made break for today's modern holidaymaker.

Author: Simon Heptinstall
Published: May 2008
ISBN: 978 1 85458 426 7

Author: Lesley Anne Rose
Published: May 2008
ISBN: 978 1 85458 425 0

Author: Susan Griffith
Published: May 2008
ISBN: 978 1 85458 423 6

Author: Victoria Pybus
Published: May 2008
ISBN: 978 1 85458 422 9

Author: Lesley Gillilan
Published: February 2009
ISBN: 978 1 85458 424 3

THE BRECON BEACONS

The Brecon Beacons are recognised globally as a phenomenon. They are geologically ancient, have supremely temperamental meteorological conditions and they are stunningly beautiful. They are part of the Brecon Beacons National Park, which covers approximately 500 well-soaked, and in parts very watery, square miles reaching from Black Mountain in the west to, confusingly, the plural Black Mountains in the east. In between the two Black Mountains is the Fforest Fawr (Great Forest), which was designated a Unesco European and Global Geopark in 2005, along with major features of the Brecon Beacons themselves. These include underground cave networks and the wildly romantic ruin of the mountain top castle of Carreg Cennen. The whole of the western part of the Brecon Beacons National Park is designated a Geopark, including the highest Beacon, Pen-y-Fan (2,906ft). The flat-topped Brecon Beacons are named from the fact that they were once used for sighting signal fires to warn of imminent attacks from the English. Geologically, their flattened shapes are the result of softer layers of sandstone being worn away over millions of years. The Brecon Beacons are an hour's drive from Cardiff and the haunt of serious walkers from Britain and all over the world. You can lose yourself in the Beacons National Park, metaphorically, and literally if the weather suddenly changes and you are not properly equipped. The fact that the Special Air Service (SAS) hold training exercises in the Beacons is some indication of how tough the going can get. Many official organisations support the Brecon Beacons, but they also have their own society, The Brecon Beacons Park Society (www. breconbeaconsparksociety.org), which organises walks, talks and more and whose membership is a snip at £10.

The Brecon Beacons are ringed with interesting small towns, including Llandovery and Llandeilo to the west, Sennybridge and Brecon to the north and Hay-on-Wye and Abergavenny to the east. To the south are the industrial vales of South Wales.

Abergavenny

Abergavenny is a Welsh border town set against the backdrop of the Black Mountains, on the River Usk in Monmouthshire, at the eastern edge of the Brecon Beacons National Park. A small wooden Roman fort called Gobbanium was probably the first structure on the site. After the Norman Conquest, a castle and Benedictine priory were built by Hamelyn de Ballon. In medieval times, the Welsh prince Owain Glyndwr bore down from the north and laid the English-held town in ruins. Bloodletting in Abergavenny never again reached the same crescendo and the town was left free to prosper. In the 16th and 17th centuries Abergavenny grew from its market and local industries, including flannel making and weaving, and its wealth was conspicuous in its expanding streets. Many improvements were made to the town from the 1760s to the end of the 19th century, including the Market Hall, designed by John Nash before he reached peak celebrity fame as George IV's favourite architect. The Market Hall today is used for antiques fairs, craft exhibitions, farmers' markets and similar events, and annually in September it is the stylish venue for a celebrated international food festival. One Abergavenny retirement complex, Pegasus Court, incorporates 18th century Tan House, a former master tanner's home, when leather production was an important local industry.

My experience...

Michael Gurney, now 79 and formerly an accountant, moved to Abergavenny with his wife from Salisbury in 2004.

My wife was always keen to move and we had the idea we'd move when we were free to do so. We had a link with this area in that we and another family had a cottage not far from Abergavenny; the other side of Brecon. My wife was very keen on this cottage, but I didn't want to live in it, so we started looking for a house in Brecon, but Abergavenny attracted us because of the rail links. We'd always driven through it and knew it anyway; got a nice feel about it, but since moving here we have learned what a really lovely place it is. We found a house conveniently placed; the train station is 15 minutes away and the centre of town is 10 minutes' walk. There's a good train line coming up from Newport. It's a lovely line for enjoying the sheer pleasure of travelling. The countryside around here is generally lovely and good for walking. There is a nice little theatre that has visiting shows and the shops are adequate for daily needs. There's a thriving U3A in Abergavenny, it's very successful and I was told about it as soon as I arrived. There's also a very good college known as the Hill College, which is a marvelous place for meeting. There's a lot of activity locally, local history group, general history, etymology, etc.

The best thing about Abergavenny is that it's not too big, but it has a good variety of local shops: bakery, butchers, grocers and so on. If it's a John Lewis situation then we go to the Mall at Cribbs Causeway, just off the M5 near Bristol, or Hereford, which is 12 miles. The weather can get you down as it rains a lot and you are a long way from London, but then this is Wales and that goes with the territory.

Abergavenny fact file

Access: A40; A465; A4042. Newport, 19 miles.

Average property price: £198,000

Airports: Cardiff, 47 miles; Bristol, 57 miles

Bus services: Lots including summertime services to the Brecon Beacons (www.traveline-cymru.org.uk)

Climate: It rains a lot

Councils: Abergavenny Town Council (www.abergavenny.net/council) Monmouthshire County Council (www.torfaen.gov.uk)

Council tax: Band D £1,055.60; band E £1,290.17

Crime: Drug problems and antisocial youth

Economic activity: Low income area

Ferries: Fishguard (Pembrokeshire) to Rosslare Ireland (Stena Line)

Hospitals: Nevill Hall Hospital, Abergavenny (A&E) (www.wales.nhs.uk)

Percentage of people over 65: 22.7%

Population: Approximately 14,000

Property prices: One-bedroom £109,447; two-bedroom £157,775; three-bedroom £202,126

Railway station: Abergavenny

Residents' on-street parking permit: £30 per year

Specialised retirement property: Priory Gardens, 37 one and two-bedroom apartments (www.hanover.org.uk). Barratt Homes have a forthcoming retirement development (White Castle) of apartments and houses in Abergavenny (0845 688 6799).

WALES

Brecon

Brecon (Aberhonddu in Welsh) is an important Welsh town in south Powys, sheltered by the mountains (Brecon Beacons to the south and the desolate Mynydd Eppynt range to the north) and sited at the confluence of the Usk and Honddu rivers. Towns circling Brecon include Builth Wells, Hay-on-Wye, Abergavenny, Merthyr Tydfil, Aberdare and Sennybridge. The area was once on an important Roman route to Chester and there are Roman remains near the town. It is believed that in the fifth century it was ruled by a local chieftain Brychan, after whom the territory was called Brycheiniog. These are the origins of the English names Brecknock and Brecknockshire, by which the town and area were known until the reorganisation of county boundaries in the 1970s. Brecon town was founded by no less a personage than Bernard de Neufmarché (half-brother of William the Conqueror) who built a castle and a priory there. Later a town wall was constructed, parts of which are still standing. It is believed that ancient stones utilised for the construction of Brecon's fortifications came from the sacked Romano-British fort three miles west of the present town. Brecon, however, proved to be not easily defendable because of its low position. So in an act typical of the days when female royals were used as dynastic and political chess pieces, Bernard married a local Welsh princess to cement the peace with the Welsh.

For several centuries Brecon prospered as a market town. In the 17th century Daniel Defoe, writer and businessman, quipped, 'The English jestingly call it Breakneckshire: 'tis mountainous to an extremity'.

During Jacobean and Georgian times Brecon had its greatest period of expansion. At the end of the 18th century, the Brecon and Abergavenny canal was begun, to link Brecon with Newport and thence Bristol. The canal was completed in 1811 and was a conduit for the export of leather, wool and agricultural produce. Restoration, including the magnificent viaduct that carries the canal over the River Usk, has now been completed over 37 miles of this waterway for recreational use.

WALES

My experience...

Mary Cummings moved to Brecon from Dorset in 1997, with her husband, a former clergyman.

We decided to leave Dorset because we'd had two nasty burglaries and with my husband being 10 years older, I didn't feel I could stay in the country if he died. We'd never thought of Wales, but we'd spent many holidays there visiting my daughter and we loved the countryside here. We're both very much outdoor people and we are people-people, so we wanted somewhere good for walking, and somewhere where there are people around.

For the first six months after we bought our bungalow in Brecon I was miserable. I had been very well-known where we were before; we'd lived there 26 years. I felt lonely because I think there is a different culture in Wales. People know each other well, but they don't invite people into their homes so much and I wasn't used to that. However, once we joined the U3A and were members of the Cathedral it was fine. We now have a huge number of friends, and you can talk to anyone here; on the bus or in shops. People are very friendly. I run two walking groups and my husband is very musical and started a couple of music groups and a philosophy one in the U3A. I've actually made more friends here than I had in Dorset. Apart from the U3A, there are also choirs, flower arranging groups and I belong to a gardening club. But the U3A's definitely the liveliest thing in Brecon. We're lucky that we meet every week (most U3As meet monthly), so you're always meeting people.

The town has three supermarkets and amenities are adequate but there's no Marks & Spencer or B&Q. There is an excellent cinema and theatre. There are beautiful places to go walking. I've run walking groups twice a month for eight years, and I've only repeated four walks. Brecon is quite isolated and I did miss having large shops nearby. We have to go to Cardiff for big shopping and I tend to make impulse buys because you can't just pop back next week. But the good things are that we have friends and family here, it's clean and a friendly town to live in. I am very happy here.

Brecon fact file

Access: A470, A40, B4520 (from Builth Wells). Cardiff, 34 miles (takes about an hour).

Average property price: £180,000

Airports: Cardiff (www.cwlfly.com), 45 miles; also Bristol, 57 miles

Bus services: Brecon is a hub for bus services to the Brecon Beacons National Park and the major towns: Hereford, Hay-on-Wye, Abergavenny, Cardiff

Climate: High rainfall, variable cloudiness and hill fogs in the mountains

Council: Brecon Town Council (www.brecon.co.uk); Powys County Council (www.powys.gov.uk)

Council tax: Band D £813.73

Crime: Generally safe area

Economic activity: Tourism in particular

Hospitals: Brecon Hospital has a minor injuries unit. Nearest large hospitals are Nevill Hall in Abergavenny or Prince Charles in Merthyr Tydfil. (www.wales nhs.uk)

Percentage of people over 65: 20%+

Population: Approximately 8,000

Property prices: Detached £240,000; semi-detached £222,550; terrace £174,518; flat £153,749

Railway station: Nearest is Abergavenny

Specialised retirement property: Gwenwillian Morgan Court retirement flats, McCarthy & Stone (01874 622602) (www.mccarthyandstone.co.uk). From £131,450.

WALES

SWANSEA BAY

By the time you reach the western end of Swansea Bay in the south-west of Wales you have left behind the former industrial heartland of South Wales, and find yourself at the eastern end of the 19-mile long Gower Peninsula. The Area of Outstanding Natural Beauty is one of Wales' most beautiful wild places and the beginning of the tourist coast of south-west Wales. At the eastern end of Swansea Bay, Swansea town is a once great commercial port and former home of Wales' metallurgical industry.

The wide, five-mile sweep of Swansea Bay leaves Swansea town and reaches to the Victorian resort of The Mumbles with its quaint streets, and the Mumbles headland with its lighthouse and two tiny companion offshore islands. From the 17th to the 20th century the Mumbles area was known by its alternative name of Oystermouth. It was famous for its multitudinous biscuspids which had been enjoyed as far back as Roman times, until first over-harvesting and then disease wiped out the last oyster beds in the 1920s, and the oyster boats were left to decay on the beach. As you would surmise, the area of the Bay and the Gower Peninsula offer spectacular walking. Along the Bay itself, the tidal reach (the distance between high and low tide) is immense and the area of Black Pill, about half way along is an Site of Special Scientific Interest (SSSI) for its marine life and seabirds. Unfortunately, there is growing concern about the falling levels of sand in Swansea Bay and on the 34 miles of beaches on the Gower. Many blame industrial-scale dredging, others say that the sand moves around and some bays have more than usual and others less depending on when you take its measure. It is unlikely, however, that these sands of time will run out before the end of your retirement, should you choose to move there.

Swansea

Swansea, which the poet Dylan Thomas called 'ugly, lovely town', marks the border between industrial South Wales, and the Wales of outstanding coasts and scenic beauty. Thus it has the best of both worlds: all the convenience of the city and only the shortest of journeys to escape from it. Abertawe, the Welsh name for Swansea, reflects its location at the mouth of the River Tawe. For most of its history Swansea was much more accessible via the sea than by land, and the sea is the source of Swansea's fortunes then as now. It occupies a spot largely bypassed by the Romans, but the Vikings had a trading post thereabouts, and the name comes possibly from the Nordic 'Sveinne' (a person's name) and the word for island. The Normans made their appearance in 1099 when the Gower was taken and a Marcher lordship established. Swansea castle, the ruin of which rises incongruously near the modern town centre, dates from this time. By the 16th century, when the English and the Welsh had buried the hatchet, Swansea experienced an inflowing of Welsh immigrants into what had been primarily an Anglo-Norman settlement. By the 17th century it was a thriving port, thanks largely to the increasing importance of coal, which, in those days, without proper roads or railways, could only be transported in bulk via the sea. Between 1700 and 1740 it has been estimated that 16 collieries were operating in the vicinity of Swansea, and metallurgy in the form of smelting had become a major local industry. Steel making, with which Swansea was latterly associated, did not start until 1867.

Swansea had a pre-Depression in the 1920s caused by the decline of its traditional metallurgy industries in the face of cheaper foreign imports. By the 1930s when the Great Depression reached Britain's industrial areas, 150 years of Welsh prosperity came to halt, and from 1925 to 1939, 390,000 Welsh people emigrated from their homeland, many of them from Swansea and the Swansea area. In 1931 it is estimated that one third of the Welsh population lived within 25 miles of Swansea. The population of Wales did not recover to its pre-1925 levels until 1973. Thus it is the case that many of the current inhabitants of south-west Wales, including Swansea, are returning after they or their forbears sought a better life in other countries around the world. Wales, and in particular Swansea, has reinvented itself boomingly for the 21st century. As a consequence, property prices in the city and Mumbles have rocketed in the last five years. Swansea became a city in 1969 and was made part of the district of West Glamorgan in 1974 and with a much enlarged area including the Gower, it became a county in 1996. It is now the City and County of Swansea.

WALES

My experience...

Former teacher **Cecily Hughes,** now aged 62, moved to Swansea from Beaconsfield, Buckinghamshire in 2002 along with her husband, a former lecturer.

We decided to move because when you live in area like the west of London, you just do not retire there because you are just sitting on your collateral and most people can't afford to retire there. We did consider Ireland, where my husband's from, or the South Coast, because it had to be near the sea; for me that was it really; but eventually we settled on Swansea. I lived there when I was young, but we didn't return because of family or anything, as I only have one relative in Swansea that I occasionally see. We wanted a university town, where my husband could do part-time lecturing and I could do some supply teaching. The great thing about Swansea is the mix of age groups. You have the student population and working people and you don't have this predominance of older people that afflicts some good

(Continued on following page)

(Continued)

retirement spots. We settled in the village of Mumbles, which I love. It's close to the centre of Swansea. Because of the difference in prices, we were able to afford an old bed and breakfast place with four storeys and a huge basement. We also have the bonus of a beach hut and from April onwards we cycle down to our hut and have breakfast on the beach, which is lovely. Swansea is good for theatres; there's one in the university, one in the city itself and the Dylan Thomas Theatre. There's a fantastic choice of restaurants. There's a shuttle bus between Swansea and Cardiff every half an hour, which is used by commuters. From Mumbles there's a frequent bus service to Swansea. Mumbles has little individual shops and a delicatessen. You don't have to go to a supermarket if you don't want to.

There are so many activities you can get involved in that it's difficult to choose. I'm chair of the Dylan Thomas Society and a member of the U3A where I run a wine appreciation group in my basement and two reading groups. The U3A in Swansea is very lucky because it is attached to the University; the Vice President is also Chancellor of the University. I also belong to the Swansea Little Theatre. My husband belongs to several bridge clubs and is a member of a golf club. It's very friendly and cosmopolitan here; there don't seem to be any prejudices against incomers, but then Swansea and Mumbles are not a very 'Welsh' area. The best thing about living here is that you have all the advantages of the city and yet you've got the Gower Peninsula, which was the first Area of Outstanding Natural Beauty owned by the National Trust. The only disadvantage is that it's an hour and a half's drive to the Severn Bridge and you get the feeling that you are a bit isolated from England. But then you can always hop on a bus or a train and be very quickly out of Wales.

Swansea fact file

Access: M4 (London and South-east). M50, M5 and M6 (Midlands and North). Birmingham, 146 miles; Bristol, 81 miles; Cardiff, 42 miles; London, 189 miles.

Average property price: £151,346

Airports: Cardiff, 40 miles along M4

Bus services: Frequent bus services to and from Swansea and all other principal towns of South Wales

Climate: Sheltered, mild but rainfall is high. In October 2006, Swansea was flooded after the worst deluge for 20 years.

Council: City and County of Swansea (www.swansea.gov.uk)

Council tax: Band D £849.52; band E £1,038.30

Crime: The South Wales police force area, which includes Swansea, has one of the highest crime rates in Britain

Economic activity: Thriving city with huge services industry responsible for 86% of employment and the site of national and international company headquarters

Ferries: Swansea to Cork, Ireland (www.swanseacorkferries.com).

Hospitals: Two large hospitals: Morriston (has main A&E; www.morristonhospital.co.uk) and Singleton (www.wales.nhs.uk)

Percentage of people over 65: 18.5%

Population: 225,500

Property prices: Detached £237,761; semi-detached £140,049; terrace £113,203; flat £143,345

Railway station: Swansea. Hourly service to London Paddington (First Great Western).

Residents' on-street parking permit: £20 (£35 for second car)

Specialised retirement property: Swansea waterfront is the subject of intensive redevelopment including residential retirement apartments. May not be suitable for all retirees – and pricey – but worth a look.

WALES

PEMBROKESHIRE COAST

West of the Gower Peninsula is Carmarthen Bay and Pendine Sands, where the land speed record was broken in 1924 and 1927 by Sir Malcolm Campbell, who reached 174.22mph in the famous *Bluebird*. At the western end of Pendine beach the Pembrokeshire Coast begins. The famous Pembrokeshire Coast Path, 186 miles of it, begins at Amroth, just east of Saundersfoot, and continues all the way to Poppit Sands, north of the Preseli Hills on the border with Ceredigion. The Preselis are the source of blue stone, which has many uses in stonecraft. The huge stones of neolithic Stonehenge come from the Preselis, and precisely what method was employed to move them 250 miles (before the wheel was invented), from north Pembrokeshire to the middle of Salisbury Plain exercises the minds of archaeologists and lateral thinkers. The Pembrokeshire Coast is also a National Park, the only one in Britain that is predominantly coastal. The original conception of the Pembrokeshire National Park in 1952, was as a geological treasure house of some of the oldest rock in Britain, formed at least 600 million years ago in the pre-Cambrian phase. But the Pembrokeshire coast is not only earthly Paradise for geologists; walkers and birdwatchers see their own version of heaven in the shape of the rugged cliffs, sheltered coves, sandy beaches, wooded estuaries, sea caves, island nature reserves and much more. The Pembrokeshire coast is an astonishing mixture of beautiful views and beaches, and ancient Christian and pagan lore. The southern part of the Pembrokeshire coast is mostly English speaking; Welsh is spoken by about 50% of people in the north. The climate is surprising mild, although it rains a great deal and bitterly cold winds blow in winter.

Tenby and Saundersfoot

Tenby is small historic town and seaside resort on the Pembrokeshire Coast that is usually linked with nearby Saundersfoot, a pretty village also very popular for holidays and sailing. After the Normans had conquered and colonised this part of Wales in the 11th century, the Earls of Pembrokeshire built first a castle in the 12th century and then magnificent city walls in the 13th century, to protect the settlement of Tenby from Welsh insurgents. Although the Normans developed the settlement, the name Dinbych-y-Pysgod (Welsh for 'town of the fishes'), from which Tenby is derived, already existed in the ninth century and reflects its origins as a fishing village, a trade in which it prospered during the 14th century. By 1329 Tenby's population was in the region 1,500; sizeable for those times. During the English Civil War (1642–1646), Tenby was hammered by the Parliament side as it held out as a Royalist stronghold, but it subsequently succumbed to an enemy you couldn't see coming. The bubonic plague struck in 1650, the same disease that was to decimate London 14 years later. This and rising commercial competition affected Tenby's prosperity for years to come. By

1670 the population had dwindled by nearly half to 850, where it remained until Tenby's fortunes were completely revitalised in Victorian times by the seaside health boom. By 1830 the population was over 2,000. Seaside pursuits have continued to make the town prosper well into our times. However, modern seaside enjoyment is somewhat removed from the Victorians'. In 1999 men's magazine *Maxim* declared Tenby to be one of the top stag and hen weekend venues in the world and the town was hit by regular weekend waves of 20-somethings getting legless and abominable. It was perceived that this was damaging Tenby's regular holiday trade and the Wild West effect has been tamed (to an extent) by pub and police cooperation. The nearest towns to Tenby are Narberth, Haverfordwest and Pembroke/Pembroke Dock (15 miles).

Saundersfoot is a pretty seaside village with a magnificent sandy beach four miles north-east from Tenby and you can walk there via the coastal path. Its development is steeped in the 19th-century coal trade, when the coal was delivered to the harbour side from six collieries by small steam trains and then loaded into coal boats. Saundersfoot is a very lively and popular spot in summer and quiet to near desolation in the winter, although the climate tends to remain mild. Many former hotels have been and are still being converted into high-class flats suitable for retirees, but are also bought by those wanting a holiday home or an investment. Property prices in Tenby and Saundersfoot have more than doubled since 2001 and property is far from cheap.

Tenby Harbour

WALES

My experience...

Michael Thorne, a town planner, and his wife moved to Tenby from Newbury, Berkshire in 1998, when he was 54.

I took an early retirement package from Newbury local authority when they were restructuring. The terms were generous and I thought it would be nice to do something else. We chose Tenby because I was born near here in Fishguard and my grandparents were based in Fishguard. My parents first met on the beach at Tenby; there's a romantic association for you! Tenby is a beautiful place and we thought the grandchildren would love to visit us here.

Tenby doesn't change much because the town walls stop most development. The main change is the conversion of the old hotels into luxury apartments by property developers, but they are very expensive and local people cannot afford them. The majority of people who come here to retire are from South Wales and the Midlands. Tenby is a town of small businesses and hardworking people. There are probably 50 restaurants, cafés and bars here. I did have a dream to open one myself, but I soon realised the market is flooded.

Tenby can seem a bit remote. Our children live in London, which is five hours by car or train. The train service to London from Swansea takes three hours and the train from Tenby to Swansea is agonisingly slow and takes two hours. You could manage without a car as public transport is adequate, but life would be difficult. Health provision is quite good. Tenby Cottage Hospital is a new small hospital that caters well for minor injuries and older people. For anything they can't deal with, you usually go to Withybush in Haverfordwest.

I got heavily involved with voluntary work in Tenby. As people know that I am a town planner by profession I was used to being asked for help on a voluntary basis. I also do paid consultancy work for private clients and also the local authority. My wife does supply teaching. The U3A here is very active and the Ramblers too. I would say that the membership of the Ramblers here is predominantly over-50, or even 60. There is a council-run leisure centre and gym, but it is usually full of children. We find the gym attached to the Heywood Hotel preferable and it is open to the public via a membership scheme. There is fantastic walking and sea swimming. The local arts scene is not brilliant but we do have a cinema and theatre.

WALES

Tenby and Saundersfoot fact file

Access: A477, A478, B4316 (to Saundersfoot). Haverfordwest, approximately 15 miles; Swansea, approximately 57 miles.

Average property price: £249,950

Airport: Cardiff, 65 miles

Bus services: Infrequent bus services from Tenby

Climate: Mild and on the rainy side

Council: Pembrokeshire County Council (www.pembrokeshire.gov.uk)

Council tax: Band D £826.09; band E £1,009.67

Crime: Higher in the summer months, targeting tourists

Economic activity: Summer tourism business generates the bulk of Pembrokeshire's tourism revenue

Ferries: Pembroke Dock to Rosslare (Irish Ferries, www.irishferries.com)

Hospital: Tenby Cottage Hospital (outpatients, minor injury unit and daycare); nearest general hospital Withybush in Haverfordwest, or Carmarthen (www. wales.nhs.uk)

Percentage of people over 65: 19%

Population: Tenby 5,000; Saundersfoot 3,000

Property prices: Detached £329,975, semi-detached £240,000; terrace £287,475; flat £185,000

Railway stations: Tenby; Saundersfoot. Pembroke Dock–Carmarthen–Tenby–Swansea every two hours. For London Paddington you change at Swansea where trains leave for London every half hour at peak times.

Residents' on-street parking permit: £30 per year

Specialised retirement property: Shillingford Park Homes Park, Kilgetty near Saundersfoot

WALES

Scotland

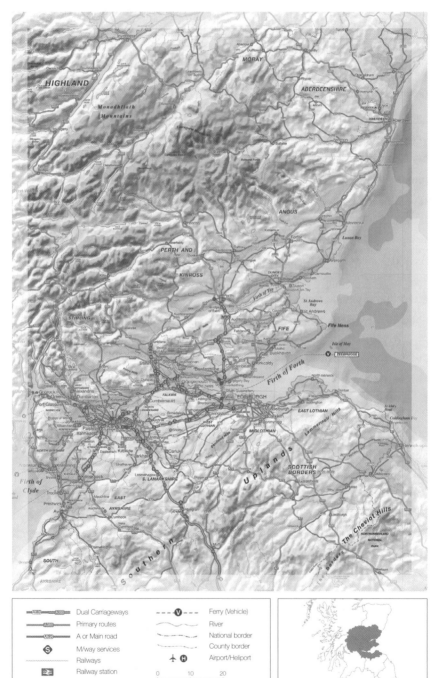

SCOTLAND

Legend:

Dual Carriageways	Ferry (Vehicle)
Primary routes	River
A or Main road	National border
M/way services	County border
Railways	Airport/Heliport
Railway station	
Towns	

0   10   20
Miles

THE LOWLANDS

The Scottish Lowlands reach from the border with England as far north as the narrow waist of Scotland, including the country's central belt of counties: Ayrshire, Dunbartonshire, Stirlingshire and Fife, the principal cities of Glasgow and Edinburgh and the Clyde Estuary and Firth of Forth. This central area is the most populated part of the country and it is where most of Scotland's industry is traditionally based. It is also geologically different from the Highlands, being made up of red sandstone dotted with extinct volcanoes, including the one on which Edinburgh is built. North of the Lowlands stretch the empty, desolate, and wildly beautiful Highlands and Islands. For retirement purposes, therefore, the Lowlands are within reach of sophisticated urban pleasures and international transport connections, and at the same time they are a gateway to wilder Scotland and activities from sailing and canal boating to fantastic walking, hiking and mountaineering. Some potential retirees will be put off by the cooler climate and more frequent rainfall that distinguishes any part of Scotland from the warmer parts of England or Wales. There are compensations, though. These include hauntingly beautiful scenery, heritage, history, arts festivals and space. If the winter months of January and February are too dark and depressing, you are close enough to two major airports to jet off to somewhere warmer.

Stirling

Like Edinburgh, Stirling grew up around a castle built on an extinct volcano and is one of the oldest towns in Scotland. It is situated in Stirlingshire at what was once the lowest crossing point on the River Forth, which gave it early strategic significance and was the cause of its origin. It subsequently became the scene of many key events in Scottish history. Thanks to Mel Gibson's film *Braveheart* (1995), the name of William Wallace is now more widely known outside his native land. Stirling has a William Wallace monument commemorating the hero (Wallace not Gibson!) and his victory over the English at Stirling Bridge in 1297. In 1314 Robert the Bruce won a decisive battle against the English, just outside Stirling at Bannockburn, and thus secured the independence of Scotland. Two Scottish kings were born in Stirling and one was crowned there. The towns around Stirling include Dunblane, Bannockburn, Bridge of Allan (site of the modern University of Stirling) and Callander. The Campsie Fells mountains are south-west of Stirling, and the Trossachs and several lochs including Katrine and the 26-mile long Loch Lomond, the longest loch in Scotland, are to the north-west. Stirling lies almost midway between Glasgow and Edinburgh, which are 40 minutes' and 50 minutes' drive respectively from Stirling. In 2002 Stirling was upgraded to city status as part of the Queen's Golden Jubilee celebrations.

The town is generally attractive, with an old part, a Victorian part and a modern part, which includes the monstrously large Thistle Centre, temple to the high street shopping gods. This shopping mall has a more recent annexe, the Thistle Marches, which includes better-known chains, including Waterstones.

My experience...

Margaret Risk, a former clinical psychologist now aged 71, moved to Stirling from Kirkcaldy, Fife in 2001.

We'd always been associated with Stirling. I'd been brought up near here and my mother lived here and I visited regularly. Before she died, I had already made a decision to move here, as I wanted to move back to the place where I was brought up. It had memories and although we'd been back regularly, in some respects it was like moving here as a stranger as I hadn't established friendships here or anything.

Stirling is a nice town and it's central with good railway connections. You're not far from either Glasgow or Edinburgh and it's a relatively short journey by either train or bus. There are also a lot of motorways leading out of the town and it's easy to get to other places by car from Stirling. Where I live, in the family house, it's not far from the bus and railway station and close to a park with a golf course. It's all turned out better than I expected. It's a friendly area and I found that people were amazingly welcoming.

For me there is plenty around Stirling, various cultural things and a college for classes. I'm mainly interested in cultural and educational things and there are plenty of opportunities for those in Stirling.

I'm less than a mile from the town centre, which I walk to. We have the MacRobert Theatre at the university and there are courses you can do at the university. There are also a number of local leisure centres. The council-run centre has things like Pilates, yoga and swimming, and it's cheap for pensioners. If you want to go up market, there are other leisure classes such as art clubs for developing skills. I've also been involved with helping set up as a kind of founder member, a branch of the U3A. The best thing about Stirling is the situation, for transport connections and places to go. For me personally, I'm glad that I'm close enough to town to get there on foot.

Stirling fact file

Access: Glasgow, 30 miles; and Edinburgh under 40 miles via M80 and M9

Average property price: £166,357 (Scottish average is £141,000)

Airports: Glasgow and Edinburgh, both approximately 35 miles

Bus services: Bus service hub

Climate: Cool, and Scotland tends to be wet

Council: Stirling Council (www.stirling.gov.uk)

Council tax: Band D £1,222.79; band E £1,494.52

Crime: CCTV is omnipresent. Crime rate is lower than Scottish national average.

Economic activity: Includes high-tech innovations park linked to Stirling University

Ferries: Rosyth to Zeebrugge (18 hours) with Superfast Ferries (www.superfast.com). Rosyth is 30 minutes' drive from Edinburgh. P&O Irish Ferries (www.poirishsea.com) Troon (Ayrshire, SW of Glasgow) to Larne (Ireland) takes 2 hours.

Hospital: Stirling Royal Infirmary (www.nhsforthvalley.com). Despite a lengthy campaign to retain it, Stirling Hospital is to be closed in 2009/2010 and services moved to a new hospital at Larbert near Falkirk (about 30 minutes away).

Percentage of people over 65: Approximately 19%

Population: 82,450

Property prices: Detached £244,016, semi-detached £136,197; terrace £126,217; flat £96,000

Railway station: Stirling. Fast frequent services to Glasgow, Edinburgh, Dundee, Aberdeen, Inverness and the rest of the UK.

Specialised retirement property: Many flats in the town, although not specifically for the retired. There are retirement flats in Dunblane (Glenallan Court) and Falkirk (Newcarron Court), 7 miles and 14 miles respectively.

SCOTLAND

THE KINGDOM OF FIFE

Fife, which forms a peninsula on the eastern coast of Scotland between the Firth of Tay and the Firth of Forth, is a county that Fifers call a kingdom. For hundreds of years, before the bridges were built across the Firth of Forth, travellers talked of leaving Scotland and going to Fife, which seemed a land on its own. It is still possible to get that feeling today, even with modern transport connections. Quite apart from its ancient status as a regional Pictish kingdom, Fife has many associations with the Scottish monarchy; the ancient Scottish capital of Dunfermline lies within its borders and Mary Queen of Scots, among other Scottish royals, considered it her home. Many of the towns of Fife have a familiar ring to their names: Cupar, seat of the thanes (earls) of Macduff, Auchtermuchty (the setting for the television series, *Dr Finlay's Casebook*), Kirkcaldy (birthplace of the economist Adam Smith in 1723), Kincardine (extra bridge across the Firth of Forth opened in 1936) Rosyth (former Royal Dockyard and now port for Superfast ferries to Belgium) and St Andrews (golfing capital of the world and site of Scotland's oldest seat of learning and largest religious building). It does seem to happen that the most attractive places in Britain often have some of the best place names, and the Kingdom of Fife fits this category; Balmerino, Ceres, Collessie, Dairsie, Elie, Moonzie, Scoonie, Torryburn and Kippo Burn are some of the Fife place names which leave one to ponder their origin and etymology. The land of Fife is mostly fertile and a mixture of low-lying ground and uplands. The Lomond, Cleish and Penarty Hills are the highest part of the county and form the boundary between Fife and Perth, and Kinross to the west. The Lomonds are also the location of Falkland Palace, the Renaissance-style country home of the Stuarts for 200 hundred years. In the East Neuk (as the most easterly part of Fife is known) many extremely picturesque fishing villages include Buckhaven, Crail, Cellardyke, Pittenweem and Anstruther. All of them are historic with their own particular history, lording it over miles of sandy beaches that form a golden border where the land meets the sea.

For Scotland's smallest county (507 square miles) Fife has more than its fair share of sights and amenities, including historic houses and gardens and more than 40 golf courses. Another attractive feature of Fife is the range of old houses, small and large, which are of very individual character. These say something about the nature of Fifers. Fife is one of the few places in Britain where the Vikings landed and were despatched to Valhalla in bulk by the locals. Fife also gained the reputation of producing some of the world's toughest sea dogs, proof against the English navy, pirates and pretty much anything the sea could throw at them. Agriculture and trade were the mainstays of the economy until the 18th century when boatbuilding, papermaking and mining boosted the economy further. In the 20th century linoleum, North Sea oil and gas and high technology brought more wealth into the economy of the region

SCOTLAND

and saw the death of the mining industry, which once employed thousands in western Fife.

These days many commuters from Scotland's lowland cities choose to live in Fife so they can have the best of both worlds; the stimulating city job and somewhere they can afford to live and enjoy themselves surrounded by beauty. Make no mistake, Fife is one of Scotland's secrets; tourists pass it by in favour of the Highlands without knowing what they've missed. Glenrothes is the main town and seat of the county council and Kirkcaldy is the largest town and main manufacturing centre. There is room for plenty more people to move there, retired or otherwise.

Dunfermline

Dunfermline city is sited five miles from the banks of the Firth of Forth and the Forth Road Bridge. Its ancient palace and abbey were founded in the 11th century and its Scottish Royal connections are too many and various to expound here. The 12th-century abbey is the final resting place of Robert the Bruce (minus his heart; that was carried to Melrose Abbey in the Borders). The Royal Palace has been the birthplace of seven kings (including Charles I of the United Kingdom), one queen and the royal burial place of nearly a dozen others. It lost its status as the royal capital of Scotland in 1603 with the Union of the Crowns (the formation of the United Kingdom). The city was devastated by fire in 1624, so most buildings date from after this time.

Dunfermline's most revered son is far from royal: Andrew Carnegie, the millionaire philanthropist who was born in a humble cottage in Dunfermline in 1935, emigrated to the United States in 1843. By 1901, he was a Pennysylvania steel magnate and regarded as the richest man in the world. He then gave it all away. Among benevolent acts towards the citizens of his birthplace was his purchase of the 80 acres of Pittencrief Park in 1902, where as a child he had been banned from playing by the local laird. These acres of unspoiled grass and trees, streams and waterfalls were his gift to the people of Dunfermline and today they are still a place of tranquility for the city. Dunfermline is an ancient attractive city with narrow cobbled streets in the centre, but which is being expanded and modernised. Barratt Homes, Bellway and Redrow have all built new estates there within the last four years, which have been snapped up as more people move out of Edinburgh and Glasgow to a place they can afford to live.

SCOTLAND

My experience...

Elizabeth O'Neill, a former teacher, now 65, moved to Cairneyhill, just outside Dunfermline, from Glasgow, in 2002.

I'd always planned to move from Glasgow, and when my husband died, my daughter was already living in Dunfermline so I moved here to be near her and my family. I liked the area and had spent happy holidays there as a child, and in my early married life we had a holiday house further along the south coast where we went for eight years. Fife, I suppose as with any peninsular area, has a varied landscape with hills and a flat coastal part. Within a 15-mile radius there's really anything you could want. Dunfermline's like the centre of a wheel insofar as there are interesting towns in all directions, such as Perth, Stirling and Glasgow. The climate is quite mild and the property is cheaper than in Glasgow. After I had made the decision to move here I sold the flat in Glasgow and with the money from that I could afford a three-bedroom house in Cairneyhill, just south-west of Dunfermline. We're lucky that the village has a post office, grocers, hairdresser and a garage. Dunfermline has the Carnegie Theatre, a ten-screen cinema complex and a swimming pool. There are a lot of folk and music clubs here and lots of things to do. I'm a member of the Ramblers and was a WI member. I belong to a Church group in Oakley, three miles from here and a heritage group.

We have a very good bus service because this is the Central Belt. The buses are very frequent. The bus from Glasgow to St Andrews goes through our village. The best thing about living here is the location. I like the fact that I can do shopping for big items in Dunfermline at the Kingsgate shopping mall, and within five minutes I can be down by the coast. I like the freedom of the area; there are so many pastimes and hobbies to pursue and people are very friendly. I love the beauty of the place. I'm actually hard-pressed to think of anything I don't like.

Dunfermline fact file

Access: M90; A985; A823. Edinburgh, 25 miles.

Average property price: £141,623 (Edinburgh £205,189)

Airports: Edinburgh, 15 miles; Glasgow, 47 miles

Bus services: Excellent and numerous

Climate: Less rain than western Scottish regions. Maximum rainfall anywhere in Fife is 35 inches per year.

Council: Fife Council (www.fife.gov.uk)

Council tax: Band D £1,483.85; band E £1,813.59

Crime: There are areas where you should not wander after dark

Economic activity: Expanding city and economy

Ferries: Superfast Ferries from Rosyth to Zeebrugge

Hospital: Queen Margaret, Dunfermline – opened 1993, due to be downgraded 2011 and the subject of huge local controversy as important services including A&E will be moved to Kirkcaldy www.nhsfife.scot.nhs.uk

Percentage of people over 65: 33% over-55

Population: 55,000 (including Rosyth)

Property prices: Detached £232,300; semi-detached £145,235; terrace £117,910; flat £80,444

Railway station: Dunfermline; more frequent services at Inverkeithing (7 miles)

SCOTLAND

ANCIENT COUNTY OF PERTH

Sir Walter Scott could not allow himself to be heard preferring Perth to his beloved Borders, so he praised it in the third person, 'If an intelligent stranger were asked to describe the most varied and most beautiful province in Scotland, it is probable that he would name the county of Perth'.

Situated right in the heart of Scotland, geographically and historically, the ancient county of Perth has its feet in the lowlands and its head in the highlands, thanks to the Highland Fault that separates these two geologically distinct parts of Scotland and which runs mostly through Perth. Much of eastern Perth is the catchment area for one of Scotland's great rivers, the Tay, on which Perth city is sited before the river widens into the Firth of Tay. The ancient county of Perth's immense area was sub-divided into some of Scotland's vast earldoms; roughly north to south these are: Atholl, Breadalbane, Gowrie, Balquhidder, Strathearn and Menteith and these are commemorated in Perth's town names. Such a spread of privately owned land, plus the nature of the land itself, meant that Perth has never spawned any great industrial cities. Instead of metropolises, it has many extremely interesting individual towns with a wealth of the aforementioned historical connections, rich and fertile agricultural areas, lochs and hills, great fortified houses, castles and Pictish carved stones. The early Irish Christian missionaries arrived in the form of the Brethren of Columba, especially around the Strathearn region, and produced the first Christian king of a united Scotland, the schizophrenically named Pict, Constantine mac Fergus (790–820). From then on, the cavalcade of Scottish history passed through ancient Perth in such volume that it is a 'who's who' of main protagonists from Rob Roy MacGregor to the Duke of Montrose and from Bonnie Prince Charlie to William Wallace. Before the local government reorganisation of 1975 when the county of Perth and Kinross was formed, the ancient county of Perth extended further south and west, and included the towns of Aberfoyle, Callander, Dunblane, Doune, Killen and the area of the Trossachs. As an up-and-coming area, Perth is attracting inward migration of approximately 1,500 a year and is becoming a popular retirement area. The population of the county is currently about 150,000. There is a Pensioners' Forum, set up in 2001 with charitable status to represent the needs of older people in the county (www.perthandkinrosspensioners.org).

Perth

The compact town of Perth is the county town of Perth and Kinross, and is referred to sometimes as 'St John's city' or 'the fair city'. It claims city status by virtue of its having a cathedral (the 19th-century definition of a city), but it is not officially recognised as such. It has always been associated with agriculture as the source of its prosperity, rather than the traditional industries of Scotland. Wealth is reflected in the splendid Georgian architecture that predominates in the terraced streets around the town centre. Confusingly, like Dunfermline, it calls itself the ancient capital of Scotland, as it was a royal residence throughout the Middle Ages. More importantly, Scone, just outside Perth was where all Scottish kings were crowned until the crowns of England and Scotland were united in 1603. Strategically sited on the lower reaches of the River Tay, Perth has had flooding problems throughout its history. As recently as 1993, parts of the town were inundated. Since then, £25m-worth of flood defences have been constructed, and they withstood the first test of their effectiveness in 2005 when unusually high rainfall caused flooding elsewhere in Perthshire. Although Perth is a busy city, much of the traffic flows around it via the bypass, making life more pleasant for its residents and those with business there. In recent years, Perth has been expanding westwards, but this does not detract from the medieval grid pattern centre where building is constrained by the river and the

SCOTLAND

two famous parks, the North and South Inches. For anyone retiring to Perth the area has much to offer in the way of walking and touring around. It also has golf course and a racecourse.

My experience...

Paul MacDonald moved to Perth from Staffordshire in 2005. Formerly he was a postal worker.

I'd always wanted to move somewhere else when I retired, and I just liked Perth. I'd holidayed up here a few times and thought it was a nice area; nicer up here than down there. I only considered Perth, nowhere else. I do a lot of walking and the countryside around here was probably the main reason why I moved. There is forest walking and lochs, everything you want. The countryside here is far more interesting and varied than where I was living before. It took only six months to move here after I'd made the decision. I live in a semi-detached house with three large bedrooms so there's plenty of room. I chose this house for the fantastic views, I can see for miles. Within two minutes, I'm in woodland and it's about a mile into town. I always walk it. The bus service goes from right outside my house if I want to use it for going to town and back. Perth is an attractive place. It's got cafés and a shopping centre. Almost all of the high street names are here and there's cinema and theatre, a hospital and a train station. I go rambling a couple of times a week, I swim and play badminton. I belong to a Church as well and go there on Sunday and one evening a week. I keep busy and there is a lot to do and see. Scone Palace is nearby and Falkland palace is spectacular and not too far from here. Edinburgh, Glasgow and Dundee are all less than an hour away. Perth is nicely located for the coast and you can get to St Andrew's in about 50 minutes. I go to the coast quite a lot in summer.

The best thing about living in Perth is probably the variety of the landscape. On Tuesday, we were walking on the coast and the following day we were up in the hills. It also isn't as busy as where I used to live, there's a lot less traffic. It amuses me when the locals say 'isn't it busy' and there's just no comparison.

SCOTLAND

Perth fact file

Access: A9, A85, A93, A94, A90, M90. Edinburgh, 45 miles; Dundee, 22 miles; Glasgow, 65 miles.

Average property price: £158,811

Airports: Edinburgh, 38.7 miles; Glasgow, 69 miles

Bus services: An area-wide public transport map for residents and visitors is available in libraries, tourist information offices or on 01738 476538; publictransport@pkc.gov.uk

Climate: Prolonged wet springs and cool summers have established a pattern for recent years

Council: Perth and Kinross Council (www.pkc.gov.uk)

Council tax: Band D £1,523.85; band E £1,862.48

Crime: There are areas where you should not wander after dark

Economic activity: Rural economy, rural estate renting and businesses. Perth is growing economically, especially wholesale/retail and hotels.

Ferries: Rosyth (about 20 miles south down M90) to Zeebrugge; Stranraer to Belfast (Stranraer is aproximately 2 hours by train from Glasgow)

Hospital: Perth Royal Infirmary (www.nhstayside.scot.nhs.uk)

Percentage of people over 65: Approximately 16%. In the whole of Perth and Kinross 37.49 are aged 50+.

Population: Approximately 55,000

Property prices: Detached £252,866; semi-detached £166,857; terrace £154,179; flat £107,981

Railway station: Perth. Perth–Edinburgh 1 hour 15 mins; Perth–Glasgow 1 hour. Details of all services on www.firstgroup.com/scotrail.

Residents' on-street parking permit: £85 per year to park near your house (£150 if you want to add free city centre car parking)

Specialised retirement property: McCarthy & Stone (0845 249 1178) Glenearn Court retirement apartments in Crieff (south-west of Perth) from £107,450

SCOTLAND

THE SHETLAND ISLES

From John O'Groats, sail the northern oceans in a north-easterly direction past the Orkney Islands (Mainland and its larger acolytes of Hoy, Shapinsay, South Ronaldsay, Rousay, Eday, Stronsay, Sanday, Westray and North Ronaldsay) and after 130 miles you will reach the Shetland Isles; strung out, lengthy and inleted fragments of land, known to some as 'The Auld Rock'. Their extraordinarily eaten-away coastline is the result of millions of years of erosion by rivers, glaciers and the sea, the result of which is that nowhere in the islands is more than three miles from the sea. For over 600 years, the Shetlands were dominated by Norway and only became part of Scotland in 1468. It is not unexpected, therefore, to find that Norse culture is strongly blended with the Scottish tones. The traditions of the Shetland Isles include music and festivals, storytelling, crafts, seamanship and crofting. For hundreds of years Shetland sucked its prosperity from the fertility of the seas around it, rather than from the land, where strip cultivation produced only subsistence produce. A trade was built up with merchants of the Hanseatic League of northern Germany who resourced Europe's prize commodity of salted fish from the Shetlands, in return for cash and commodities including cloth, corn and beer. After the Treaty of Union united Britain and Scotland in 1707, the British government saw off the Hanseatic traders and inexpert Scottish merchant lairds took over – with disastrous economic consequences. Their ruinous incompetence reduced the islanders to bondsmen, fishing to earn a living from their lords. The hated lairds were agents of the British Crown, which obliged them to supply a quota of Shetland sailors for the British navy. The tradition of Shetlanders going into the navy and later the Merchant Navy continued up to and including the Second World War, with a wearing effect on the population as casualties tended to be high. In the 1920s and 1930s dire poverty caused migration from the Shetlands to Canada, Australia and New Zealand. After the Second World War, which produced a brief boom from the thousands of service personnel stationed there, the Shetlands continued haemorrhaging its population through emigration. By the 1960s, the decline was beginning to be reversed as the Shetlands reinvented industries based on their natural resources: agriculture, fishing, knitwear and the expanding interest in tourism, but the population had plummeted to an all-time low of 17,000 (in 1861 it had been 30,000). The discovery of oil in 1972 brought Shetland wider attention, as it became a temporary home for thousands of construction workers and those in the oil business. The oil fields Brent and Ninian are off to the north-east of Shetland, but the oil is brought right home to the oil terminal at Sullom Voe in the north of Mainland, via underwater pipelines. Some of the oil workers liked the islands so much they brought their families and became permanent residents. The population nowadays is a mix of indigenous families and incomers from several countries including Norway and Russia and also retired people.

SCOTLAND

Startling as it seems, Shetland was voted one of the top 10 places to retire in Britain by readers of *Yours* magazine in 2005, a reflection perhaps that distance from the mainland of Britain is no bar to enjoying a comfortable and far from deprived lifestyle on a well-run and community based archipelago with stunning scenery, even if it is battered on all sides by the Atlantic and the North Sea and is devoid of trees.

Shetland

Shetland is an archipelago of over 100 islands on the 60th parallel level with the tip of Greenland, Anchorage (Alaska), St Petersburg (Russia) and Oslo (Norway). The relatively warm seas and weather pattern of the islands are the result of the North Atlantic Drift, part of the Gulf Stream, sweeping up past Shetland before the icy Arctic currents take over. The islands fall naturally into two groups, the northern isles (Yell, Fetlar and Unst) and the Mainland islands, Fair Isle and Foula. The most westerly island, Foula, and the most southerly, Fair Isle, are somewhat isolated from the rest. Unst is the most northerly island. The population lives on 15 of the islands and 80% lives on the largest, Mainland. Lerwick, the capital of Shetland had its beginnings as a market place for Dutch herring fleets. These days the harbour is more likely to contain luxury yachts and a cruise liner or two. Lerwick town has a foreign feel to it with granite buildings and winding narrow streets. Scalloway, six miles to the west of Lerwick was the capital in the 17th century when Patrick (Earl) Stewart built Scalloway Castle (now roofless) and made it the centre of administration. Oil, fishing, fish farming and tourism activities are providing the Shetlanders with comfortable living. Oil revenues in particular have provided additional resources for the islands in improved infrastructure and amenities, including leisure centres and public transport, particularly ferry services. Shetland islanders are resourceful and forward-looking. For them the hard times of history seem to be over and the future looks set to improve with improved transport links and newer industries such as organic meat production gaining ground. Shetland also has a higher than average proportion of young people among its population, testimony to its excellent schools and perception of it as a good and unpolluted place to bring up children. House prices, which were at bargain rates, are now rising fast and before long they will be like prices in many other desirable retirement places. There is currently quite a lot of new housing development in Norwegian-style architecture. Care for the elderly is reckoned excellent and the sense of community is very strong. Shetland apparently has hundreds of voluntary organisations. In a survey conducted by the Bank of Scotland in 2006, Shetland came out as the top place in Scotland for quality of life. The only downside is the winter weather; it gets awfully cold.

SCOTLAND

My experience...

Mabel Freeland, now in her nineties, moved to Shetland from Buckinghamshire in 1976, just after she was retired.

A friend and myself came up in the 1960s, thinking we'd spend a few days looking around Shetland, but liked the area and we had such a welcome, we thought 'we must come back'. A few years later, I advertised for a cottage and I found this croft at Dunrossness that really suited me. I'm not crowded in by other people and I look out over unspoilt views. There's a hill behind me that gives a bit of shelter and I'm on a slope that goes down to a loch just below me.

When I first moved here, it was like stepping back 50 years. People came out of the hotels to see you off on the bus to church and my next door neighbour was still cutting his corn with a scythe, but it's changed tremendously since I've been here, which is good in some ways, but not in others. There are no trees here, just beautiful coastal scenery and beautiful beaches with hardly a soul on them. I'm about five miles from the airport which I took advantage of until a couple of years ago. We have a community bus about once a week that takes us to the local shop about two miles away, but that's it. It's a well-stocked shop and there's also a hairdresser, wine shop, gardening shop. A fish van and the mobile library call round to the house.

I've got very nice folk around me, although unfortunately most of the friends I made when I first moved here have passed on. I've never lived anywhere where I've received so much kindness. We had snow last year, and half a dozen people phoned me to ask whether I needed anything. I'm a member of the Senior Citizens' Club and I go to the WI and we also have a gardening club in Lerwick, where good friends take me. There's never enough time for everything and you have to keep active. The best things about the place are that it is so peaceful and crime is rare. The only reason I lock my door when I go out, is if you don't and someone got in, your insurance would be invalidated, but at one time, nobody dreamt of locking their doors.

SCOTLAND

Shetland fact file

Access: Aberdeen by plane 1 hour. London, 600 miles; Arctic Circle, 400 miles; Norway (Bergen), 200 miles

Average property price: £103,860

Airports: Sumburgh (southern tip of Shetland). Lerwick, 25 miles.

Bus services: To/from Sumburgh

Climate: Long days, comfortable warmth and sunshine and extra daylight hours (up to 15) in summer. Winters are dark (five-hour days), wet, and windy with the odd hurricane.

Council: Shetlands Island Council

Council tax: Band D £1,418.85; band E £1,734.15

Crime: Very low crime, but alcohol abuse and associated violence on the rise

Economic activity: Oil, tourism, crafts, fish farming, organic agriculture. 90% employment among the population.

Ferries: Lerwick Ferry Terminal/ Aberdeen (Northlink Ships) 13-hour crossing operates 7 nights a week, all year round. Shetlands Island Council operates a fleet of 12 inter-island ferries linking 8 islands. Smyril Line sails from Lerwick to Denmark, Norway, the Faroes and Iceland.

Hospital: Gilbert Bain in Lerwick has A&E and 108 beds (www.shb.scot.nhs.uk). Visiting consultants from Grampian University Hospital Trust provide outpatient clinics and day case surgery. Anything they can't handle means going to Aberdeen Royal Infirmary. Emergencies are airlifted there.

Percentage of people over 65: 48% of Shetland's population are over 40

Population: Human population approximately 22,740 (greatly outnumbered by seabirds, rabbits and sheep)

Property prices: It is difficult to give a meaningful average as properties are very individual. They may be very large, very small, or have a croft attached, all of which distort prices. The best policy is to make enquiries through Shetland solicitors and estate agents that you can find via the internet. Most houses sold are on the mainland. They are cheaper on other Shetland Isles for obvious reasons. The most expensive property is in Lerwick.

Railway station: Thurso on the mainland of Scotland. Trains go to Inverness (www.travelinescotland.com).

SCOTLAND

Index

www.crimsonpublishing.co.uk